THE EUROPEAN UNION SERIES

General Editors: Neill Nugent, William E. Paterson

The European Union series provides an authoritative library on the European Union, ranging from general introductory texts to definitive assessments of key institutions and actors, issues, policies and policy processes, and the role of member states.

Books in the series are written by leading scholars in their fields and reflect the most up-to-date research and debate. Particular attention is paid to accessibility and clear presentation for a wide audience of students, practitioners and interested general readers.

The series editors are **Neill Nugent**, Visiting Professor, College of Europe, Bruges and Honorary Professor, University of Salford, UK, and **William E. Paterson**, Honorary Professor in German and European Studies, University of Aston, UK. Their co-editor until his death in July 1999, **Vincent Wright**, was a Fellow of Nuffield College, Nuffield College, University of Oxford, UK.

Feedback on the series and book proposals are always welcome and should be sent to Steven Kennedy, Palgrave Macmillan, Houndmills, Basingstoke, Hampshire RG21 6XS, UK, or by e-mail to s.kennedy@palgrave.com

---

General textbooks

Published

Forthcoming

Also planned

The major institutions and actors

Published

Renaud Dehousse **The European Court of Justice**
Justin Greenwood **Interest Representation in the European Union (3rd edn)**
Fiona Hayes-Renshaw and Helen Wallace **The Council of Ministers (2nd edn)**
Simon Hix and Christopher Lord **Political Parties in the European Union**
David Judge and David Earnshaw **The European Parliament (2nd edn)**
Neill Nugent **The European Commission**
Anne Stevens with Handley Stevens **Brussels Bureaucrats? The Administration of the European Union**

Forthcoming

Wolfgang Wessels **The European Council**

The main areas of policy

Published

Michelle Chang **Monetary Integration In the European Union**
Michelle Cini and Lee McGowan **Competition Policy In the European Union (2nd edn)**
Wyn Grant **The Common Agricultural Policy**
Martin Holland and Mathew Doidge **Development Policy of the European Union**
Jolyon Howorth **Security and Defence Policy in the European Union**
Johanna Kantola **Gender and the European Union**
Stephan Keukeleire and Tom Delreux **The Foreign Policy of the European Union (2nd edn)**
Brigid Laffan **The Finances of the European Union**
Malcolm Levitt and Christopher Lord **The Political Economy of Monetary Union**
Janne Haaland Matláry **Energy Policy in the European Union**
John McCormick **Environmental Policy In the European Union**
John Peterson and Margaret Sharp **Technology Policy In the European Union**
Handley Stevens **Transport Policy in the European Union**

Forthcoming

Karen Anderson **Social Policy In the European Union**
Michael Baun and Dan Marek **Cohesion Policy in the European Union**
Hans Bruyninckx and Tom Delreux **Environmental Policy and Politics in the European Union**
Sieglinde Gstöhl and Dirk de Bièvre **The Trade Policy of the European Union**
Christian Kaunert and Sarah Leonard **Justice and Home Affairs in the European Union**

Paul Stephenson, Esther Versluis and Mendeltje van Keulen **Implementing and Evaluating Policy in the European Union**

Also planned

Political Union
The External Policies of the European Union

The member states and the Union

Published

Carlos Closa and Paul Heywood **Spain and the European Union**
Andrew Geddes **Britain and the European Union**
Alain Guyomarch, Howard Machin and Ella Ritchie **France in the European Union**
Brigid Laffan and Jane O'Mahoney **Ireland and the European Union**

Forthcoming

Simon Bulmer and William E. Paterson **Germany and the European Union**
Brigid Laffan **The European Union and Its Member States**

Issues

Published

Derek Beach **The Dynamics of European Integration: Why and When EU Institutions Matter**
Christina Boswell and Andrew Geddes **Migration and Mobility in the European Union**
Thomas Christiansen and Christine Reh **Constitutionalizing the European Union**
Robert Ladrech **Europeanization and National Politics**
Cécile Leconte **Understanding Euroscepticism**
Steven McGuire and Michael Smith **The European Union and the United States**
Wyn Rees **The US–EU Security Relationship: The Tensions between a European and a Global Agenda**

Forthcoming

Graham Avery **Enlarging the European Union**
Emiliano Alessandri and Nathalie Tocci **Turkey and the European Union**
Thomas Christiansen, Emil Kirchner and Uwe Wissenbach **The European Union and China**
Tuomas Forsberg and Hiski Haukkala **The European Union and Russia**

Understanding the European Union

A Concise Introduction

Sixth Edition

John McCormick

First published 1999
Second edition 2002
Third edition 2005
Fourth edition 2008
Fifth edition 2011

This edition published 2014 by
PALGRAVE

Palgrave in the UK is an imprint of Macmillan Publishers Limited, registered in England, company number 785998, of 4 Crinan Street, London, N1 9XW.

Palgrave Macmillan in the US is a division of St Martin's Press LLC, 175 Fifth Avenue, New York, NY 10010.

Palgrave is a global imprint of the above companies and is represented throughout the world.

Palgrave® and Macmillan® are registered trademarks in the United States, the United Kingdom, Europe and other countries

ISBN: 978-1-137-36233-9   hardback
ISBN: 978-1-137-36232-2   paperback

This book is printed on paper suitable for recycling and made from fully managed and sustained forest sources. Logging, pulping and manufacturing processes are expected to conform to the environmental regulations of the country of origin.

A catalogue record for this book is available from the British Library.

A catalog record for this book is available from the Library of Congress.

Printed in China

Contents

List of Boxes, Tables, Figures and Maps

Boxes

Tables

Figures

Maps

List of Abbreviations and Acronyms

ACP	Africa, the Caribbean and the Pacific
CAP	Common Agricultural Policy
CFSP	Common Foreign and Security Policy
CSDP	Common Security and Defence Policy
CO_2	carbon dioxide
EC	European Community
ECB	European Central Bank
ECSC	European Coal and Steel Community
EDC	European Defence Community
EEA	European Economic Area
EEAS	European External Action Service
EEC	European Economic Community
EFTA	European Free Trade Association
EMS	European Monetary System
EMU	economic and monetary union
EP	European Parliament
EPC	European Political Cooperation *and* European Political Community
ERDF	European Regional Development Fund
ERM	Exchange Rate Mechanism
ESDP	European Security and Defence Policy
EU	European Union
EU-15	the 15 member states of the EU prior to the 2004 enlargement
EU-27	the 27 member states of the EU following the 2004–07 enlargement
FDI	foreign direct investment
GATT	General Agreement on Tariffs and Trade
GDP	gross domestic product
GNI	gross national income
IGC	intergovernmental conference
IGO	intergovernmental organization
IO	international organization
IR	international relations
JHA	justice and home affairs
MEP	Member of the European Parliament
NAFTA	North American Free Trade Agreement

NATO	North Atlantic Treaty Organization
NGO	non-governmental organization
OECD	Organization for Economic Cooperation and Development
PR	proportional representation
QMV	qualified majority vote
RIA	regional integration association
SEA	Single European Act
SME	small and medium enterprise
TEN	trans-European network
UN	United Nations
VAT	value-added tax
WTO	World Trade Organization

The member states:

AT	Austria	IE	Ireland
BE	Belgium	IT	Italy
BG	Bulgaria	LT	Lithuania
CY	Cyprus	LU	Luxembourg
CZ	Czech Republic	LV	Latvia
DE	Germany	MT	Malta
DK	Denmark	NL	Netherlands
EE	Estonia	PL	Poland
EL	Greece	PT	Portugal
ES	Spain	RO	Romania
FI	Finland	SE	Sweden
FR	France	SI	Slovenia
HR	Croatia	SK	Slovakia
HU	Hungary	UK	United Kingdom

Introduction

This is a book about the European Union (EU), whose impact on the lives of Europeans and non-Europeans has been substantial, and yet which still has a remarkable capacity to confuse, bemuse and confound. At no time has that capacity been more evident than it is today, as the EU continues to wrestle with the fallout from the greatest existential crisis in its history. Even as it briefly celebrated the award of the Nobel Peace Prize in 2012, it found itself deep in a political and economic maelstrom that began in 2009 with a sovereign debt crisis both inside and outside the eurozone. A vicious combination of domestic and international economic woes raised deeply troubling questions about the future of the euro, while polls indicated declining faith in the EU, and eurosceptical political parties won new support at elections. This combination of developments led in turn to suggestions from the most pessimistic commentators that the days of the EU itself might be numbered. But four critical points are worth making.

First, while the eurozone crisis is undoubtedly the worst ever to have afflicted the European project, it is hardly the first. The EU has faced everything from economic decline to false starts on monetary integration, shock votes against European treaties, concerns about democracy and efficiency, and worries about how little most Europeans know or care about the EU. When the proposed EU constitutional treaty was voted down by French and Dutch voters in 2005, pundits responded by asking how the EU could possibly survive. And yet it did. It is also worth noting that while the eurozone crisis has fed in to an alarming decline in faith in the European project (the proportion of Europeans who trust the EU institutions fell from a high of 57 per cent in the spring of 2007 to new lows in the range of 31–33 per cent in 2012), trust in national institutions has fallen as well, and has always been lower than trust in the EU (Eurobarometer 78, Autumn 2012:14). This is not to excuse one by pointing to the other, but rather to emphasize that faith in government in general – and not just the EU – has been falling.

Second, while it is hard to be sure where responsibility for the crisis in the eurozone lies, to blame the single currency alone was always too simple and too easy. To be sure, there were design flaws in the euro, notably the mistake of failing to give the European Central Bank control over fiscal policy (national budgets). But those flaws were created and sustained by the governments of the eurozone members, who made matters worse by often breaking their own rules on the management of the euro, and by allowing their responses to the crisis to be driven more by sectional public opinion at home than by the broader and longer-term interests of Europe. Had the euro been designed and managed more effectively, history would likely have played out quite differently. It is also worth noting that even as faith in the EU has been declining, support for the euro remains strong (Pew Research Centre Global Attitudes Survey, 13 May 2013).

Third, the EU is routinely criticized for suffering from a lack of leadership, and yet there is strong opposition to giving its institutions the kinds of powers and authority that would allow it to exert that leadership. And its powers are considerably overstated: critics like to blame 'Brussels' for numerous crimes and ills, and to discuss it as though it had independent powers – but it does not. Not only are the EU institutions limited in what they can do by the treaties, but two of them (the European Council and the Council of the EU) consist of members of the democratically elected national governments of EU states; it is particularly ironic to see those representatives pointing the finger of blame for Europe's woes at institutions of which they are members. The third of those institutions (the European Parliament) is directly elected by EU voters, while the fourth and the fifth (the European Commission and the European Court of Justice) are the servants of the others in the sense that their jobs are, respectively, to make sure that the content of the treaties is turned into practical policies and to make sure that the treaties are closely observed and respected.

Finally, it should come as no surprise that the EU has had problems, because it is a unique project that has always been sailing uncharted waters. One of its founders, the French bureaucrat Jean Monnet, warned in his 1978 memoirs that 'Europe would be built through crises' and would be 'the sum of their solutions' (Monnet, 1978:417). He also argued (introducing what came to be known as Monnet's law) that 'people only accept change when they are faced with necessity, and only recognize necessity when a crisis is upon them' (Monnet, 1978:109). That the EU has faced so many problems is less remarkable than the fact that it has survived so many.

Clearly nothing will be the same in the wake of the eurozone crisis. Numerous questions had already been asked about the EU before the crisis broke, feeding into the euroscepticism that has been on the rise since the early 1990s. The crisis sparked substantial changes to the rules of the EU, intended to make sure that problems of this scale do not arise again, and questions continue to be asked about the purposes and organizational style of the EU, the answers to which will continue to evolve for years to come. But it is important to remember that while confidence in the EU has been shaken since 2009, it has long been much more than an exercise in economic integration, and the ties that bind Europeans will be hard to unravel. There has been an invisible hand of integration at work, and even if the entire edifice of the EU could somehow be closed down tomorrow, the economic, political and social links that have come to bind Europeans over the last few decades would continue to have their own internal logic and motive force.

Few of the laws that once limited free movement and trade among European states are likely to return. The physical and psychological barriers that for so long reminded Europeans of their differences have come down, and while national and regional identities are still alive and well, Europeans are no longer willing to fight each other to assert those identities. Twenty or thirty years ago, the EU was only a marginal factor in the lives of most Europeans, but today – with the near-completion of the single market, policy cooperation on a wide range of issues, the development of a system of European law, the adoption of the euro, eastern enlargement, moves towards a common foreign policy, and important global challenges that demand responses from its leaders – Europe has become impossible to ignore.

The eurozone crisis has once again made clear how hard it is to pin down the character and personality of the EU. It is much more than a standard intergovernmental organization, because its powers, roles and responsibilities go far beyond those of any other intergovernmental organization that has ever existed. But it has not yet become a European superstate, or a United States of Europe, and there are many in Europe who are keen to make sure that this never happens. Just where this leaves it on the continuum between an intergovernmental organization and a superstate remains contested.

In addition to the basic challenge of defining the EU, we are also faced with a host of organizational questions. What role does the EU play in the daily life of politics, economics and society in its 28 member states? Is it a bona fide political system, and if so, how do we explain and characterize its relationship with the 28 member states? Are they independent actors, or should we think of them as part of a club, whose rules, norms and expectations they must follow? What does the EU mean for policy making in Europe? And what has been the impact of the EU on the identity and meaning of Europe? Is it any longer realistic or useful to make a distinction between Europe and the EU?

What of Europe's place in the world? What difference has the EU made to how Europe deals with the rest of the world, and to how the rest of the world deals with Europe? Are the statistics as impressive as they seem? (The EU is the wealthiest marketplace in the world, controller of one of the world's two leading international currencies, the biggest trading power in the world, the biggest market for mergers and acquisitions in the world, and the biggest source of foreign direct investment and official development assistance in the world.) Or are there still too many problems and divisions among Europeans to allow Europe to flex its international political and economic muscle?

And what of the future? How will the EU emerge from the crisis in the eurozone, and what will be the effect of opposition to the directions being taken by integration? Will the accumulation of doubts and crises prove too much, or will European leaders continue to adapt and make the EU both more stable and more widely accepted?

The number of responses to these questions has grown with time, but agreement on the best is as remote as ever. We cannot even agree on whether the EU is a good idea, and a project worth pursuing, or whether it has involved the surrender of too much state sovereignty and identity, and has aspirations above its station. Opinion polls find that only about half of Europeans approve of the EU, while the other half either disapproves or is not sure what to think. Polls also find that most Europeans do not know how it works, begging the obvious question of how far we can rely on public opinion about the EU. Critics disapprove of the authority given to European institutions that they consider secretive, elitist and unaccountable. They also question the extent to which integration can be credited with the peace, economic growth and prosperity that have come to Europe since 1945. But supporters take the opposite view, see many political and economic advantages in integration and are ready to credit much of Europe's renewal and revival to the opportunities provided by integration, and to think of themselves more as Europeans than as citizens of particular states.

This is an introductory book about the EU, written for anyone who wants to understand how it works and what it means for the more than half a billion people who live under its jurisdiction. It sets out to introduce the EU from first principles: to look at the debates over what it is and how it has evolved, to describe and assess the way it works and reaches decisions, to examine its impact on the individual states of Europe and their citizens, to review the effects of European integration on a range of critical policy issues, and to discuss its changing global role. The analysis in the chapters that follow has been coloured by two core influences.

First, the emphasis is on brevity. This book has never been intended to be a detailed analysis of the EU, but nor has it ever been designed as a mere whistle-stop description of the EU, reciting key facts, names and dates. Instead, it sets out to review and synthesize the major points in the analytical debate about the EU, the key steps in its history, the work of its major institutions, the ways in which ordinary Europeans relate to its work, and its key policy outputs, all the while engaging and challenging its readers, and tying up the basic facts with reflection, analysis and context. While some textbooks on the EU now top 600 pages, *Understanding the European Union* has never been more than

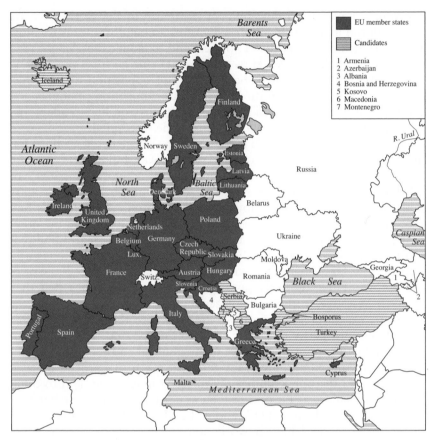

Map 0.1   *The European Union*

half that length, and this new edition brings the story up to date while also being exactly the same length as the last edition. Anyone looking for a more in-depth treatment might want to consider my other textbook, *European Union Politics*, also published by Palgrave Macmillan, of which *Understanding the European Union* is – in essence – a brief but also somewhat wider-ranging version.

Second, much of the academic writing on the EU – particularly at the introductory level – has done us a disservice by shrouding the EU in a fog of theoretical debates, treaty articles, arcane jargon, acronyms and convoluted philosophical theses that have helped make one of the most fascinating developments in European history sound dull and bureaucratic, and has too often divorced European integration from the real, daily life of Europeans. Events at the European level are just as full of drama, of success and failure, of bold initiatives and weakness, and of visionary leadership and mercenary intrigue as events at the national level, and it is important in books such as this to show clearly why the EU changes our lives in real and substantial ways.

The first edition of *Understanding the European Union* was published in 1999, and happily struck a note; new editions followed in 2002, 2005, 2008 and 2011, and this sixth edition follows in short order. There is something of a myth in the academic world that new editions of textbooks rarely involve many changes, but while that may be so in some fields of study, light tinkering is not an option for those of us dealing with the EU: it constantly evolves, its rules are amended, its personality keeps changing, and new layers of analysis and interpretation are regularly added to the debate over integration. Above all, however, the personality of the book has been altered by the fallout from the eurozone crisis and the rise of euroscepticism.

While the sixth edition preserves the overall goals and structure of its predecessors, it has been substantially updated to take account of recent developments, shortened wherever possible, the arguments tightened and adjusted as needed, new boxes, figures and tables have been inserted to present information more visually and new sources have been used in order to show how the study of the EU has evolved. As a result it looks quite different in several places.

Chapter 1 on theory remains relatively unchanged, the reorganization and revisions made to the fourth and fifth editions holding firm: explanations of how the EU evolved (which come mainly out of the study of international relations) are distinguished from explanations of what the EU has become (which come mainly out of comparative politics and public policy).

Chapter 2 on the meaning of Europe has been shortened but otherwise remains relatively unchanged, the goal being to review the changing identity of the region, to address the knotty issue of the outer limits of Europe, and to discuss what it means to be European by defining the political, economic and social norms and values that distinguish the region and its inhabitants.

Chapter 3 on the history of the EU has been revised to cut back on some of the early developments in order to make room for an analysis of the eurozone crisis and its long-term implications.

Chapter 4 on institutions has been revised and updated in light of the Treaty of Lisbon and the accession of Croatia, and with a view to clarifying the often confusing decision-making processes of the EU.

Chapter 5 on the EU and its citizens includes updated information on changes in public opinion, and expanded coverage of euroscepticism, reviewing its sources, varieties and implications for the debate over Europe.

Chapter 6 began life in earlier editions as a study of the relationship between the EU and the member states, and continues its transition in the sixth edition into a full-blown study of the policy process.

Chapter 7 on economic policy has been substantially updated in order to provide more detail on the achievements and problems of the single market, a new section has been inserted on the effects of the single market on European business, and the coverage of the euro has been rewritten to offer more analysis on the causes of the eurozone crisis and the political response.

Chapter 8 has been reformulated so that where in past editions it focused heavily on cohesion policy and efforts to create a level EU playing field, it has been renamed 'Internal Policies' and now reviews all the major EU policy areas other than the single market, the euro and external policies. An extended section has been inserted on justice and home affairs.

Chapter 9 focuses on external policies, with sections on foreign policy, security policy, trade policy and relations with the United States and the neighbourhood. The chapter has been restructured and updated in order to make it more distinctive from Chapter 8, and there is more speculation about the EU's role in the changing international system.

This edition has in many ways been the hardest of the six to complete, because it was written against a background of hardening pessimism about the future of the European experiment. Opinion about the EU has diverged of late, with increasingly strong views held by supporters and critics, an overall decline in faith in the EU, and a steady stream of bad economic news combined with more intensified criticism of the political responses of EU and national leaders. The last few years have not been a happy time for the EU, a point made forcefully by one of the editors of the Palgrave Macmillan EU Series when he noted during preparations for this book that the eurozone crisis was not just any issue, but one which meant a choice between the survival of the EU and its demise. It is not often that authors of textbooks are faced with the possibility that the subject of their writing may be on the verge of collapse, and it was hard for me – as I wrote this new edition during 2013 – to avoid becoming infected by the aura of gloom in which the EU was wreathed. My only option was to heed the advice of the recently revived wartime British government slogan: 'Keep calm and carry on.'

The purpose of textbooks is to support the learning process, and to provide students with a survey of factual details held together with a representative selection of the analyses that give those details meaning (including, of course, a substantial dose of my own analyses). I hope that students will find what follows to be a helpful and balanced introduction to the work of the EU, and to its implications and the debates over its future. I would like to thank the four anonymous reviewers who provided feedback and suggestions on my proposal for this new edition, series editors Neill Nugent and Willie Patterson for their guidance, Stephen Wenham for his fine work as publisher, Steven Kennedy for the constant energy, reassurance and excellent judgement that he provides, and the staff at Palgrave Macmillan for their work on the production. And my love and thanks as always to my wife Leanne and to my sons Ian and Stuart.

JOHN MCCORMICK

Chapter 1

What is the European Union?

At the heart of the debate about the European Union is the problem of how best to define it. The EU is more than a standard international organization, because it has involved more pooling or transfer of authority than membership of – for example – the United Nations (UN) or the World Trade Organization (WTO). But it also falls short of being a federal United States of Europe, or a European superstate. This leaves it in limbo somewhere between these two points of reference, with multiple opinions about how it is best understood. Scholars have applied terms such as *multi-level governance* and *consociationalism* in their efforts to define it, but none has yet gained traction. Others who study the EU have described it simply as *sui generis* (unique), but this is less a descriptive term than a surrender to the uncertainty. Perhaps, as former Commission president Jacques Delors once quipped, it is simply an unidentified political object.

The problem with our failure to agree a label for the EU, or at least to agree its political and economic personality, is that many of the conclusions that we draw about the EU depend on how we understand it. Take, for example, the question of the democratic deficit (discussed further in Chapter 5). Critics often argue that the EU institutions are insufficiently responsible and transparent, and that they develop laws and policies without being held accountable to public opinion. But those same critics will often resist attempts to create more elected offices in those institutions for fear that the result will be a federal Europe. Conversely, there are some who argue that the democratic deficit is a fiction because the EU is not a federal superstate, and its institutions are held accountable to voters through the governments of the member states. In short, the size (or even existence) of the democratic deficit depends on how we define the EU as a system of authority.

Most of the early analyses of European integration came out of the study of international relations, because the EU (and the European Community before it) was long approached by most scholars of integration – and by European political leaders – as an international organization. But since the 1990s there has been growing support for understanding the EU as a political system in its own right, and for looking at explanations coming out of the fields of comparative politics and public policy. There is still no grand theory of European inte-

1

gration, and no agreement about how best to understand and describe the EU today, but the parameters of the debate are changing.

This chapter looks at the different theoretical and conceptual approaches to understanding the EU. It argues that because the EU is both more than an international organization and less than a federal European superstate, it is best regarded as a confederal system with some federal qualities. In other words, it is for the most part a union of independent states that have pooled or transferred authority in those areas of policy where cooperation makes the most sense. There is no European government with independent powers, and the EU is still very much an intergovernmental system in which decisions are made by the governments of its member states working together, but there has been a federalizing tendency in several areas of policy, such as the single market, trade, agriculture and the environment.

The EU in the international system

The best point of reference for understanding the EU is the state, the most common approach to structuring large political systems, and one with which we are all familiar. World maps show continents divided by state frontiers, marking out territories under the administration of sovereign governments and subject to independent systems of law. When we travel from one state to another, we must usually show passports or other documents, and are reminded that we are in transit until we return to our 'home' state: the one to which we legally 'belong' and with which we feel a sense of identity.

A state is a legal entity which has four key qualities:

- It operates within a fixed *territory* marked by borders, and controls the movement of people, money, goods and services across those borders.
- It has *sovereignty* over that territory and over the people and resources within its borders, and has the sole right to impose domestic laws and taxes.
- It is legally and politically *independent*, and both creates and operates the system of government under which its residents live.
- It has *legitimacy*, meaning that it is recognized both by its people and by other states as having jurisdiction and authority within its territory.

None of these qualities is absolute: there may be political disputes that create uncertainties about the borders of a territory; there may be legal, economic or political difficulties that limit the sovereignty of a state; the independence of states is qualified by external economic and political pressures; and levels of legitimacy vary according to the extent to which the citizens of a state (and the governments of other states) respect the powers and authority of that state (see Gill, 2003; Hay, Lister and Marsh, 2006). Furthermore, the viability of the state system has come under increased scrutiny of late, and there are some (see Strange, 1996; van Creveld, 1999) who argue that the state is in retreat – or is perhaps simply being transformed (Sørensen, 2004) – as a result of three critical developments.

First, public loyalty to the state – and the strength of state identity – has long been compromised by economic, social and political divisions. In Europe, most states are home to multiple different nations, or groups of people linked by history, language and culture. Occasionally, a nation will coincide with a state (for example, most of the residents of Portugal are Portuguese), but most European states are home to multiple nationalities. Thus Spain is a state, but its population is divided among Andalusians, Aragonese, Basques, Cantabrians, Castilians, Catalans, Galicians, Navarrese, Valencians and others. In many parts of the world, the focus of people's allegiance has changed as national minorities have become more assertive and demanded greater self-determination, and even separation in some cases, as with the Scots in Britain, or the division of Belgium into new Flemish and Wallonian states.

Second, international borders have been weakened by the building of political and economic ties among states, driven mainly by the need to trade, to expand markets, to develop security alliances and to borrow money. Perhaps nothing today poses as much of a threat to the state as globalization: increased economic interdependence, changes in technology and communications, the rising power of multinational corporations, the growth of international markets, the spread of a global culture and the harmonization of public policies in the face of shared or common problems such as terrorism, transboundary pollution, illegal immigration and the spread of disease. At the same time, people have become more mobile: complex new patterns of emigration have been driven by a combination of political instability, economic need and personal choice, and mass tourism has broken down many of the psychological borders among states.

Third, states have not always been able to meet the demands of their residents for security, justice, prosperity and human rights. States have frequently gone to war with each other, their democratic records have been mixed, many have failed to manage their economies and national resources to the benefit of all their residents, and even the wealthiest and most progressive of states still often struggle with poverty and social division. Many states have also failed to meet the needs of their consumers for goods and services, a problem that has combined with the rise of multinational corporations in search of new markets and

State	A free-standing entity with territory, sovereignty, independence and legitimacy.
International organization	A body that allows and encourages cooperation among states or state-based bodies, founded on voluntary cooperation, communal management, and joint decision-making. Intergovernmental in character.
Regional integration association	An organization based on the transfer, sharing or pooling of authority, that is administered by bodies with shared power, and that work to encourage collective action and the development of common rules and policies. Both intergovernmental and supranational in character.

Figure 1.1   *Types of political organization*

profits to change the nature of production, and to make state boundaries more porous.

The decline (or transformation) of the state has run in tandem with growing interstate cooperation on matters of mutual interest, ranging from the narrowly focused to the broadly idealistic. Cooperation has been most clearly obvious in the work of international organizations (IOs), bodies that promote voluntary cooperation and coordination between or among their members, but have neither autonomous powers nor the authority to impose their rulings on members. Some IOs have national governments as members; they include intergovernmental organizations (IGOs) such as the UN, the WTO and the North Atlantic Treaty Organization (NATO). Others are non-governmental organizations (NGOs), including multinational corporations (such as Walmart, Royal Dutch Shell, Toyota or ING) or private organizations with specific interests (such as Amnesty International, Doctors Without Borders, Friends of the Earth or Oxfam).

In few places has the prestige and hold of the state been more actively challenged than in Europe, where centuries of conflict and tension reached a climax with the horrors of two world wars, driving home the dangers of nationalism and emphasizing the urgency of interstate cooperation. Political divisions were further emphasized by the cold war, which made many realize that states seemed unable to guarantee the safety of their citizens except through a balance of violence with other states, and which found Europe caught in the middle of a political and ideological competition between the superpowers, the west obliged to follow the lead of the United States, and the east trapped in the Soviet bloc.

One of the responses to these developments was the creation of two new European IGOs: the European Coal and Steel Community (ECSC) in 1952, and the European Economic Community (EEC) in 1958. In both cases, decision making was primarily intergovernmental: like most IGOs, they were fora within which government representatives could meet, share views, negotiate and work to reach agreement. Membership was voluntary, management was communal, decisions were the result of the joint will of their members, and both organizations depended for revenue on member contributions. They lacked independent powers, they did not have the means or authority to enforce their decisions, and they could not impose sanctions on recalcitrant members other than those agreed by the membership as a whole.

But the focus of European cooperation quickly moved from the work of these two IGOs to the development of a regional integration association (RIA). This happens when a group of states agree to take collective action and develop common rules and policies on shared interests. Regional integration goes beyond cooperation by involving the transfer, sharing or pooling of sovereignty and the creation of regional institutions within which rules and regulations are developed in policy areas where the members have agreed to cooperate. The final say on the adoption of those rules and regulations is left to the member states, and the regional institutions have few if any direct powers of execution, a job left to the governments of the member states.

In many respects the EU is still a standard IGO in which decisions are taken as a result of negotiations among the leaders of the states, and its institutions mainly carry out the wishes of the member states. But in other respects it has moved into the realms of supranationalism: a form of cooperation which results in the creation of a new level of authority whose interests and powers are independent of those of participating member states. In policy areas where the member states have ceded or transferred authority to the EU institutions, those institutions can make laws and policies that are binding on the member states. In some areas, such as trade, the EU has been given the authority to negotiate on behalf of the member states collectively, and other countries work with the EU institutions rather than with the governments of the member states. In several other policy areas, such as agriculture, the environment and competition, decisions are taken at the level of the EU rather than of the member states.

Matters are complicated, however, by the different personalities of EU institutions. Some (notably the European Council and the Council of the EU) are more clearly intergovernmental, because they are meeting places for the representatives of the governments of the EU member states, and decisions are reached as a result of compromises based on competing state interests. Other institutions (notably the European Commission and the European Court of Justice, or ECJ) are more clearly supranational, because they focus on the broader interests of the EU, and their decision makers are not national representatives. But the debate about the logic and personality of the EU has provided few hard answers, in part because of competing opinions about how the EU has evolved, but also because of questions about whether it is even a good idea to begin with (see Box 1.1). Under the circumstances, pinning down the character of the EU is fraught with difficulty.

The dynamics of regional integration

The pressures and motives for states to cooperate come from a variety of sources:

- States may be brought together by force, as they were in Europe by Napoleon and Hitler.
- They may come together out of the need for security in the face of a common external threat, as did the members of NATO during the cold war.
- They may share common values and goals, and agree to cooperate or share resources in selected areas, as have the Nordic states on transport, education and passports.
- They may decide that they can promote peace and improve their quality of life more successfully by working together rather than separately, as have the members of the UN.
- Cooperation can encourage efficiency by removing troublesome rules and barriers, and avoiding duplication.

Interstate relations in Europe were long influenced and driven by the first two of these motives, but since 1945 there has been a shift to the last three. In other words, compulsion has been replaced by encouragement, but just why and how this has happened remains a matter of debate. At first, there was an idealistic notion that out of the ruins of postwar Europe, and before state governments could reassert themselves, there was an opportunity to break with the past and create a new European federation. Federalists worried that if the prewar system was rebuilt there would be a return to nationalism and further conflict, and hoped that political integration would be followed by economic, social and cultural integration. With this optimistic idea in mind, the European Union of Federalists was created in 1946, but it was able to agree only on the creation of the Council of Europe, with its modest goal of intra-European cooperation.

Sparked by the tensions arising out of the nuclear age, postwar thinking about international relations instead came to be dominated by the more pessimistic notion of realism. This argues that states are the

Box 1.1 The pros and cons of regional integration

Particularly since the early 1990s, when the Maastricht treaty led to the European Community being superseded by the EU, there has been a growing backlash against European integration which has sparked a vigorous debate about its advantages and disadvantages. For supporters of the EU, its benefits include the following:

1. Cooperation makes war and conflict less likely as self-interest is replaced with shared interests, and exclusion is replaced with inclusion.
2. Member states working together enjoy new global power and influence.
3. The single market offers European businesses a larger pool of consumers, and encourages innovation, opportunity, competition and more choice.
4. Mergers and takeovers create world-class European corporations, helping the EU better compete in the global marketplace.
5. Greater freedom of cross-border movement within the EU eases travel.
6. The pooling of the economic and social resources of multiple member states has widespread benefits.
7. Less advanced member states 'rise' to standards maintained by more progressive states.
8. Funds and investments create new opportunities in the poorer parts of the EU.
9. Cooperation and integration encourage democracy, human rights and free markets.

For critics of the EU, its costs include the following:

1. Loss of sovereignty, national independence and the freedom of national governments to make decisions.
2. Loss of national identity as laws, regulations and standards are harmonized.
3. Charges that the EU institutions are undemocratic, elitist and inefficient, and that they generate burdensome new regulations.
4. The creation of a new level of distant and impersonal European 'government'.
5. Concern that the EU is headed down the dangerous path of becoming a federal European superstate at the expense of the self-determination of its member states.
6. Increased competition and job losses brought by the removal of market protection.
7. Handicaps on progressive states as standards are reduced to help integrate states with lower standards.
8. Increased cross-border crime and illegal immigration arising from the removal of internal border controls.
9. Problems related to controversial initiatives such as recent bailouts of economically troubled eurozone states.

most important actors on the world stage (because there is no higher sovereign power), that they strive to protect their interests relative to each other in a hostile global environment, and that they use both conflict and cooperation to ensure their security through a balance of power with other states (see Waltz, 2008). Under this analysis, the EU today would be best understood as a gathering of sovereign states, which retain authority over their own affairs, transfer authority to new cooperative bodies only when it suits them, and reserve the right to take back that authority at any time. In short, realists argue that the EU exists only because the governments of the member states have decided that it is in their best interests. But realism was unable to explain the rising tide of cooperation that followed the Second World War, left many unanswered questions about the motives behind international relations, and has recently lost some support.

An alternative view was offered by functionalism, based on the idea of incrementally bridging the gaps between states by building functionally specific organizations (see Box 1.2). Instead of trying to coordinate big issues such as economic or defence policy, functionalists believed they could 'sneak up on peace' (Lindberg and Scheingold, 1971:6) by integrating relatively non-controversial areas such as the postal service, or a particular sector of industry, or by harmonizing technical issues such as weights and measures. While realists spoke of competition, conflict and self-interest, functionalists focused on cooperation. While realists were concerned with relations among governments, functionalists focused on cooperation promoted by technical experts, and argued that European integration had a logic that participating states would find hard to resist.

The first in-depth study of European integration, by Ernst Haas in 1958, led to the expansion of these ideas as neofunctionalism. This argued that preconditions were needed before integration could occur, including a switch in public attitudes away from nationalism and towards cooperation, a desire by elites to promote integration for pragmatic rather than altruistic reasons, and the delegation of real power to a new supranational authority (see Haas, 1958, and Rosamond, 2000, Chapter 3). Once these changes took place there would be an expansion of integration caused by spillover, described by Lindberg (1963:10) as a process by which 'a given action, related to a specific goal, creates a situation in which the original goal can be assured only by taking further actions, which in turn create a further condition and a need for more action'. For example, the integration of agriculture would only really work if related sectors – say, transport and agricultural support services – were integrated as well. Equally, the integration of an international rail system would inevitably increase the pressure to integrate road systems and air routes as well.

Box 1.2   A working peace system

At the core of thinking about the mechanics of regional integration are the ideas of the Romanian-born British social scientist David Mitrany (1888–1975). His treatise *A Working Peace System* (first published in 1943) became the basis of functionalism, defined as an attempt to link 'authority to a specific activity [and] to break away from the traditional link between authority and a definite territory' (Mitrany, 1966:27). He argued that transnational bodies would not only be more efficient providers of welfare than national governments, but that they would help transfer popular loyalty away from the state, and so reduce the chances of international conflict (Rosamond, 2000:33). He argued for the creation of separate bodies with authority over functionally specific fields, such as security, transport and communication. This focus on particular functions would encourage international cooperation more quickly and effectively than grand gestures, and the dimensions and structures of these international organizations would be self-determined (Mitrany, 1966:27–31, 72).

Once these functional organizations were created, Mitrany argued, they would have to work with each other. For example, rail, road and air agencies would need to collaborate on technical matters, such as the coordination of timetables and agreement on how to deal with different volumes of passenger and freight traffic. As different groups of functional agencies worked together, there would he coordinated international planning. This would result not so much in the creation of a new system as in the rationalization of existing systems through a process of natural selection and evolution. States could join or leave, drop out of some functions and stay in others, or try their own political and social experiments. This would eventually lead to 'a rounded political system ... the functional arrangements might indeed he regarded as organic elements of federalism by instalments' (Mitrany, 1966:3–84).

Mitrany was not much interested in regional unification, which he felt would simply expand the problems of the state system and replace interstate tensions with interregional tensions, and nor did he support the idea of world government, which he felt would threaten human freedom. Nonetheless, his ideas were at the heart of the thinking of the two men most often described as the founders of the EU, French bureaucrat Jean Monnet and French foreign minister Robert Schuman (see Chapter 3). They believed that the integration of a specific area (the coal and steel industry) would encourage integration in other areas. As Schuman put it, 'Europe will not be made all at once or according to a single plan. It will be built through concrete achievements which first create a *de facto* solidarity' (Schuman Declaration, reproduced in Weigall and Stirk, 1992:58–9).

Spillover is a valuable analytical concept, but it is broad and ambiguous, and is better understood when it is broken down into more specific varieties, of which there are at least three:

- *Functional spillover* implies that economies are so interconnected that if states integrate one sector of their economies (for example), it will lead to the integration of other sectors (Bache et al., 2011:10). So many functional bodies would have to be created to oversee this process, and so many links built among states, that the power of national government institutions would decline, leading eventually to economic and political union.

- *Technical spillover* implies that disparities in standards will cause states to rise (or sink) to the level of the state with the tightest (or loosest) regulations. For example, Bulgaria and Romania – which had few environmental controls in place before they joined the EU – were encouraged to adopt such controls because of the requirements of EU law, which had in turn been driven by economic pressures from states with tight environmental controls, such as Germany and the Netherlands.

- *Political spillover* assumes that once different functional sectors are integrated, interest groups (such as corporate lobbies and labour unions) will switch from trying to influence national governments to trying to influence regional institutions (which will encourage them in an attempt to win new powers for themselves). The groups would appreciate the benefits of integration and would act as a barrier to a retreat from integration, and politics would increasingly be played out at the regional rather than the national level (Bache, George and Bulmer, 2011:10).

The forerunner of today's EU was the ECSC. It was created partly for short-term goals such as the encouragement of Franco-German cooperation, but it was also seen as the first step in a process that would eventually lead to political integration. It won little initial support or attention, but once it had been working for a few years, trade unions and political parties became more supportive because they began to better understand it, and the logic of integration in other sectors became clearer. But there was only so far it could go because its interests and goals were so limited; hence, six years after the creation of the ECSC, agreement was reached among its member states to work on broader economic integration within the EEC.

Neofunctionalist ideas dominated studies of European integration in the 1950s and 1960s, but briefly fell out of favour in the 1970s, in part because the process of integrating Europe seemed to have ground to a halt, and in part because the theory of spillover needed further elaboration. The most common criticism of neofunctionalism was that it was too linear, and needed to be expanded or modified to take account of different pressures for integration, such as changes in public and political attitudes, the impact of nationalism on integration, the influence of external events such as changes in economic and military threats from outside, and social and political changes taking place separately from the process of integration (Haas, 1958: xiv–xv).

Neofunctionalism was given a boost by Nye (1971:208–14) when he suggested taking it out of the European context and looking at nonwestern experiences. He concluded that experiments in regional integration involve an integrative potential that depends on several different conditions, including the economic equality or compatibility of the states involved, the extent to which the elite groups that control economic policy in the member states think alike and hold the same values, the breadth of interest-group activity, and the capacity of the member states to adapt and respond to public demands, which in turn depends on the level of domestic stability and the capacity – or desire – of decision makers to respond.

On all these counts the EU has always had a relatively high integrative potential: the member states are economically compatible (in the sense that their goals and values are generally the same, even if Eastern European members are still shaking off the effects of central planning), elite groups may disagree on the details but they tend to have broadly similar goals and values, interest groups have taken advantage of the rise of a new level of European decision making (see Chapter 5), and the democratic processes and structures of EU member states are responsive to public demands, even if there is sometimes a mismatch between what majority public opinion says and what political leaders do. By contrast, similar exercises in integration in other parts of the world generally have more handicaps to overcome (see Box 1.3).

A response to criticisms of neofunctionalism came in the form of intergovernmentalism, a theory which draws on realism and takes neofunctionalism to task for concentrating too much on the internal dynamics of integration without paying enough attention to the global context, and for overplaying the role of interest groups. Intergovernmentalism argues that while organized interests play an important role in integration, as do government officials and political parties, the pace and nature of integration are ultimately determined by national governments pursuing national interests; they alone have legal sovereignty, and they alone have the political legitimacy that comes from being democratically elected. Put another way, governments have more autonomy than the neofunctional view allows (Hoffman, 1964).

A variation on this theme is liberal intergovernmentalism, a theory which emerged in the 1980s and 1990s, and combined the neofunctionalist view of the importance of domestic politics with the role of the governments of the EU member states in making major political

Box 1.3   Regional integration around the world

The EU is the example of regional integration that has attracted the most international attention and that has had the most evident effects both on its member states and on states doing business with the EU. But regional integration is very much a global affair, and there are similar experiments under way on every continent. Levels of progress have been mixed, regional groupings do not always have the same levels of ambition and their integrative potential varies. Extrapolating from the arguments made by Nye (1971), the chances of success are greatest where the states involved have the most in common and where there are obvious advantages to integration. So, for example, while the five-member East African Community and the 10-member Association of Southeast Asian Nations (ASEAN) bring together countries with often common historical experiences and comparable political and economic conditions, the 53-member African Union faces enormous challenges in bringing its members together.

Since its creation in 1994, the North American Free Trade Agreement (NAFTA) has tried to open up trade among the United States, Canada and Mexico. But it has been handicapped by economic differences, minimal political support, public indifference and concerns about international terrorism and the enormous challenge of controlling illegal immigration into the United States. The United States is much wealthier than Mexico, elite groups in Mexico are more in favour of state intervention in the marketplace than those in the United States and Canada, trade unions in the United States have been critical of NAFTA, public opinion in Mexico is more tightly controlled and manipulated than in the United States and Canada, and both Mexico and Canada are wary of the political, economic and cultural power of their giant neighbour.

Elsewhere, the Union of South American Nations, the Central American Integration System, the Caribbean Community, the Economic Community of West African States, the South Asian Association for Regional Cooperation and the Pacific Islands Forum have all had teething troubles, but have made progress toward encouraging their member states to work together on issues of mutual interest, notably internal trade. With its common history, language, religion and culture, the Arab world would seem to offer strong prospects for integration, but the Arab League, the Council of Arab Economic Unity, the Gulf Cooperation Council and the Arab Maghreb Union have all been handicapped by the political and religious divisions of the region.

choices. Proponents argue that European integration has moved forward as a result of a combination of factors such as the commercial interests of economic producers, and the relative bargaining power of important governments (see Moravcsik, 1998).

Whatever the debates about how and why the EU evolved, there is no question that its institutions as a group today constitute an additional level of political authority in Europe, being involved in making decisions that impact both the governments and the residents of the member states. So while the debates over how the EU reached its present state are interesting, of more immediate interest now are attempts to understand what the EU has become, and to tie down its contemporary personality and character. Here again, there are many competing explanations and not much agreement.

Explaining the EU today

To summarize the discussion so far: there is no agreement on how best to understand the EU. It has many of the typical features of an inter-governmental organization, in that membership of the EU is voluntary, the balance of sovereignty lies with the member states, decision making is consultative and the procedures used to direct the work of the EU are based on consent rather than compulsion. At the same time, it also has some of the qualities of a state: it has internationally recognized external borders, there is an EU system of law to which all member states are subject, it has administrative institutions with authority that impacts the lives of Europeans, the balance of responsibility and power in many policy areas has shifted to the European level, and in some areas – such as trade – the EU functions as a unit.

That so much emphasis has been placed on analysing the EU as an international organization can be explained in part by the dominance in the academic debate of theories of international relations (IR). IR has made important contributions, to be sure, but it is concerned with interactions between or among states, and pays little attention to the internal characteristics and qualities of the states themselves. As long as the EU was mainly an association of states, this presented few problems, but once the EU began to develop a life and personality of its own, and its institutions accumulated stronger roles, so IR analyses became less useful. As a result, there has been growing support since the early 1990s for approaching the EU as a political system in its own right (Sbragia, 1992; Hix, 2005), and for making greater use of the analytical methods of comparative politics and public policy.

With its focus on institutions and processes, comparative politics can help us better understand how political power is exercised at the European level, how Europeans relate to EU institutions, and how EU-wide administration is influenced by political parties, elections and interest groups. In other words, instead of studying the motives and dynamics behind integration, we can try to better understand the structure of the EU using the comparative method, defined as the process by which different cases or samples are systematically studied in order to establish empirical relationships among two or more variables while the others are held constant (Lijphart, 1971). In other words, we can focus less on assessing the EU as an international organization, and more on comparing its institutions and procedures with those found in states, and in other regional groupings of states.

Meanwhile, the methods and theories of public policy can help us better understand the European decision-making process: the forces and limitations that come to bear on decision making, the relative balance of influence of the EU and the member states, and the steps involved in setting the European agenda, developing plans of action, implementing decisions and evaluating the results. There are many different models and theories of the policy process that are applicable to the EU case, including the process model, rational choice, incrementalism, group theory, elite theory and game theory – see Chapter 6 for more details.

The greatest problem with trying to encourage the use of comparative and public policy analyses is how quickly most European leaders and scholars of the EU shy away from the idea that there is a European government. The term *government* typically refers to the institutions and officials that make up the formal administrative structure of a state, and the context in which it is normally used implies that they have discrete powers to make laws and set the political agenda. But while the EU clearly has a network of 'governing' institutions and full-time officials, that network is rarely described in the language used to describe national systems of government. Instead, it is more usual to see the system of authority within the EU described as *governance*, a term which plays down the role of institutions and focuses instead on processes: governance is the exercise of authority through interactions involving a variety of actors, which in the case of the EU includes member state governments, EU institutions, interest groups and other sources of influence.

At the heart of any such discussion is the question of sovereignty, defined as the right to hold and exercise authority. A state is sovereign over its territory in that it has the power to decide what happens within that territory, and to make laws that govern the lives of the people who live there. More specifically, sovereignty is usually said to lie in the hands of the institutions that exercise control over the territory, which in democratic systems means the national executive, legislature and judiciary. Theoretically, there are no legal constraints on a sovereign power, only moral and practical ones – sovereign institutions are not answerable to any higher authority, but can only exert their powers to the extent that those under their authority will allow, and to the extent that they can practically implement their decisions.

The complaint made most often by critics of European integration is that it has involved the surrender of sovereignty. But whether or not this

International relations	The study of relations among states, focusing on alliances, diplomacy, war and peace, and based heavily on the development of theory.
Comparative politics	The study of different political systems, usually based on cases, and aimed at drawing up general rules about how those systems function.
Public policy	The study of the actions taken (or avoided) by governments and other authorities as they address the needs of society.
Sovereignty	The right to hold and exercise authority, usually associated with states and incorporating territorial integrity and political independence.

Figure 1.2   *Approaches to the study of the EU*

is true depends upon how we understand the EU and the changing role of its member states, the point being that sovereignty has not been lost so much as redistributed. Where sovereign power was once monopolized by the governments of the member states, it is now shared by those governments and by the institutions of the EU. But just how is it shared, and how do national governments interact with EU institutions?

One analytical concept that has gained popularity in recent years has been multi-level governance (MLG), which describes a system in which power is shared among the supranational, national, sub-national and local levels, with considerable interaction among them all (see Puchala, 1975; Marks, 1993; Bache and Flinders, 2004). The debate within academic circles about the value of MLG has been vigorous, but once again inconclusive. And what almost everyone has failed to acknowledge is that MLG is a conceptual cousin of two other, older concepts which also play a role in the debate. The most important of these is federalism, which has generated often heated debates among European political leaders and publics, more often being used as a red flag marking what the EU should be avoiding than as an objective measure of what it has become, or might become. Less important, but only because it has rarely been discussed in the context of the EU, is confederalism, a looser form of administration which historically has been a stepping stone to federalism.

Federalism

Although there is no fixed template for federalism (see Burgess, 2006, Chapter 1; Watts, 2008), it is best defined as an administrative system in which there are at least two levels of government (usually national and regional), each of which has independent powers but neither of which has supreme authority over the other. A federation usually consists of an elected general government with sole power over monetary, foreign and security policy, and separately elected local governments with powers over such issues as education and policing. There is a single state currency and a common defence force, a written constitution that spells out the relative powers of the different levels of government, a court that can arbitrate disputes between them, and at least two major sets of law, government, bureaucracy and taxation. The local units will also have their own constitutions and governments, and the cumulative interests of the local units help define the interests of the general government, which deals mainly with those matters better addressed at the state rather than the local level.

There are about two dozen federations in the world, including Australia, Canada, Germany, India, Mexico and Nigeria, but the best known and most thoroughly studied is the United States. It has been a federal republic since 1789, when the Articles of Confederation were replaced with a federal union by which states voluntarily gave up power over such areas as security, retaining their own sets of laws and a large measure of control over local government. American states today can raise their own taxes, and have independent powers over such policy areas as education, land use, the police and roads. But they are not allowed to make treaties with other states or foreign nations, or to have their own currencies, to levy taxes on imports and exports, or to maintain their own armies. Meanwhile, the federal government in Washington DC cannot unilaterally redraw the borders of a state, impose different levels of tax by state, give states different levels of representation in the US Senate (where each state has two representatives) or amend the US constitution without the support of two-thirds of the states. Meanwhile – an important point – the US constitution (in the Tenth Amendment) reserves to the states or the people all the powers not delegated to the national government by the constitution or prohibited by it to the states.

EU member states can still do almost everything that the states in the US model *cannot* do: they can make treaties, still have a near-monopoly over tax policy, maintain independent militaries, and have had no obligation to adopt the euro. The EU institutions, meanwhile, have few of the powers of the federal government in the US model: they cannot levy taxes, they can make few independent decisions on law and policy, they do not yet enjoy the undivided loyalty of most Europeans, and they do not have sole power to negotiate all agreements on behalf of the member states with the rest of the world. Despite this, the EU has several of the features of a federal system:

- It has a complex system of treaties and laws that are the functional equivalent of a constitution, are uniformly applicable throughout the EU, apply to all the member states and their citizens, are interpreted and protected by the European Court of Justice and coexist with national laws and constitutions.

- It has several levels of administration, ranging from the European to the local, that each have some autonomy in different areas of policy.
- In those policy areas where the member states have agreed to pool some or all authority – including trade, competition, agriculture and social policy – EU law supersedes national law.
- It has a directly elected representative legislature in the form of the European Parliament, which has growing powers over the process by which European laws are made. As those powers grow, so the powers of national legislatures are declining.
- Although still small by comparison to most national budgets, the EU budget gives the EU institutions an element of financial independence.
- The European Commission has the authority to oversee negotiations with third parties on behalf of all the member states, in those areas where it has been given authority by the member states.
- Eighteen of the EU member states have their own currency, the euro, meaning that they have transferred monetary policy from their own national central banks to the European Central Bank (ECB) in Frankfurt. In the wake of the eurozone crisis there has also been more transfer of responsibility for fiscal policy.

One way of looking at the practice of European federalism is to picture the EU as a network in which individual member states are increasingly defined not by themselves but in relation to their EU partners, and in which they prefer to interact with one another rather than with third parties because those interactions create incentives for self-interested cooperation (Keohane and Hoffmann, 1991:13–14). It has been argued that the EU has become 'cooptive', meaning that its participants have more to gain by working within the system than by going it alone (Heisler and Kvavik, 1973). Once they are involved, governments of the member states must take some of the responsibility for actions taken by the EU as a whole. (In practice, though, many are more than happy to blame the EU for Europe's problems, even though the EU has few autonomous powers, and its institutions are either directly or indirectly accountable to the governments and voters of the member states.)

Federalism is not an absolute or a static concept, and it has taken different forms in different situations and at different times according to the relative strength and nature of local political, economic, social, historical and cultural pressures. For example, the US model of federalism was in place long before that country began its westward expansion, explicitly includes a system in which the powers of the major federal government institutions are separated, checked and balanced, and was adopted more to avoid the dangers of chaos and tyranny than to account for social divisions. Furthermore, it has changed over time as a result of an ongoing debate over the relative powers of federal and state government. In India, by contrast, federalism was seen as a solution to the difficulty of governing a state that was already in place, and that had deep ethnic and cultural divisions; the union (federal) government has a fused executive and legislature on the British model, and while India is a federal republic like the United States, political reality has ensured that powers have often been more centralized in the hands of the union government.

The most committed European integrationists would like to see a federal United States of Europe in which today's national governments would become more like local governments, with the same kinds of powers as *Länder* governments in Germany or state governments in the United States. Before this could happen, however, there would need to be – at the very least – a directly elected EU government, a constitution, a common tax system, a substantial EU budget, a single currency and fiscal policy, a common military, and EU institutions and their leaders would have to be able to act on behalf of all the member states in foreign relations. But the political resistance to a shift of powers on this scale would be substantial, and just how far the process of integration would have to go before there was a federal Europe is debatable. There are several quasi-federations in existence – including Argentina, Britain, Spain and South Africa – which have some of the features of a federal system without having formally declared themselves as federations. In many ways the EU could be added to this list, and there is no reason why European federalism (should it ever come) would need to look like the US, Indian or even German models.

To complicate matters, the European model of integration has never been uniform across all the member states. The British and the French, for example, have long taken the lead on defence and security cooperation, while the EU's neutral or smaller member states have been less committed. In spite of efforts to remove barriers to the free movement of people, such barriers remain but are targeted mainly at stopping citizens of poorer EU states moving to richer states. Not all EU states have yet adopted the euro, and progress on the development of common monetary and fiscal policies has varied. These and examples like them have spawned multiple labels – Europe *à la carte*, multi-speed Europe, enhanced cooperation and differentiated integration, among them – which all have approximately the same meaning: member states that wish to proceed more rapidly with cooperation in a given policy area may do so, with no obligation on the others and without a formal extension of the powers of the EU (see Andersen and Sitter, 2006). It is one thing to understand a group of countries engaged on a shared project, but quite another when they pick and choose among the poli-

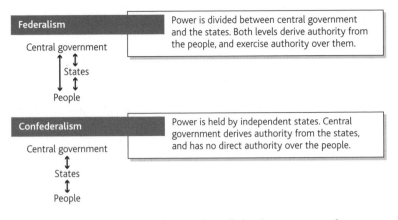

Figure 1.3 *Federalism and confederalism compared*

cies that most or least interest them. The result is what might be termed patchwork federalism.

Confederalism

While federalism is found only within states, confederalism is a looser system of administration that exists between or among states. In other words, two or more states retain their separate legal existence but give limited and specified powers to a central authority for reasons of convenience, mutual security or efficiency. Lister (1996, especially pp. 22–3) argues that if a federation is a union of peoples living within a single state, then a confederation is a union of states. The balance of power in a confederation is tilted towards the member states, central authorities are kept subordinate, the shifting of powers to those authorities must be approved by the states, ultimate control remains firmly fixed with the governments of the member states (which exercise it jointly in the various confederal decision-making bodies) and the loyalty of individuals remains focused on their home states. 'In a confederal setting,' Lister argues, 'the central institutions are both the agents of the member states and the instruments that enable those states to attain the degree of political union that is provided for in their treaty-constitutions' (Lister, 1996:83).

Expressed differently, the member states in a confederation are sovereign and independent, and the central authority is relatively weak, existing at the discretion of the members, and doing only what they allow it to do. If states were to form a confederation, then the citizens of those states would continue to relate directly to their own governments, and only indirectly to the higher authority (see Figure 1.3). Unlike a federal system, where government exercises power over both its constituent units and its citizens, and there is a direct relationship between citizens and each level of government, the higher authority in a confederation does not exercise power directly over individuals.

One example of confederalism in practice was the United States in 1781–88. Following the end of the War of Independence, the original 13 states cooperated under a loose agreement known as the Articles of Confederation, or a 'league of friendship'. Central government could declare war, coin money and conclude treaties, but could not levy taxes or regulate commerce, and founded its system of 'national' defence on a network of state militias. The Articles could not be amended without the approval of all 13 states, and treaties needed the consent of at least nine states. There was no national executive or judiciary, and the powers of the confederation lay in the hands of an elected Congress in which each state had one vote. Congress rarely met, and had no permanent home, so its powers were exercised by committees with variable membership. The assumption was that the states might cooperate enough eventually to form a common system of government, but they did not. It was only in 1787 that work began on developing the federal system of government that we find in the United States today.

Confederalism was also used in Germany in 1815–71, when a 39-member confederation was created under the domination of Austria and Prussia following the Congress of Vienna in 1815. Based on the old Holy Roman Empire, it was more an empire than a new state. Few restrictions were placed on the powers of the member kingdoms, duchies and cities, whose representatives met sporadically (just 16 times in the history of the confederation) in a diet (assembly) in Frankfurt. Amendments to the constitution needed near-unanimity, and most other measures required a two-thirds majority. Regular business was conducted by an inner committee in which the 11 largest states had one vote each, and the smallest had six among them. There were no common trade or communications policies, and the development of a common army was frustrated by the refusal of smaller states to cooperate (Carr, 1987:4–5).

Switzerland, too, was confederal until 1798, and although it now calls itself a federation, it has given up fewer powers to the national government than has been the case with other federations, such as Germany, the United States or Russia. Its 1874 constitution allocates specific powers to the federal government, the rest being reserved to the 20 cantons and six half-cantons. The Swiss encourage direct democracy by holding national referenda, have a Federal Assembly elected by proportional representation, and are governed by a seven-member Federal Council elected by the Assembly. Comparable arrangements can be found today in Bosnia and Hercegovina. Even though it is formally described as a federation, and the federal government has accumulated more powers with time, the two partner states – the Bosnian Muslim-

Croat Federation of Bosnia and Hercegovina and the Bosnian Republika Srpska – still have a high degree of independence. Each has its own system of government, with a president, a legislature, a court, a police force and other institutions, but they come together under a joint Bosnian government with a presidency that rotates every eight months between a Serb, a Bosnian Muslim and a Croat.

The EU has several of the features of a confederal system:

- The citizens of the member states do not relate directly to any of the EU institutions except Parliament (which they elect), instead relating to them mainly through their national governments. Despite their powers of making and implementing policy, the key institutions of the EU – the European Commission, the Council of the EU, the European Council and the ECJ – derive their authority not from the citizens of the member states, but from the leaders and governments of the member states. They are run either directly by national government leaders (the Council of the EU and the European Council), or are appointed by those leaders (the Commission and the ECJ).
- The member states still have their own separate identities, have their own systems of law, can sign bilateral treaties with other states, can act unilaterally in most areas of foreign policy and can argue that the EU institutions exist at their discretion. There is no European government in the sense that the EU has obvious leaders – such as a president, a foreign minister or a cabinet – with substantial power to make or direct policy for the EU member states. The most important political leaders in the EU are still the heads of government of the individual member states.
- There is no generalized European tax system. The EU raises funds in part through levies and customs duties, which are a form of tax, but the vast majority of taxes – income, corporate, property, sales, estate, capital gains, and so on – are raised by national or local units of government, which also make tax policy.
- There is no European military or defence system. The armies, navies and air forces of the member states still answer to the governments of the member states, although contingents have come together as the seeds of a European security force (see Chapter 9).
- The EU may have its own flag and anthem, but most of the citizens of the member states still have a greater sense of allegiance to their own national flags, anthems and other symbols, and there has been only limited progress towards building a sense of a European identity (see Chapter 2).

Interestingly, the concept of confederalism is rarely mentioned in conjunction with the EU (see Majone, 2006 and Moravcsik, 2007 for exceptions), in spite of how much it clearly offers to the debate. There are several possible reasons for this: federalism is more often found in practice and has been more thoroughly studied, federalism has been at the heart of the criticisms directed by eurosceptics at the EU, confederalism falls short of what the most enthusiastic European federalists would like for Europe, and in those few cases where confederalism has been tried in practice it has always evolved ultimately into a federal system. In his 1981 study of confederation and the EEC, Forsyth argued that studies of federalism seemed to have little connection with the realities of European integration, and that if we were to look more closely at historical examples of confederations, we would find that the EEC was clearly an economic confederation in both content and form (Forsyth, 1981:x, 183). Lister agrees, describing the EU as a 'jumbo confederation' whose member states and governments continue to dominate the EU's institutions (Lister, 1996: ch. 2).

Conclusions

What, then, is the EU? The answer depends upon who you ask, and what preferences and perspectives they bring to their analysis. It is clearly more than a conventional international organization, but it has not yet been comfortably slotted in to discussions about the state. It often works in the company of states, as in peacekeeping operations in world trouble spots, where EU soldiers might be operating alongside those from individual states, or in negotiations held under the auspices of the WTO, where there is a single EU trade representative who speaks on behalf of all 28 EU member states.

In spite of the time and energy devoted to first understanding the process of European integration, and then to understanding the personality of the EU, all that has been agreed is that nothing in the political lexicon captures the essence of the EU. It is, in other words, *sui generis*, or unique. To describe it as such is to avoid taking a position, and yet to take a position, and to describe the EU as federal, confederal, quasi-federal, an exercise in multi-level governance, or something else, is to invite immediate criticism. This is one of the great frustrations of studying the EU. No one can quite agree what it is, it constantly changes form, it is on the path to an end-state whose features are unknown, everyone has different opinions about when the end-state will be reached and it is unlikely that we will even know we have reached that end-state until many years after the event. Political scientist Michael Burgess summarizes the dilemma best when he argues that the most we can say is that 'the EU works in practice but not in theory' (Burgess, 2006:245).

But whatever theories and concepts we apply to its evolution, and however we choose to understand the EU today, there is little question that the laws and decisions that govern the lives of Europeans are being made less at the local or national level, and increasingly as a result of negotiations and compromises among the EU member states. Developments at the EU level have become as important for Europeans to understand as those in their national capitals. Not long ago an 'informed citizen' was someone who knew how their national system of government worked, how their national economy functioned and how their national society was structured. To be 'informed' now demands a broader horizon, and familiarity with a new set of institutions, processes and political, economic and social forces. As we will see, however, most Europeans still do not understand the EU or its effects, and much of what they have seen and heard of late – whether negative votes on national referenda, alarmed debates about the trials of the eurozone, or the often strident claims of eurosceptic political parties and media – has not been encouraging.

Opinions on the value of regional integration – and its long-term prospects – will remain divided as long as discussions are confused and obscured by questions and doubts about the conditions that encourage integration, the logic of the steps taken towards integration, and the end product. Comparing the EU with a conventional state can give us more insight, but we are still some way from agreement on what drives the process, and from understanding what we have created. The next three chapters will attempt to address some of the confusion by looking at the personality, evolution and structure of the EU.

Chapter 2
==============

The Idea of Europe

We live in a European world. It is a multicultural and multiracial world, to be sure, but most of it has been colonized at some point by one European power or another, and most people today live in societies that are either based on the European (that is, Western) political and cultural tradition or influenced by the norms and values of that tradition. The 'world culture' described by the American political scientist Lucien Pye (1966) is ultimately European in origin, and the terms *Western* and *European* are ultimately synonymous.

It is all the more ironic, then, that the idea of Europe remains hard to pin down. Its political and cultural qualities are hard to define (beyond being an accumulation of national identities), its geographical boundaries are debatable, and there is little agreement on what 'Europe' represents. Europeans have had much to unite them over the centuries, but they have had much more to divide them. They know little about each other, they speak many different languages, they have struggled with religious and social divisions, their views of their place in the world have changed, wars have broken out among them with depressing frequency, and the map of Europe has frequently had to be redrawn as a consequence.

But all is now changing. Although Europeans after the Second World War were too focused on rebuilding their economies and political systems to think much outside their own states and communities, they could not ignore their perilous location astride the divisions of the cold war. First the western part of the continent built ties through the European Community (followed by the EU), and then the end of the cold war brought the east into the equation. Through a complex process of trial and error, Europeans have learned more about each other, and have discovered their common interests, goals and values. Outsiders have also had to review their perception of Europe, which is now less a collection of sovereign states and more a regional collective. North American and Asian business and government leaders see the EU as a new source of competition for economic and political influence, while most Eastern Europeans and Russians see it as an assertive new force for democratic and free-market change.

This chapter attempts to get to grips with the idea of Europe. It reviews the changing identity of the region, pointing out that the concept of European cooperation is far from new. Many have written and spoken over the centuries of unity as a means of defending Europe against itself and outsiders, the difference today being that we see the practical application of these ideas. The chapter then tackles the troubling but critical question of defining the outer limits of Europe. Finally, it looks at the internal identity of Europe, the doubts about which are often used to question the achievements of European integration. What does Europe represent in political, economic, social and cultural terms, and how can its qualities help us better understand the significance and impact of European integration? Is there a European political, economic and social model, and a distinctively European way of interpreting domestic and international problems, and of addressing those problems? In short, what is the idea of Europe, and what – if anything – do Europeans have in common?

Europe's changing identity

Defining *Europe* and *European* has never been simple, thanks to disagreements about the outer limits of the region and the inner personality of its residents. The rise of the EU has added a new dimension to the challenge, obliging us to think of the inhabitants of the region not just as Greeks or Belgians or Poles or Latvians, but also as Europeans. And to add yet more spice to the debate, macro-integration has been accompanied by a micro-level loosening of ties as national minorities in several countries – such as the Scots in Britain, the Catalans in Spain, the Flemings and Walloons in Belgium, and multiple nationalities in the Balkans – express themselves more vocally, and remind us that European identity is being re-formed not only from above but also from below.

Europe has never been united, and its long history has been one of repeated fragmentation, conflict and the reordering of political boundaries. Parts of Europe have been brought together at different times for different reasons – beginning with the Romans and moving through the Franks to the Habsburgs, Napoleon and Hitler – but while many have dreamed of unification, it has only been since the Second World War that the idea of setting aside nationalism in the interests of regional cooperation has been put into practice. For the first time in its history, almost all of Europe has been engaged in a joint integrative exercise that has encouraged its inhabitants to think collectively rather than as members of smaller cultural or national groups that happen to inhabit the same land mass. But Europeans have often been better at defining themselves in relation to outsiders than in relation to each other.

The word *Europe* is thought to come from Greek mythology: Europa was a Phoenician princess who was seduced by Zeus disguised as a white bull, and was taken from her homeland in what is now Lebanon to Crete, where she later married the King of Crete. It is unclear when the term *European* was first applied to a specific territory or its inhabitants, but it may have been when the expansion of the Persian Empire led to war in the fifth century BC. Greek authors such as Aristotle began to make a distinction between the languages, customs and values of Greeks, the inhabitants of Asia (as represented by the Persians), and the 'barbarians' of Europe, an area vaguely defined as being to the north. Maps drawn up by classical scholars subsequently showed the world divided into Asia, Europe and Africa, with the boundary between Europe and Asia marked by the River Don and the Sea of Azov (Delanty, 1995:18–19; den Boer, 1995).

The Roman Empire – at its peak from approximately 200 BC to AD 400 – brought much of Europe for the first time under what has been described as a 'single cultural complex' (Cornell and Matthews, 1982). The Roman hegemony came with a common language (Latin), a common legal and administrative system, and – following the adoption of Christianity in AD 391 – a common religion. However, the Roman Empire included North Africa and parts of the Middle East, and because the Romans presided over an empire, there was no prevailing sense that everyone living under Roman rule was part of a region with a common identity. Roman hegemony ended in the last part of the fourth century AD, when Rome was invaded by the northern 'barbarians' and Europe broke up into feuding kingdoms.

The birth of Europe is often dated to the Early Middle Ages (500–1050), which saw the emergence of a common civilization with Christianity as its religion, Rome as its spiritual capital and Latin as the language of education. The new sense of a European identity was strengthened by a rift between the western and eastern branches of Christianity, the expansion of Frankish power from the area of what are now Belgium and the Netherlands, and the development of a stronger territorial identity in the face of external threats, notably from the Middle East. The retreat of Europeans in the face of Arab expansionism into Spain and southern France ended only in 732 with the epic victory over the Arabs by Charles Martel near Poitiers, in west-central France.

The term *European* was used by contemporary chroniclers to describe the forces under the command of Martel (Hay, 1957:25), but it would not become more widely used until after 800, when his grandson Charlemagne was crowned Emperor of the Romans by Pope Leo III and hailed in poems as the king and father of Europe. His Frankish Empire covered most of what are now France, Switzerland, Austria, southern Germany and the Benelux countries (an area that supporters of European unity in the 1950s liked to point out coincided with the territory of the six founding member states of the EEC).

Although the Frankish Empire helped promote the spread of Christianity, and passed on to his son after Charlemagne's death in 814, it was later subdivided and ultimately evolved into the Holy Roman Empire.

It was not until the fifteenth century that it became more usual for scholars to use the term *Europe*, which to outsiders was synonymous with *Christendom*. The power of monarchs rose, and challenges to the authority of the papacy led to the Reformation and the emergence of the modern state system. Religious divisions strengthened as Protestant churches expressed their independence from the Roman Catholic Church, and for much of the sixteenth and early seventeenth century Europe was destabilized by religious warfare. But this did not stop Europeans from embarking on voyages of overseas discovery, there was an expansion of education based on the classical works of Greek and Latin authors, and a revolution in science was sparked by the findings of Copernicus, Newton and others. These developments combined to give Europeans a new confidence and a new sense of their place in the world.

The earliest proponents of European unity were moved in part by their belief in a united Christian Europe and by concern about Europe's insecurity in the face of gains by the Turks in Asia Minor. But then the Renaissance (roughly 1350–1550) saw loyalty shift away from the Church, with growing support for individualism and republicanism, and the Church had become so divided by the end of the sixteenth century that the idea of a united Christian Europe was abandoned. Those who still championed the idea of regional unity (see Box 2.1 for examples) saw it as based less on a common religion than on addressing the religious causes of conflict and the growing threat of Habsburg power. But the borders of European states were achieving new permanence, and with the Peace of Westphalia in 1648, and two treaties bringing an end to the Thirty Years War and the Eight Years War and leaving many territorial adjustments in its wake, the grip of the state strengthened.

The tumult of the French Revolution and the Napoleonic wars encouraged several prominent thinkers and philosophers to explore the notion of European peace through unity. Jean-Jacques Rousseau wrote in favour of a European federation; Jeremy Bentham, in *A Plan for an Universal and Perpetual Peace* (1789), wrote of his ideas for a European assembly and a common army; Immanuel Kant's *Thoughts on Perpetual Peace* (1795) included suggestions for the achievement of world peace; and the Comte de Saint-Simon published a pamphlet in 1814 titled *The Reorganization of the European Community*, in which he argued in support of a federal Europe with common institutions, but within which national independence would be maintained and respected.

Box 2.1 Early thoughts on European cooperation

The challenge of how best to encourage Europeans to set aside their differences has exercised the minds of many thinkers over the centuries, some of their suggestions looking remarkably like elements of today's EU:

- Pierre Dubois (1255–1312), a French lawyer, suggested that the princes and cities of Europe form a confederal 'Christian Republic', overseen by a permanent assembly of princes working to ensure peace through the application of Christian principles. In the event of a dispute, a panel of nine judges could be brought together to arbitrate, with the Pope acting as a final court of appeal (Heater, 1992:10; Urwin, 1995:2).
- King George of Bohemia (1420–71) and his diplomatist Antoine Marini proposed a European confederation in response to the threat posed by the Turks in the mid-fifteenth century. Their plan involved an assembly meeting regularly and moving its seat every five years, a college of permanent members using a system of majoritarian decision making, a council of kings and princes and a court to adjudicate disputes (de Rougemont, 1966:71).
- The Duc de Sully (1560–1641) proposed a redrawing of administrative lines throughout Europe so as to achieve equilibrium of power, and the creation of a European Senate with 66 members serving three-year terms (Heater, 1992:30–5).
- William Penn (1644–1718) published in 1693 his *Essay Towards the Present Peace of Europe*, proposing a European diet or parliament that could be used for dispute resolution, and suggesting that quarrels might be settled by a three-quarters majority vote, weighted according to the economic power of the participating states: Germany would have twelve votes, France ten, England six, and so on (Heater, 1992:53–6; Salmon and Nicoll, 1997:3–6).
- The Abbé de Saint-Pierre (1658–1743) published in 1717 his *Project for Settling an Everlasting Peace in Europe*, arguing for free trade and a European Senate. His ideas inspired the German poet Friedrich von Schiller to write his 'Ode to Joy' in 1785, which – sung to the main theme of Beethoven's Ninth Symphony – is today the European anthem: 'Thy magic reunites those whom stern custom has parted, All men will become brothers under thy gentle wing'.

Those who attempted unity through conquest found themselves foiled by the sheer size of the task and by resistance from key actors to changes in the balance of power. The attempts by Charlemagne, Philip II of Spain and the Habsburgs to establish a European hegemony all failed, argues Urwin (1995:2), because of the 'complex fragmented mosaic of the continent ... [and] the inadequate technical resources of the would-be conquerors to establish and maintain effective control by force over large areas of territory against the wishes of the local populations'. Napoleon also failed. He saw himself as the 'intermediary' between the old order and the new, and hoped for a European association with a common body of law, a common court of appeal, a single currency and a uniform system of weights and measures. While he was able to bring what are now France, Belgium, the Netherlands, Luxembourg and parts of Germany and Italy under his direct rule, his ambitions ended at Waterloo in 1815.

Despite rapid economic, social and technological change, nineteenth-century Europe was driven by nationalism, boosted by the effects of the 1815 Congress of Vienna on great-power rivalry, and tracing its evolution through to the unification of Italy in the 1860s, of Germany in 1871, and beyond. It also prompted rivalry among European states in the competition to build colonial empires. Dreams of a United States of Europe nonetheless continued to inspire nineteenth-century intellectuals such as the French poet and novelist Victor Hugo, who in 1848 declared that the nations of Europe, 'without losing [their] distinctive qualities or ... glorious individuality, will merge closely into a higher unity and will form the fraternity of Europe ... . Two huge groups will be seen, the United States of America and the United States of Europe, holding out their hands to one another across the ocean.'

Nationalism fed into militarization and the outbreak in 1914 of the First World War, when all the competing tensions within Europe finally boiled over in what was effectively a European civil war. One of the consequences was chaos in much of central Europe, and the peace arranged under the 1919 Treaty of Versailles did little more than fan the fires of nationalism, particularly in Germany. The horrors of the war helped create a more receptive audience to notions of European integration and unity, the new debates involving not just intellectuals but politicians as well. The strongest support came from the leaders of smaller states that were tired of being caught up in big-power rivalry, and several made practical moves towards economic cooperation. Thus Belgium and Luxembourg created a limited economic union in 1922, including fixing the exchange rates of their currencies relative to each other, and in 1930 joined several Scandinavian states in an agreement to limit tariffs.

One of the champions of European unity was Count Richard Coudenhove-Kalergi (1894–1972), the son of an Austrian diplomat and his Japanese wife, and co-founder in 1922 of the Pan-European Union. In his 1923 manifesto *Paneuropa*, Coudenhove-Kalergi argued in favour of large-scale cooperation within a network of five 'global power fields': the Americas (excluding Canada), the Soviet Union, Eastern Asia (China and Japan), Paneuropa (including continental Europe's colonies in Africa and Southeast Asia) and Britain and its empire. He proposed a four-stage process for the achievement of European union: a conference of representatives from the 26 European states, the agreement of treaties for the settlement of European disputes, the development of a customs union and the drafting of a federal European constitution. His ideas failed to generate a mass following, but they impressed several leading figures in the arts, as well as several contemporary or future political leaders, including Georges Pompidou, Thomas Masaryk, Konrad Adenauer, Winston Churchill and two French prime ministers, Edouard Herriot and Aristide Briand.

The prevailing view in France was that European cooperation was an impossible dream, and that the best hope for peace lay in French strength and German weakness (Bugge, 1995:102). Herriot disagreed, and in 1924 he called for the creation of a United States of Europe, to grow out of the postwar cooperation promoted by the League of Nations. For his part, Briand called for a European confederation working within the League of Nations, and in May 1930 distributed a memorandum to governments outlining his ideas (Salmon and Nicoll, 1997:9–14). In it he wrote of the need for 'a permanent regime of solidarity based on international agreements for the rational organization of Europe'. He used such terms as 'common market' and 'European Union', and even listed specific policy needs, such as the development of trans-European transport networks, and anticipated what would later become the regional and social policies of the EU. But all thought of European cooperation was now swept aside in the gathering storm of tensions sparked by the rise of Nazism.

Adolf Hitler was obsessed with correcting the 'wrongs' of Versailles and creating a German 'living space'. He spoke of a 'European house', but only in terms of the importance of German rule over the continent in the face of the perceived threat from communists and 'inferior elements' within and outside Europe. The nationalist tensions that had not been resolved by the First World War now boiled over once again into pan-European conflict. Almost every European state was dragged in, and Hitler was able to expand his Reich to include Austria, Bohemia, Alsace-Lorraine and most of Poland, and to occupy much of the rest of continental Europe.

With the end of the Second World War in 1945, the need to deal with the pre-existing economic and social divisions of Europe was joined in European calculations by the question of how to deal with the ideological rift between a capitalist west and a socialist east. Ironically, it was the very depth of the threats posed to Europe by the cold-war dominance of the United States and the Soviet Union that was to allow the dreamers of unity to begin taking the substantive actions needed to move beyond theory and philosophy into the realms of practical political, economic and social change. At no time in its history had Europe been so divided, or had its future been so patently out of its control.

The dismay at the depths to which it had been reduced by centuries of conflict now sparked a new interest in European cooperation and independence; the first modest step was taken in 1952 with the creation of the ECSC, and the second in 1958 by the creation of the EEC (see Chapter 3).

Western Europeans continued to build ties among themselves during the 1960s and 1970s, so that by the time the cold war came to an end in 1990–91, the foundations for the economic integration of the entire continent were firmly in place. There are still many divisions: Eastern Europe (or Central Europe, as some prefer to call it) has not yet entirely rid itself of the heritage of state socialism, Germans still distinguish between those from the east and those from the west, Italy is culturally and economically divided into north and south, and Britain is an amalgam of English, Scottish, Welsh and Northern Irish influences. Cultural and economic differences also continue to complicate European identity: the Mediterranean states to the south are distinctive from the maritime states to the west or the Scandinavian states to the north. And the rivalries, suspicions and stereotypes that have their roots in centuries of conflict still surface periodically.

But compared with just a generation ago, what unites Europeans has become more distinct and important than what divides them. Europeans are more individually mobile, the communications revolution has made Europe a smaller place, there has been a growth in intra-European trade, and there is a new awareness of what Europeans have in common and of how their values and priorities differ from those of the United States, China and Russia. The EU may be suffering the effects of rising euroscepticism and the crisis in the eurozone, but at no time in its history has Europe been so integrated, so peaceful and so aware of itself as a single region as it is today.

Where is Europe?

In spite of the dramatic recent changes in the meaning of the terms *Europe* and *European,* differences remain. First, few European states are culturally homogeneous, and there is no such thing as a European people or race. The repeated reordering of territorial lines over the centuries has bequeathed to almost every European state a multinational society, and has left several national groups – such as the Germans, the Poles, the Basques and the Irish – divided by national frontiers. Many states have also seen large influxes of immigrants since the 1950s, including Algerians to France, Turks to Germany and South Asians to Britain. Not only is there no dominant culture, but most Europeans rightly shudder at the thought of their separate identities being subor-

Table 2.1   *Official languages of the EU*

Bulgarian	French	Maltese
Croatian	German	Polish
Czech	Greek	Portuguese
Danish	Hungarian	Romanian
Dutch	Irish	Slovak
English	Italian	Slovene
Estonian	Latvian	Spanish
Finnish	Lithuanian	Swedish

dinated to some kind of homogenized Euroculture; at least part of the resistance to integration is generated by concerns about threats to national identity.

Second, the linguistic divisions of Europe are substantial: its natives speak more than 40 languages, which are defended as symbols of national identity. Multilingualism in Europe also means that all official EU documents are translated into the 24 official languages of the member states (see Table 2.1), although the work of EU institutions is increasingly carried out in English and French. Supported by its rapid spread as the language of global commerce and diplomacy, the dominance of English grows, and it is slowly becoming the language of Europe. This worries the French in particular and other Europeans to some extent, but it at least gives Europeans a way of talking to each other, and helps reduce the cultural differences that divide them.

Third, while the histories of European states overlapped for centuries as they colonized, went to war or formed alliances with each other, those overlaps often emphasized their differences rather than giving them the sense of a shared past. When it came, European integration grew in part out of the reactive idea of ending the conflicts that arose from those differences. Historical divisions were further emphasized by the external colonial interests of European powers, which encouraged them to develop competing sets of external priorities at the expense of cultivating closer ties with their immediate neighbours. Even now, Britain, France, Spain and Portugal have close ties with their former colonies, while Eastern European states have still not entirely shrugged off the heritage of Soviet-style state socialism.

Finally, it is not clear exactly where Europe physically begins and ends. It is often described as a 'continent', but continents are defined by geographers as large, unbroken and discrete land masses that are almost entirely surrounded by water. Strictly speaking, Europe is no more than part of the Asian continent, but Europeans are not Asians. The western, northern and southern boundaries of Europe are conveniently demarcated by the Atlantic, the Arctic and the Mediterranean, but there is no handy geographical feature to mark Europe's eastern boundary. It is usually defined as running down the Ural Mountains, across the Caspian Sea, along the southern edge of the Caucasus Mountains, across the Black Sea and through the Bosporus Strait. But these are no more than convenient physical features that have been adopted despite political and social realities.

The Urals are considered a boundary of Europe only because they were nominated as such by an eighteenth-century Russian cartographer, Vasily Tatishchev, so that Russia could claim to be an Asian as well as a European power. If we accept them as a boundary, then six former Soviet republics – Belarus, Moldova, Ukraine and the three Baltic states (Estonia, Latvia and Lithuania) – are part of Europe. The Baltic states offer no problems, because they have historically been bound to Europe, and are now members of the EU and NATO. But Belarus, Moldova and Ukraine are all still caught in a residual struggle for influence between Russia and Europe. Belarus is a political outlier, having resisted the wave of democracy that has swept over most of its neighbours. Ukraine underwent its famous Orange Revolution in 2004, but an initial interest in EU membership has been replaced with a reorientation since 2010 towards Russia. In Moldova, meanwhile, political leaders have hinted at an interest in EU membership, but the country is poor and has strong historical and cultural links with Russia.

The major problem with the Urals is that they are deep in the heart of Russia. Russians are sometimes defined as European, and Russia west of the Urals was long known as Eurasia because of the distinctions imposed on the region by Europeans, but opinion on Russia's identity remains mixed: some Russians see their country as part of Europe and the West, others distrust the West and see Russia as distinctive from both Europe and Asia, and yet others see it as a bridge between the two (Smith, 1999:50). The most obvious problem with defining Russia as European is that three-quarters of its land area is east of the Urals in Siberia, and most Siberians – including Buryats, Yakuts and Siberian Tatars – are unquestionably non-European. Further south, meanwhile, the Caucasus Mountains present similar problems as a boundary; should the republics of Armenia, Azerbaijan and Georgia be considered European? They are all members of the Council of Europe, after all, and there have been hints here, too, of EU and NATO membership down the line. But are they too politically and economically tied to Russia?

In central Europe, changes in the balance of power long meant that the Poles, the Czechs and the Slovaks were caught in the crossfire of great-power competition, which is why this region was known as the 'lands between'. The west looked on the area as a buffer against Russia, a perception that was helped by the failure of its people to form lasting states identified with dominant national groups. During

the cold war the distinctiveness of Eastern Europe was further emphasized by the ideological divisions between east and west, despite the
historical ties that meant Poland was actually closer to Western Europe
than to Russia. But the end of the cold war meant a rapid reorientation
of central Europe towards the west, and all states in the region are now
members of the EU and NATO.

For their part, the Balkans occupy an ambiguous position between
Europe and Asia, being a geographical part of the former but historically drawn towards the latter. They were long regarded as an extension of Asia Minor, and until relatively recently were still described by
Europeans as the Near East (Hobsbawm, 1991:17). Frequent changes
of authority – whether it was the Macedonians, the Romans, the
eastern Roman empire, Slavic tribes, Christianity, the Kingdom of
Hungary, the Venetians or the Ottoman Turks – has helped create what
Delanty (1995:51–2) describes as 'frontier societies in the intermediary
lands' between great powers. The Slavs in particular were split between
those who accepted Catholicism, Greek Orthodoxy or Islam, which
resulted in cultural heterogeneity in spite of the greater linguistic
homogeneity that existed among Slavs than among the peoples of
Western Europe (Delanty, 1995:54). Slavs continue to have affiliations
with Russia, which is part of the reason why NATO was wary of
becoming too deeply involved in the conflicts in Bosnia and Kosovo in
the 1990s. Since the break-up of Yugoslavia there has been a trend for
Balkan national groups to look to the EU; the Slovenians were the first
to become members in 2004, Croatia followed in 2013, Macedonia,
Montenegro and Serbia have been accepted as candidate countries and
other Balkan republics have broached the prospect of eventual EU
membership.

By far the most troubling question in the debate about the boundaries of Europe relates to Turkey. The Bosporus is usually regarded as
the border between Europe and Asia, which means that about 4 per
cent of the land area of Turkey lies inside Europe. Turkey indicated its
interest in joining the EEC as early as 1963, and is currently considered
a candidate country, meaning that its application for membership has
been accepted and negotiations on the terms of membership are under
way. But numerous problems stand in the way, including its relative
poverty, doubts about its democratic record, its large size, and the fact
that it is a Muslim state (see Box 2.2.)

So where, then, is Europe? If its borders with Turkey, the Caucasus
and Russia are taken as its eastern limits, then it consists today of 40
countries: the 28 members of the EU, three other Western European
states (Iceland, Norway and Switzerland) and nine Eastern European
states. If a broader definition of Europe's boundaries is accepted, then
it includes four more countries: Armenia, Azerbaijan, Georgia and
Turkey. Stretching the limits of credibility, some (such as former Italian

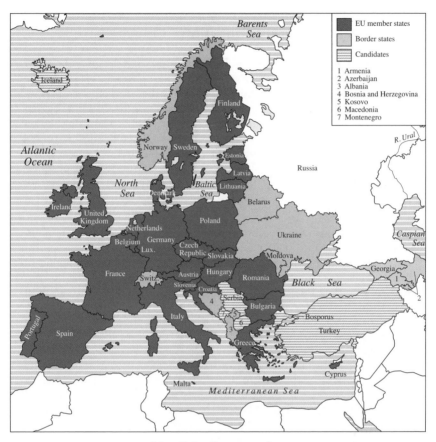

Map 2.1   *Europe today*

prime minister Silvio Berlusconi) have even suggested that Israel should be considered European, and might qualify for EU membership, but this view has little support.

Whatever Europe's external boundaries, its inner personality has been driven by two critical developments. First, the cold-war division of Europe has faded into the mists of history as the political, economic and ideological differences between Western and Eastern Europeans have diminished and the bonds among them have tightened and strengthened. Political and economic investments have flowed from west to east, and workers in search of new opportunities have moved from east to west. Second, enlargement of the EU has helped reduce the distinctions between 'Europe' and the 'European Union'. As recently as 2004, less than half the states of Europe were members of the EU, which was home to only two-thirds of Europeans. Today, and taking the 40-state definition of Europe, the EU includes 70 per cent of

Box 2.2 The Turkish question

When it comes to defining the borders of Europe, and deciding the limits of EU enlargement, the Turkish question has a special place in the debate. The EEC agreed as long ago as 1963 that Turkish membership was possible, and it became an associate member of the Community that same year. It applied for full membership in 1987, a customs union between the EU and Turkey came into force in December 1995, Turkey was formally recognized as an applicant country in 1999 and negotiations on EU membership opened in 2006. But a string of difficult questions continues to muddy the waters, not least being the matter of whether or not Turkey is a European country. If EU member Cyprus is European, then presumably so is Turkey, in geographical terms at least.

But the problems with Turkey are less geographical than they are political, economic and religious. The EU has agreed three criteria for aspiring members, known as the Copenhagen conditions: an applicant must be democratic, capitalist and willing to adopt the existing body of EU laws. Turkey is clearly capitalist, and has made great efforts to meet the third of these requirements, most notably abolishing the death penalty in 2004. But while it is capitalist it is also poor, with a per capita gross domestic product (GDP) less than one-third that of the EU (although greater than that of EU members Romania and Bulgaria). Current EU members fear not only that billions of euros in subsidies and investments will be diverted to Turkey if it joins the EU, but that large numbers of Turks will move to wealthier parts of the EU in search of jobs. As to Turkish democracy, its record on human rights has been poor, with concerns – for example – about the role of the military in politics, about the treatment of the Kurdish minority, and about women's rights. There is also the unresolved question of the division of Cyprus into Turkish and Greek sectors.

But the most telling – if usually unspoken – concern about prospective Turkish membership of the EU is religious. Turkey is a Muslim state, and even though its brand of Islam is mainly secular and western-oriented, the potential difficulties of integrating 73 million Turkish Muslims into a club that often emphasizes its Christian credentials, and that has been struggling with accommodating its own existing Muslim minorities, are substantial. If Turkey was small, poor and Muslim (like Albania) it might be less of a problem, but its size means that it would become the second largest member state of the EU by population after Germany. The resulting doubts have divided European public and political opinion, which tends to focus on the challenges rather than the opportunities offered by Turkish membership. Among the latter are a large new market and labour pool, and the importance of Turkey in helping Europe strengthen its geopolitical relationship with the Middle East and the Muslim world. (For further discussion, see Morris, 2005.)

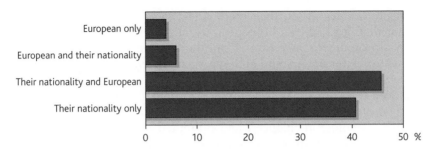

Figure 2.1 *Changing European identities*
How Europeans self-identify. Data from European Commission, *Eurobarometer* 61, Spring 2004.

the states of Europe, covers 74 per cent of the land area of Europe, is home to 85 per cent of Europeans and accounts for 92 per cent of the economic wealth of Europe. We may still quibble about the eastern borders of Europe, but the differences between the EU and Europe are fast disappearing.

All these changes have reordered the way in which Europeans regard one another and approach their understanding of the division of policy interests. Even in spite of the recent troubles of the EU, Europeans are slowly transferring their loyalty from individual states to a more broadly defined European identity, and are thinking of themselves less as Germans or Belgians or Slovaks and more as Europeans. It has been a slow process, to be sure, but recent opinion polls have found that slightly more than half of Europeans think of themselves as European in addition to their own nationality (see Figure 2.1) and that about 60 per cent feel proud to be European. Fligstein (2008:250) divides Europeans into three camps: one (making up about 10–15 per cent of the population) has deep economic and social ties to Europe, from which it benefits materially and culturally; a second (40–50 per cent) is aware of what is going on across borders but is still wedded to national language, culture, and politics; the third (40–50 per cent), made up mainly of older, poorer, and less educated Europeans, is more wedded to home, does not travel or consume culture from other societies, and is more fearful of European integration.

Critics of integration have long argued that one of the greatest dangers posed by integration is the homogenization that comes as member states lose their individuality in the move towards Europe-wide standards and regulations. They argue that authority is shifting from national governments mandated by the people towards a European superstate that lacks such a mandate. But this depends upon how the EU is understood; if it is a European federation, then many problems remain. But if it is a confederation, in which citizens have the closest ties to their home states, and national governments set the pace of regional integration, then there is less to be concerned about. And rather than leading to a homogenized Europe, integration has actually helped promote a reassertion of cultural differences as Europeans have grown to better understand and appreciate the variety of the regions in which they live.

Indeed it is sometimes argued that a Europe of the regions may come to rival or even replace a Europe of the states. In the interests of correcting economic imbalances, and prompted by growing demands for greater decentralization, European states began to regionalize their administrative systems in the 1960s, and as a result regions have emerged as important actors in politics and policy (Keating and Hooghe, 1996). They have come to see the EU as an important source of investment and of support for minority cultures, and in some cases this has given more confidence to nationalist movements (such as those in Scotland and Catalonia), as they feel less dependent on the support of the state governments. It has also reduced the overall importance of interstate relations within the EU, and drawn new attention to interregional relations. The logical conclusion is that forces of this kind will lead to Europe centralizing and decentralizing at the same time, with the member states as we know them today squeezed in the middle.

What is a European?

There is an old and well-worn joke that heaven is where the police are British, the cooks are French, the mechanics are German, the lovers are Italian and everything is organized by the Swiss. Meanwhile, hell is where the police are German, the cooks are British, the mechanics are French, the lovers are Swiss and everything is organized by the Italians. National stereotypes such as these abound in Europe (as they do everywhere), some based on a modicum of truth, some with no redeeming qualities, and most nonetheless perpetuated by the media and popular culture (see Connelly, 2009). But even if such stereotypes are typically wrong (or wrong-headed), what they tell us is that Europe is a region of diversity, with every European state claiming to have a distinctive personality arising out of a combination of history, culture, norms and values, while also often having strong opinions about their neighbours.

The effects were reflected in a 2013 poll carried out by the Pew Research Centre (see Table 2.2), which asked the residents of eight European countries which of their neighbouring states they found most and least trustworthy, arrogant and compassionate. The dominance of Germany is noteworthy, particularly the extent to which it is regarded as the most trustworthy by all except Greece (unsurprisingly, given tensions over addressing the sovereign debt crisis). Opinion was divided on who was the least trustworthy, but – interestingly – Poles regarded

Table 2.2 *Stereotyping in Europe*

Views in:	Most trustworthy	Least trustworthy	Most arrogant	Least arrogant	Most compassionate	Least compassionate
Britain	Germany	France	France	Britain	Britain	Germany
France	Germany	Greece	France	France	France	Britain
Germany	Germany	Greece/Italy	France	Germany	Germany	Britain
Italy	Germany	Italy	Germany	Spain	Italy	Germany
Spain	Germany	Italy	Germany	Spain	Spain	Germany
Greece	Greece	Germany	Germany	Greece	Greece	Germany
Poland	Germany	Germany	Germany	Poland	Poland	Germany
Czech Rep.	Germany	Greece	Germany	Slovakia	Czech Rep.	Germany

Source: Pew Research Centre Global Attitudes Survey (2013), 'The New Sick Man of Europe: the European Union'. At http://www.pewglobal.org.

Germans as both most and least trustworthy. The Germans and the French were regarded as the most arrogant, with even the French regarding themselves as arrogant, while there was a tendency for each country to consider itself both the least arrogant and the most compassionate, and Germany won the stakes for being least compassionate.

How is it possible, out of this melange of competing identities and opinions, to pin down a distinctive European personality? Surely the histories, cultures and social structures of European states are too deeply ingrained to make such an exercise credible? And those who doubt the wisdom and effects of European integration are more than ready to point to the many instances where EU member states still squabble and disagree. The open disagreement over the US-led invasion of Iraq in 2003 is a prime example, often touted as evidence of the underlying weaknesses of the European experiment, notably in the area of foreign policy. But what almost all the analysts and observers failed to mention was that the disagreement was primarily between European governments, and not between Europeans themselves. Indeed, opinion polls found a near-uniformity of opinion across Europe, with 70–90 per cent of those polled expressing opposition to the war, even in countries whose governments supported the war, including Britain, Spain, Italy, Denmark and the Netherlands.

At the same time, a growing body of research indicates that there are many common values and opinions across the EU on a broad array of issues, ranging from welfarism to capital punishment, immigration, international relations, environmental protection and the relationship between Church and State. Much remains to be done to better understand and clarify the commonalities, and to move the analysis beyond the fascination with what divides rather than unites Europe, but the outlines have achieved a new clarity in recent years, particularly since the end of the cold war finally allowed Europeans from east and west to begin expressing and exerting themselves without being limited by the constraints of rivalry between the Americans and the Soviets. (For more details on the arguments that follow, see McCormick, 2010. See also Fligstein, 2008.)

The term *Europeanism* is usually understood to mean support for the process of European integration, but it is also used to signify the collective values and principles associated with Europe and Europeans. An initial attempt was made to pin down those values in 2003, when – inspired by the massive demonstrations against the impending invasion of Iraq that were held in every major European city on 15 February – the German and French philosophers Jürgen Habermas and Jacques Derrida hailed the birth of a 'European public sphere', noted that there had been a reaction to nationalism that had helped give contemporary Europe 'its own face' and argued that a 'core Europe' (excluding Britain and Eastern Europe) should be built as a counterweight to US influence in the world. They listed several features of what they described as a common European 'political mentality', including secularization, support for the welfare state, a low threshold of tolerance for the use of force and support for multilateralism (Habermas and Derrida, 2003 [2005]).

During the cold war, the outlines of a distinctive European identity had been hard to find, divided as the subcontinent was by the lines of the conflict, and subject as most European states were to the political lead of the United States (in the west) or of the Soviet Union (in the east). Since then, however, and encouraged by the twin effects of European integration and the removal of cold-war ideological and social divisions, there has been an emerging sense that Europeans have much in common, and a set of values that give them a unified and distinctive identity. The key elements of Europeanism can be found in four major areas: political values, economic values, social values and attitudes towards international relations (see Table 2.3).

On the political front, Europeans are clearly champions of democracy, human rights and the rule of law, but they also have a particularly European view of the nature and purposes of democracy. Institutionally, the structure and distribution of power is driven by the principles of parliamentary government, which – while not peculiar to Europe – were born in Europe and today form the basis of all national European political systems, albeit with local variations. One effect of the system is that political parties play a more central role in European

Table 2.3   *Shared European values*

Democracy	Cosmopolitanism	Welfarism
Human rights	Multiculturalism	Secularism
The rule of law	Communitarianism	Multilateralism
Declining state identity	Positive rights	Smart power
Declining patriotism	Capitalism	Civilian power

Based on McCormick, 2010.

politics than they do in much of the rest of the world (in spite of the many suggestions that European party systems are on the decline), the distribution of seats in national legislatures determining the make-up of governments, and the variety and ideological spread of parties reflecting and driving the diversity of voter opinion (Mair, 2001). The arithmetic of elections tends to produce coalition governments, which in turn means that Europeans are familiar with the pressures and demands of political compromise.

In terms of how they identify themselves politically, Europeans live in the part of the world where the modern state system first emerged and where many now argue that it is most rapidly declining. As state borders have become more porous and Europeans move and travel in greater numbers to neighbouring states, so identification with states has declined and a sense of patriotism (love of country) has also declined, to be replaced by a belief in democratic ideas, otherwise known as constitutional patriotism (see Müller, 2007). Europeans have become more aware of their national and European identities, and this has encouraged them to adopt views of the world, and of their place in it, that are driven more by cosmopolitanism and multiculturalism. The first is the idea that humans can associate themselves more with universal ideas and that they belong to a single moral community that exists above the level of states and nations (for background, see Rumford, 2007, and Beck and Grande, 2007). The second suggests that Europeans have become more used to contacts and integration with other cultures and no longer see the world exclusively from their own national or cultural perspective. But this is only a factor in relation to other Europeans; when it comes to racial or religious tolerance the European record is not so strong.

In terms of how they conceive political rights, Europeans stand in particular distinction to Americans; while the latter emphasize individual rights and place an emphasis on self-reliance, Europeans are more communitarian in their approach: they support more of a balance between individual and community interests, and are more tolerant of the argument that in some cases society may be a better judge of what is best for individuals than vice versa (for more on the qualities of communitarianism, see Etzioni, 1998). At the heart of this concept are positive rights, meaning those which permit or oblige action, perhaps making way for the offering of services by the state, and which stand in contrast to negative rights, which prevent actions by others (in areas such as freedom of speech and religion, for example). Hutton (2003:54–8) argues that while the American liberal definition of rights does not extend beyond the political to the economic and social, the European conception of rights is broader, including free health care, free education, the right to employment insurance, and so on.

On the economic front, Europeans are committed capitalists and sup-porters of the free market, but they place a premium on the redistribu-tion of wealth and opportunity, and on the responsibility of government to maintain a level playing field. As Prestowitz puts it, a key difference between the American and European economic models is that 'Americans emphasize equality of opportunity, [while] Europeans focus more on equality of results' (Prestowitz, 2003:236–7). Europeans have a high level of tolerance for the collective society: the idea that key services (such as education and health care) should be managed and offered by the government and paid for out of taxes. One American observer – Jeremy Rifkin – contrasts the American emphasis on economic growth, personal wealth and individual self-interest with the European emphasis on quality of life and community (Rifkin, 2004). Europeans have not yet been able to address the prob-lems of persistent poverty and unemployment (just as no one has), but their welfarist approach places an emphasis on self-reliance and on the private delivery of key services.

On the social front, there may not yet be a distinctive European society, and regional integration has not been able to overcome the considerable barriers posed by language differences, by the absence of pan-European media, and by cultural differences (see Box 2.3), and yet there are many trends which suggest substantial agreement among Europeans on a variety of issues. For example, they are willing to concede that government may have a role in making moral decisions or defining the social choices of individuals; this can be seen in relation to issues such as abortion, capital punishment, gun control, censorship, doctor-assisted suicide and same-sex civil unions and marriage.

In few social areas is there a more distinctive European identity than in religion; the evidence suggests that Europe is the only part of the world where belonging to a religion is on the decline, and much of the explanation for this can be found in history. Despite the central role that the Church has played in European public and political life over the centuries, it has never been a uniting force (Dunkerley *et al.*, 2002:115). First there was the division between the Latin and Orthodox Churches, then the division between the Catholic and Protestant Churches, and more recently there has been the rise of religious diversity as new immigrants have brought Islam, Hinduism, Buddhism, Sikhism and other religions into the equation. During the discussions over the European constitutional treaty, it was suggested that the preamble should include reference to the Christian heritage of Europe, but this was turned down on the grounds that it would not reflect the religious diversity of the new Europe, and would send a particularly worrying message to Muslims and Jews (see discussion in Schlesinger and Foret, 2006).

European society is also distinguished by important demographic changes that are routinely quoted as sources of concern and as indicating weaknesses in the future success of Europe, and yet are at the core of European identity. Prime among these is a declining birth rate, which has helped bring about a fundamental redefinition of the family: fewer Europeans are marrying (or, at least, more are delaying marriage), divorce rates are growing, fewer Europeans are having children and one-parent or childless households are common. At the same time, Europeans are working fewer hours and are taking more time off (a 40-hour week and five weeks of paid holiday are now the norm), which is changing their attitudes towards both work and leisure. But how far they can continue to sustain an ageing population while working fewer hours is currently the topic of much debate.

In international relations, Europeans have a preference for multilateralism, the use of smart power (a balance between soft power – encouragement and opportunity – and hard power – coercion and force; see Chapter 9) and for using civilian means for dealing with conflict. They take the liberal view of the international system, arguing that states can and must cooperate and work together on matters of shared interest, and placing an emphasis on the importance of international organizations and international law. The European view once again stands in particular contrast to that of the United States, which has a reputation for the promotion of national interests, an emphasis on military solutions to problems, and a distrust of international organizations. Where many Europeans see themselves as members of an international system, and prefer to act multilaterally, there are still many Americans for whom there are only two realistic options: American leadership, or isolationism.

These four sets of features can help us pin down the nature of Europeanism, and of what it means to be a European, but – just as with Europe's eastern borders – it is not easy to draw firm lines around those features, many of which are shared with other parts of the world. It is also important to emphasize that these features or not absolutes, but are only tendencies. In geographical, political, economic and social terms it has never been easy to pin down Europe, particularly given its enormous internal diversity. But one of the effects of integration has been to encourage more efforts to understand what Europeans have in

Box 2.3   Promoting European culture

The stability of a state is usually predicated upon a high degree of legitimacy (public acceptance), which is in turn predicated upon a strong sense of national identity, in which a sense of a common culture plays a critical role. Conversely, the instability of states often arises out of social and cultural divisions, which weaken the sense of a common national identity. France is an example of a state with a high level of cultural unity, while British national identity is weakened by divisions among the English, the Scots, the Welsh and the Northern Irish, and Belgium is weakened by divisions between its Flemish and Wallonian communities.

Historically and culturally speaking, Europeans have long been insular and inward-looking, often knowing little about the history or culture of even their closest neighbours. The EU has tried to address this problem by promoting the idea of a common European culture (even though such promotion may be anathema to some – how can culture be legislated or 'promoted' as a policy goal?). Despite the results of Eurobarometer polls showing a majority in favour of cultural policy being left to the member states, since the early 1990s the EU has been committed to contributing to 'the flowering of the cultures of the Member States' with a view to improving knowledge about the culture and history of Europe, conserving European cultural heritage, and supporting and supplementing non-commercial cultural exchanges and 'artistic and literary creation'.

What this has so far meant in practice has been support for the restoration of historic buildings, training schemes in conservation and restoration, preserving regional and minority languages, subsidising the translation of works by European authors (particularly into less widely spoken languages), awarding prizes in architecture, literature and music and supporting cultural events. For example, the EU has funded a Youth Orchestra and a Baroque Orchestra to bring young musicians together, and since 1985 has declared European 'Capitals of Culture' (including Essen in Germany, Marseilles in France and Riga in Latvia).

While the sentiments behind these projects are laudable, it is difficult to see how cultural exchanges and the development of a European cultural identity can work unless they are driven by Europeans themselves. It is easy to argue that Shakespeare, Michelangelo, Voltaire, Goethe, Picasso and Mozart are all part of the heritage of Europe, but the notion of a modern pan-European popular culture is a beast of an entirely different stripe. Even the most mobile of art forms – film and rock music – come up against the barrier of national preferences, and little that is not produced in English has had commercial success outside its home market.

common. There is still much resistance among political leaders, academics and Europeans themselves to the idea that generalizations can be drawn across national borders, but the common themes in both the meaning of Europe and in the values and norms that are represented by Europe are easier to identify today than ever before.

Conclusions

The idea of European unity is nothing new. The conflicts that brought instability, death and changes to the balance of power in Europe over the centuries prompted many to propose unification – or at least the development of a common system of government – as a means to the achievement of peace. The rise of the state system undermined these proposals, but interstate conflict ultimately reached a level at which it became clear that only cooperation could offer a path to peace. The two world wars of the twentieth century – which in many ways began as European civil wars – underlined the dangers of nationalism and of the continued promotion of state interests at the expense of regional interests.

New thinking has dramatically altered the idea of Europe over the past two generations, and the nature of the internal relationship among the states that make up Europe has been transformed. Not everyone is a supporter of European integration, and the criticisms of the directions it has been taking have grown, but there has been a generational shift since 1945, as memories of the horrors of the Second World War fade into history, and the idea of Europe is one associated with peace and progress. Where intellectuals and philosophers once argued in isolation that the surest path to peace in Europe was cooperation, or even integration, the costs of nationalism are now more broadly appreciated, ensuring a wider and deeper consideration of the idea of regional unity.

Europeans still have much that divides them, and those differences are obvious to anyone who travels across the region. There are different languages, cultural traditions, legal structures, education and health-care systems, social priorities, cuisines, modes of entertainment, patterns of etiquette, styles of dress, approaches to planning and building cities, ways of spending leisure time, attitudes towards the countryside and even sides of the road on which to drive (the British, Irish, Cypriots and Maltese drive on the left; everyone else on the right). Europeans also have differences in the way they govern themselves, and in what they have been able to achieve with their economies and social welfare systems.

Increasingly, however, Europeans have more in common. The economic and social integration that has taken place under the auspices of the EU and its precursors since the early 1950s has brought the needs and priorities of Europeans closer into alignment. It has also encouraged the rest of the world to see Europeans less as citizens of separate states and more as citizens of the same economic bloc, if not yet the same political bloc. Not only has there been integration from the Mediterranean to the Arctic Circle, but the 'lands between' – which spent the cold war as part of the Soviet bloc and part of the buffer created by the Soviet Union to protect its western frontier – are now becoming part of greater Europe for the first time in their history. The result has been a redefinition of the idea of Europe. In the next chapter we will look at the key steps in the evolution of the EU, the underlying motives of integration and the debates involved in the process.

Chapter 3

The Evolution of the EU

While the idea of 'Europe' has been evolving for centuries, serious efforts to encourage regional integration date back only to the end of the Second World War, when three critical needs came to the fore: economic reconstruction, security in the face of cold war tensions, and efforts to prevent European nationalism spilling over once again into conflict. At the core of political calculations was concern about the traditional hostility between France and Germany, and the belief that if these two states could cooperate it might provide the foundations for broader European integration.

A modest early step was taken in 1949 with the creation of the Council of Europe, but this did not go far enough for committed integrationists, who sought instead the creation of new institutions with supranational powers. The first move in this direction was taken in 1952 when the ECSC opened for business, bringing the coal and steel industries of its six member states (France, West Germany, Italy and the three Benelux countries) under a joint authority. The next step was the creation in 1958 of the EEC, with the same six member states but a more ambitious set of goals, including the development of a single market within which there would be free movement of people, money, and services, and common policies on agriculture, competition, trade and transport.

Other countries now became interested and applied for full or associate membership. The first enlargement came in 1973 with the accession of Britain, Denmark and Ireland, followed in the 1980s by Greece, Portugal and Spain, and in 1995 by Austria, Finland and Sweden. The single market was given a boost in 1986 with agreement of the Single European Act, setting a five-year deadline for the removal of remaining barriers. After some false starts, there was progress, too, on monetary union, with the launch in 1999 of the euro, which fully replaced 12 national currencies in 2002. The focus of enlargement then shifted eastwards; 13 new mainly Eastern European countries joined the EU in 2004–13, bringing membership to 28 and the population of the EU to just over 500 million. Along the way, common policies were developed on a wide range of issues, with varying results and levels of success.

This chapter reviews the dramatic story of experimentation, opportunism, success, failure, alarm and serendipity that has led to today's EU. It is a story that has often been marked by crisis, but at no time more than over the last two decades. National votes against new treaties in Denmark and Ireland set alarm bells ringing in the 1990s, and talk of the collapse of the European project reached new levels with the rejection of a proposed constitutional treaty in 2005 after negative public votes in France and the Netherlands. Agreement was instead reached on a new Treaty of Lisbon, but the manner in which it was adopted was widely criticized. Meanwhile, many Europeans remained ambivalent about the EU, while the ranks of its critics swelled. The global financial crisis of 2007–10 added new problems to the mix, the remaining economic weaknesses and vulnerabilities of Europe being emphasized by a new and even more serious crisis that wracked the eurozone after 2009.

Postwar Europe

The EU was born out of the ruins of the Second World War. Before the war, Europe had dominated global trade, banking and finance, its empires had stretched across the world and its military superiority had been unquestioned. But Europeans had often disagreed, their conflicts undermining the prosperity that cooperation might have brought. Pacifists hoped that the war of 1914–18 would have offered final proof of the futility and brutality of armed conflict, but it would take the Second World War to convey this message to a wider audience: the war left many millions dead and widespread devastation in its wake; cities lay in ruins, agricultural production was halved, food was rationed, and communications were disrupted. The war also dealt a near-fatal blow to Europe's global influence, heralding the beginning of the end of the imperial era and clearing the way for the emergence of the United States and the Soviet Union as superpowers.

The western postwar economic agenda had been set at a meeting held in July 1944 at Bretton Woods, New Hampshire, and attended by representatives from 44 countries. There was agreement on an Anglo-American proposal to promote free trade, non-discrimination and stable exchange rates, and support for the view that Europe's economies should be rebuilt and placed on a more stable footing. However, it soon became clear that reconstruction needed substantial capital investment, the readiest source of which was the United States, which saw Europe's progress as essential to its own economic and security interests, and made a large investment in the future of Europe through the Marshall Plan (see Box 3.1).

The second postwar priority was security, and once again the United States was to play a critical role. Winston Churchill had warned in his famous 1946 speech of an iron curtain descending on Europe, a reality whose implications were illustrated by events in 1948. When, in June

Box 3.1   The Marshall Plan

US policy after 1945 was to withdraw its military forces as quickly as possible from Europe. However, it soon became clear that the Soviets had plans to expand their sphere of influence, and the US State Department realized that it had underestimated the extent of Europe's economic destruction: despite a boom in the late 1940s, sustained growth was not forthcoming. When an economically exhausted Britain ended its financial aid to Greece and Turkey in 1947, President Truman argued the need for the United States to fill the vacuum in order to curb communist influence in the region.

US policy makers also felt that European markets needed to be rebuilt and integrated into a multilateral system of world trade, and that economic and political reconstruction might help forestall Soviet aggression and the rise of domestic communist parties (Hogan, 1987: 26–7). Thus Secretary of State George Marshall argued that the United States should provide Europe with assistance to fight 'hunger, poverty, desperation and chaos'. The original April 1947 State Department proposal made clear that one of the ultimate goals of the plan was the creation of a Western European federation (quoted in Gillingham, 1991: 118–19).

The European Recovery Programme (otherwise known as the Marshall Plan) provided just over $12.5 billion in aid to Europe between 1948 and 1951 (Milward, 1984:94) (about $120 billion in 2013 terms, adjusted for inflation). Disbursement was coordinated by the Organization for European Economic Cooperation (OEEC), a new body set up in April 1948 with headquarters in Paris. Governed by a Council of Ministers made up of one representative from each member state, the OEEC's goals included the reduction of tariffs and other barriers to trade, and consideration of the possibility of a free-trade area or customs union among its members. Opposition from several European governments (notably Britain, France, and Norway) ensured that the OEEC remained a forum for intergovernmental consultation rather than becoming a supranational body with powers of its own (Wexler, 1983:209; Milward, 1984:209–10).

Although the effects of the Marshall Plan are still debated, there is little question that it helped underpin economic and political recovery in Europe, and helped bind more closely the economic and political interests of the United States and Western Europe. It was a profitable investment for the United States, in both political and economic terms, but it also had critical influence on the idea of European integration: as Western Europe's first venture in economic cooperation, it encouraged European governments to work together and highlighted the interdependence of their economies (Urwin, 1995: 20–2). It also helped liberalize intra-European trade, and helped ensure that economic integration would be focused on Western Europe.

that year, the three western occupying powers in Germany agreed to combine their zones into a new West German state, the Soviets responded with a blockade around West Berlin, prompting a massive western airlift to supply the beleaguered city. In 1949 NATO was created, by which the United States agreed to help its European allies 'restore and maintain the security of the North Atlantic area'. But while NATO members agreed that an attack on one of them would be considered an attack on all of them, each agreed only to respond with 'such actions as it deems necessary'.

The Western Europeans overreached themselves with a 1950 proposal for the creation of a European Defence Community (EDC), and a coincidental European Political Community (EPC) that would offer a fast-track to a European federation. The EDC lacked the essential support of Britain, and many in France were nervous about the idea of German rearmament so soon after the war. A critical blow came in May 1954 with the humiliating defeat of French troops at Dien Bien Phu in French Indochina. Reeling from the effects of wounded national pride, the French National Assembly voted down the EDC treaty in August, which also meant an end to plans for the EPC. Within days of the May 1955 admission of West Germany into NATO, the Soviet bloc created the Warsaw Pact. The lines of cold-war Europe were now clearly drawn, and its implications illustrated by the Suez crisis.

In July 1956, seeking funds to help him build a dam on the Nile, Egyptian president Gamal Abdel Nasser nationalized the Suez Canal, still owned and operated by Britain and France. Their governments immediately conspired with that of Israel to launch an invasion of the canal. Coincidentally, the Hungarian government announced the end of one-party rule, the evacuation of Russian troops, and withdrawal from the Warsaw Pact. Just as Britain and France were invading Egypt, the Soviets were sending tanks into Hungary. The United States wanted to criticize the Soviet use of force, but could not while British and French paratroopers were storming the Suez Canal. In the face of US hostility, Britain and France were ostracized in the UN Security Council and the attempt to regain the canal was abandoned. The effects were profound (see Turner, 2006): Britain and France finally recognized that they were no longer world powers capable of significant independent action; Britain began to look to Europe for its economic and security interests; and it was now clear that the United States was the dominant partner in the Atlantic Alliance.

First steps towards integration (1948–55)

For many Europeans, the major obstacles to peace were nationalism and the nation state, both of which had been discredited by the war.

Economic reconstruction and military security were critical to the future of the region, but Europeans also needed a greater sense of unity and common purpose than they had been able to achieve before. The spotlight fell on Britain, which had taken the lead in fighting Nazism and was still the dominant European power. In 1942–43, Winston Churchill had suggested the development of 'a United States of Europe' operating under 'a Council of Europe' with reduced trade barriers, free movement of people, a common military and a High Court to adjudicate disputes (quoted in Palmer, 1968:111). He made the same suggestion in a speech in Zurich in 1946, but it was clear that Churchill felt this new entity should be based around France and Germany and would not necessarily include Britain – before the war he had argued that Britain was 'with Europe but not of it. We are interested and associated, but not absorbed' (Zurcher, 1958:6).

National pro-European groups decided to organize a conference focused on the cause of regional unity. The Congress of Europe, held in The Hague in May 1948, agreed the creation of the Council of Europe, founded with the signing in London in May 1949 of a statute by ten Western European states (see Box 3.2). But the Council would never be more than a loose intergovernmental organization, and was not the kind of body that European federalists wanted. Among those looking for something more substantial were the French entrepreneur and bureaucrat Jean Monnet (1888–1979) and French foreign minister Robert Schuman (1886–1963). Both felt that practical steps needed to be taken that went beyond the broad statements of organizations such as the Council of Europe, and agreed that the logical starting point should be the resolution of the perennial problem of Franco-German relations.

By 1950 it was clear to many that West Germany had to be allowed to rebuild if it was to play a useful role in the western alliance, but this would best be done under the auspices of a supranational organization that would tie West Germany into the wider process of European reconstruction. Looking for a starting point that would be meaningful but not too ambitious, Monnet opted for the coal and steel industries on the grounds that they were the building blocks of industry, the heavy industries of the Ruhr had long been the foundation of Germany's power, and integrating coal and steel would make sure that West Germany became reliant on trade with the rest of Europe, underpinning its economic reconstruction while helping the French overcome their fear of German industrial domination (Monnet, 1978:292). He proposed a new institution independent of national governments, which would be supranational rather than intergovernmental in nature.

The plan was announced by Robert Schuman at a press conference in Paris on 9 May 1950 (now celebrated each year as Europe Day). In what later became known as the Schuman Declaration, he argued that

Box 3.2   The Council of Europe

The debates about Europe and European integration tend to focus almost exclusively on the EU, and yet much of the impetus for change has come from other sources and institutions that are often overlooked. A quick online search during the writing of this book, for example, found European associations for archaeology, cancer research, cardiology, cooperative banking, health law, institutions of higher education, gender research, geochemistry, the mining industry, nuclear medicine, universities, and urology, to name just a few. So while the EU clearly dominates, it is far from the only actor in the story of European integration.

One key institution, which is both older than the EU and which has made notable contributions in critical areas, is the Council of Europe. Founded in 1949, and headquartered in Strasbourg, France, the Council is the most truly European of international organizations in the sense that every European state except Belarus is a member, along with Russia. Its particular interests lie in the fields of human rights, democracy and culture, and it structurally fits more closely with the standard features of an international organization than does the EU: it is overseen by a secretary general, has a committee of ministers made up of the foreign ministers of the member states (or their representatives) which meets twice annually, and has a 318-member Parliamentary Assembly which meets quarterly to discuss topical issues and ask the governments of the member states to take action or report.

The Council's most substantial work is undertaken by its European Court of Human Rights, whose job is to protect the 1950 European Convention on Human Rights, which covers issues such as right to life, the right to a fair trial, freedom of thought and expression, freedom of religion, the prohibition of discrimination and of the expulsion of nationals, the protection of property, and the abolition of the death penalty. The Court did not attract much attention until 1998, when it became a permanent body to which all citizens of the 47 member states had access. Where it had been receiving less than 800 applications per year, and had issued less than 70 judgements over the course of 30 years, it now began receiving an annual average of 45,000 applications and issuing about 800–1,000 judgements per year (Greer, 2006:34–40). Turkey and Italy have topped the list of violators of human rights, more than half the judgements for the former related to the right to a fair trial and the protection of property, and more than half for the latter related to the excessive length of proceedings.

Europe would not be united at once or according to a single plan, but step by step through concrete achievements. This would require the elimination of Franco-German hostility, and Schuman proposed that French and German coal and steel production be placed 'under a common High Authority, within the framework of an organization open to the participation of the other countries of Europe'. This would be 'a first step in the federation of Europe', and would make war between France and Germany 'not merely unthinkable, but materially impossible' (Schuman, quoted in Stirk and Weigall, 1999:76).

Although membership of the new body was open to all European states, only four others accepted: Italy, which sought respectability and economic and political stability, and the three Benelux countries, which were small and vulnerable, were heavily reliant on exports, and felt that the only way they could have a voice in world affairs and ensure their security was to become part of a bigger regional unit. The other European governments had different reasons for not taking part: Britain still had extensive interests outside Europe, exported little of its steel to the continent, and the new Labour government did not like the supranational character of Schuman's proposal; Ireland was tied economically to Britain; for Denmark and Norway the memories of German occupation were too fresh; Austria, Finland, and Sweden wished to protect their neutrality; Portugal and Spain were dictatorships with little interest in international cooperation; and participation by Soviet-dominated Eastern Europe was out of the question.

The lines of thinking now established, the governments of the Six opened negotiations and on 18 April 1951 signed the Treaty of Paris, creating the European Coal and Steel Community (ECSC). The new organization began work in August 1952, managed by an appointed nine-member High Authority under the presidency of Jean Monnet, with decisions being taken by a six-member Special Council of Ministers. An appointed 78-member Common Assembly helped Monnet allay the fears of national governments regarding the surrender of powers, and disputes between states were to be settled by a seven-member Court of Justice.

The ECSC had limited goals and powers, but it was notable for being the first supranational organization to which European governments had transferred significant powers. It was allowed to reduce tariff barriers, abolish subsidies, fix prices, and raise money by imposing levies on steel and coal production, its job made easier by the fact that some of the groundwork had been laid by the Benelux customs union (founded in 1948). Although the ECSC failed to achieve many of its goals (notably the creation of a single market for coal and steel (Gillingham, 1991:319)), it had ultimately been created to prove a point about the feasibility of integration. But it did not go far enough for Monnet, who resigned the presidency of the High Authority in 1955, disillusioned by the political resistance to its work and impatient to further the process of integration (Monnet, 1978:398–404).

The European Economic Community (1955–86)

Efforts to promote European integration now moved on to a more ambitious plane. A meeting of the ECSC foreign ministers at Messina in Italy in June 1955 resulted in agreement to adopt a Benelux proposal 'to work for the establishment of a united Europe by the development of common institutions, the progressive fusion of national economies, the creation of a common market, and the progressive harmonization of their social policies' (Messina Resolution, in Weigall and Stirk, 1992:94). A new round of negotiations led to the signing in March 1957 of the two Treaties of Rome, one creating the EEC and the other the European Atomic Energy Community (Euratom), both of which came into existence in January 1958. The EEC had a similar administrative structure to the ECSC, with a quasi-executive appointed Commission, a Council of Ministers with powers over decision making, and a Court of Justice. A Parliamentary Assembly was also created to cover the EEC, ECSC and Euratom, and in 1962 was renamed the European Parliament.

The EEC Treaty committed the Six to the creation of a common market within 12 years by removing all restrictions on the internal movement of people, money and services; the setting of a common external tariff for goods coming into the EEC; the development of common agricultural, trade and transport policies; and the creation of a European Social Fund and a European Investment Bank. Action would be taken in areas where there was agreement, and disagreements could be set aside for future discussion. The Euratom Treaty, meanwhile, was aimed at creating a common market for atomic energy, but it was of real interest only to France, and Euratom was to remain a junior actor in the process of integration, focused primarily on research.

The birth and early years of the EEC must be seen in the light of international developments. The threats posed by the Soviets were clear, as was the extent to which Western Europe had to rely on the security guarantees offered by the United States. Less often considered in the story of European integration are the effects of differences of opinion within the Atlantic Alliance. Western Europeans had wondered about American priorities and perceptions as early as the Korean War, which had sparked worries about a wider conflict being set off by American plans to invade the north. Then came the 1962 Cuban missile crisis, during which the two superpowers had briefly stood on the brink of nuclear war while the Americans conferred little with their European allies. Finally, the 1960s saw escalation of the conflict in Vietnam, for which no European government offered open support, and which came to generate widespread public criticism of US policy.

Amidst these wider changes in international affairs, it had also become clear that the EEC needed to expand its membership if its effects were to reach beyond an exclusive club of six. Any European state was allowed to join under the terms of the Treaty of Rome, but non-members had mixed feelings about the Community. Most obvious by its absence was Britain, which had doubts about the EEC and instead championed the looser European Free Trade Association (EFTA), founded in January 1960 with the signing of the Stockholm Convention by Austria, Britain, Denmark, Norway, Portugal, Sweden and Switzerland. But it had already become clear to Britain that influence in Europe lay with the EEC, and that it risked isolation if it stayed out: the EEC had made impressive economic and political progress and British industry wanted access to the rich EEC market.

In August 1961, barely 15 months after the creation of EFTA, Britain applied for EEC membership, along with Denmark and Ireland, joined in 1962 by Norway. Negotiations between Britain and the EEC opened in early 1962, but quickly fell foul of President Charles de Gaulle's plans for an EEC built around a Franco-German axis. He also saw Britain as a rival to French influence in the Community, resented Britain's lack of enthusiasm for integration, and felt that British membership of the EEC would give the United States too much influence in Europe. In January 1963 de Gaulle unilaterally vetoed the British application. Since it was part of a package with Denmark, Ireland and Norway, they too were rejected. Britain reapplied in 1967 and was again vetoed by de Gaulle. Following his resignation as president in 1969 Britain applied for a third time, and this time its application was accepted. Following negotiations in 1970–71, Britain, Denmark and Ireland finally joined the EEC in January 1973. Norway would have joined as well but a public referendum in September 1972 narrowly went against membership.

More enlargement in the 1980s pushed the borders of the EEC further south and west. Greece was given associate membership in 1961, and full accession might have come sooner had it not been for the Greek military coup of April 1967. With civilian government restored in 1974, negotiations opened and Greece joined in January 1981. Meanwhile, the restoration of democracy in Spain and Portugal in 1974–75 opened the prospects of membership for these two countries. Despite their relative poverty, problems over fishing rights, and concerns about Portuguese and Spanish workers moving north in search of work, the EEC felt that membership would encourage democracy in the Iberian peninsula and help link the two countries more closely to NATO and Western Europe. Negotiations opened in 1978–79 and both states joined in January 1986, the Ten thereby becoming the Twelve.

The doubling of membership increased the global influence of the EEC, changed the dynamic of Community decision making, reduced

Box 3.3   Early steps on the road of integration

The early years of integration were a mix of achievements, failures, and crises, setting a pattern still found in the EU today:

- Although the 12–year deadline for the creation of a common market was not met, internal tariffs fell quickly enough to allow the Six to agree a common external tariff in July 1968, and to declare an industrial customs union.
- Decision making was streamlined in April 1965 with the Merger treaty, which created a single institutional structure for all three communities. The summit meetings of EEC leaders were formalized in 1975 with the creation of the European Council, and the EEC was made more democratic with the introduction in 1979 of direct elections to the European Parliament.
- A dispute in 1965 over the powers of the Commission, voting in the Council of Ministers, and the Community budget led to a boycott of Council meetings by France (the empty-chair crisis), resolved when the right of national veto was affirmed.
- Integration meant the removal of the quota restrictions that member states had used to protect their domestic industries from competition from imported products, contributing to accelerated economic growth and a rapid increase in intra-EEC trade.
- In the interests of removing non-tariff barriers to the free movement of goods across borders (including different standards and regulations on health, safety and consumer protection) standards were harmonized during the 1960s and 1970s. It was not until the passage of the 1986 Single European Act, however, that a concerted effort was made to bring all EEC members into line.
- Limited progress was made during the 1960s and 1970s on lifting restrictions on the free movement of workers.
- Agreement in 1968 on a Common Agricultural Policy (CAP), creating a single market for agricultural products, and assuring EEC farmers of guaranteed prices for their produce. The CAP initially encouraged both production and productivity, but it became increasingly controversial, not least because of its cost (see Chapter 8).
- The Six worked more closely together on international trade negotiations, achieving a joint influence that would have been missing if they had worked independently. The EEC acted as one, for example, in negotiations under the General Agreement on Tariffs and Trade (GATT) (see Chapter 9).

the overall influence of France and Germany, altered the Community's relations with the United States and with developing countries, and – by bringing in the poorer Mediterranean states – altered the internal economic balance of the EEC. Rather than enlarging any further, it was

Map 3.1   *Growth of the European Community, 1952–86*

now decided to focus on deepening ties among the Twelve. Applications were made by Turkey (1987), Austria (1989), and Cyprus and Malta (1990), and although East Germany entered through the back door with German reunification in October 1990, there was to be no more enlargement until 1995.

Focus on the single market (1986–92)

By 1986 the EEC had become known simply as the European Community (EC). Its member states had a combined population of 322 million and accounted for just over one-fifth of all world trade. The EC had its own administrative structure and an independent body of law, and its citizens had direct (but limited) representation through the European Parliament. But progress towards integration remained uneven. The customs union was in place, but completion of the common market was handicapped by barriers to the free movement of people and capital, including different national technical, health and quality standards, and varying levels of indirect taxation. It was also clear that there could never be a true single market without a common European currency, a controversial idea because it would mean a significant loss of national sovereignty and a significant move towards political union. EC leaders responded to these problems with two critical initiatives: the launch of the European Monetary System, and the signature of the Single European Act.

At a December 1969 summit, Community leaders discussed the principle of economic and monetary union (EMU), and agreed to control fluctuations in the value of their currencies and to make more effort to coordinate national economic policies. In August 1971, however, the Nixon administration – wrestling with national debt problems arising in part from the costs of the war in Vietnam – signalled the end of the Bretton Woods system of fixed exchange rates by ending the convertibility of the US dollar with gold, imposing domestic wage and price controls, and placing a surcharge on imports. This led to international monetary turbulence, made worse in 1973 by the Arab-Israeli war and the attendant global energy crisis.

In 1979, a new initiative was launched in the form of the European Monetary System (EMS). Using an Exchange Rate Mechanism (ERM) based around an accounting tool known as the European currency unit (ecu), the EMS was designed to control fluctuations in exchange rates. The hope was that the ecu would become the normal means of settling debts among Community members, psychologically preparing them for the idea of a single currency. With this in mind, Commission president Jacques Delors took EMU a step further in 1989 with the elaboration of a three-stage plan aimed at fixing exchange rates and turning the ecu into a single currency. Matters were complicated, however, by speculation on the world's money markets, which caused Britain and Italy to pull out of the ERM in 1992, and Ireland, Portugal and Spain to devalue their currencies, knocking EMU off track until 1994.

Meanwhile there was concern that progress towards the single market was being handicapped by inflation and unemployment, and by the temptation of member states to protect their home industries with non-tariff barriers such as subsidies. Economic competition from the United States and Japan was also growing. In response, the European Council decided to refocus on the original core goal of creating a single market, the result being the signature in Luxembourg in February 1986 of the Single European Act (SEA). The first major change to the treaties since the signing of the Treaty of Rome, it came into force in July 1987 with the goal of completing all requirements for the single

Table 3.1   *The Single European Act*

- It created the wealthiest marketplace in the world. Many internal passport and customs controls were eased or lifted, banks and companies could do business throughout the Community, and there was little to prevent qualified EC residents living, working, opening bank accounts and drawing their pensions anywhere in the Community.
- EC competition policy was given new prominence, and monopolies on everything from electricity supply to telecommunications were broken down.
- Community institutions were given responsibility over new policy areas such as the environment, research and development, and regional policy.
- It gave new powers to the European Court of Justice, and created a Court of First Instance to hear certain kinds of cases and ease the workload of the Court of Justice.
- It gave legal status to meetings of heads of government under the European Council, and gave new powers to the Council of Ministers and the European Parliament.
- It gave legal status to European Political Cooperation (foreign policy coordination) so that member states could work more closely on foreign, defence and security issues.
- It made economic and monetary union an EC objective and promoted 'cohesion', meaning the reduction of the gap between the richer and poorer parts of the EC.

market by 31 December 1992. This meant agreeing and implementing nearly 300 new pieces of legislation aimed at removing all remaining barriers to the free movement of people, money, goods and services. These barriers were physical (such as customs and passport controls at internal borders), fiscal (mainly in the form of different levels of indirect taxation) and technical (such as conflicting standards, laws and qualifications) (see Table 3.1).

Despite the signing of the SEA, progress on opening up borders was variable, and there was no common European policy on immigration, visas and asylum. Impatient to move ahead, the governments of France, Germany and the Benelux states in 1985 signed the Schengen Agreement, under which all border controls were to be removed among signatory countries. All EU member states have since signed the agreement, along with Iceland, Norway and Switzerland, but not all have introduced truly passport-free travel (Britain has stayed out of most elements of Schengen, claiming its special problems as an island state, and Ireland has had to follow suit because of its passport union with Britain), and the terms of the agreement allow the signatories to implement special controls at any time. Nonetheless, its signature marked a substantial step towards the removal of border controls.

From Community to Union (1992–2003)

Meanwhile, remarkable changes were taking place on the wider international stage. Reforms instituted by the Gorbachev administration in the Soviet Union after 1985 led to demands for political change in East Germany, the dismantling of the Berlin Wall in 1989, the reunification of Germany in October 1990, the dissolution of the Soviet Union in December 1991, the break-up of Yugoslavia and Czechoslovakia, and the end of the cold war. Life was changed for all Europeans, but the violence in the former Yugoslavia posed an immediate security problem that the Community tried and failed to resolve, falling back once again on the Americans (who brokered the 1995 Dayton peace accords) and proving to itself and to the rest of the world just how much work remained to be done if European foreign policy cooperation was to have any real meaning.

The controversial idea of political integration had long been left on the back-burner because it was felt that there was little hope of political union without economic union, and political union in turn demanded cooperation on foreign policy. A decision was taken in 1990 to convene an intergovernmental conference (IGC) on political union, the outcome of which was the Treaty on European Union, agreed at the European Council summit in Maastricht in December 1991 (hence it is also known as the Maastricht treaty) and signed in February 1992. The treaty had to be ratified by the 12 member states before it could come into force, and a shock came when it was rejected by Danish voters in a referendum in June 1992, and only narrowly accepted by a referendum in France in September. The content of the Maastricht treaty was further discussed by the European Council, and following agreement that the Danes could opt out of the single currency, common defence arrangements, European citizenship, and cooperation on justice and home affairs, a second Danish referendum was held in May 1993 and the treaty was accepted, coming into force the following November (see Table 3.2).

The Danish rejection of Maastricht and the near-miss in France were to prove significant, indicating as they did that – for the first time – ordinary Europeans were asking hard questions about what was being done in their name. The old 'permissive consensus', when few Europeans took much interest in the work of the Community and key decisions were left to government leaders, was now being challenged. As the reach of integration expanded and more Europeans felt its effects, so the debate about its pros and cons expanded. Unfortunately, much of that debate took place against a background of public confusion and misinformation, driven by the media, interest groups, and political parties with strong positions on integration (see Chapter 5 for more details). But whatever the motivations, euroscepticism – or resist-

Table 3.2   *The Treaty on European Union*

- Reflecting the lengths to which member states were occasionally prepared to go to reach compromises, three 'pillars' were created under a structure given the new label 'European Union'. The first pillar was the renamed European Community, while the second and third pillars consisted of areas in which there was to be more formal intergovernmental cooperation: a Common Foreign and Security Policy (CFSP), and justice and home affairs. The pillar arrangement was abolished under the terms of the 2007 Treaty of Lisbon.
- The Delors three-stage plan for monetary union was confirmed.
- EU responsibility was extended into new policy areas such as consumer protection, public health policy, transport, education, and (except in Britain) social policy.
- There was to be greater intergovernmental cooperation on immigration and asylum, a European police intelligence agency (Europol) was to be created to combat organized crime and drug trafficking, a new Committee of the Regions was set up, and regional funds for poorer EU states were increased.
- New rights were provided for European citizens and an ambiguous EU 'citizenship' was created which meant, for example, the right of citizens to live wherever they liked in the EU, and to stand or vote in local and European elections.
- New powers were given to the European Parliament, including a codecision procedure under which certain kinds of legislation were subject to a third reading in the European Parliament before they could be adopted by the Council of Ministers.

ance to European integration – has since been a critical factor in the debates over Europe.

Meanwhile enlargement was still on the agenda, the end of the cold war leading to a new focus on expansion to Eastern Europe. At its June 1993 meeting in Copenhagen, the European Council agreed a formal set of requirements for membership of the EU. Known as the Copenhagen conditions, they require that an applicant state must (a) be democratic, with respect for human rights and the rule of law; (b) have a viable free market economy and the ability to respond to market forces within the EU; (c) be able to take on the obligations of the *acquis communautaire* (the body of laws and policies already adopted by the EU); and (d) adapt their administrative structures in order to meet the demands of integration. Deciding whether applicants meet these criteria has since proved difficult, not least because of the problem – discussed in Chapter 2 – of defining the boundaries of Europe.

Throughout the 1980s, discussions about enlargement centred on other Western European states, if only because they came closest to meeting the criteria for membership. In order ostensibly to prepare prospective members (or, in the view of Dinan (2004:268)), to fob them off), negotiations began in 1990 on the creation of a European Economic Area (EEA), under which the terms of the SEA would be

Map 3.2 *Growth of the EU, 1990–95*

extended to the seven EFTA members, in return for which they would accept the rules of the single market. The EEA came into force in January 1994, but quickly lost relevance because Austria, Finland, Norway and Sweden had applied for EC membership. Negotiations with these four applicants were completed in early 1994, and all but Norway (where a referendum again went against membership) joined the EU in January 1995.

Their accession left just three Western European countries outside the EU: Iceland, Norway and Switzerland. Iceland kept its distance from the EU until the 2007–10 global financial crisis set off a collapse of its banking industry, prompting it to lodge a hurried membership application in July 2009. Should it join, it would – with a population of just 320,000 – be the smallest EU member state. Norwegian opinion on membership remains divided, but Norway continues to be impacted by developments in the EU. Switzerland, which had considered applying for EC membership in 1992, rejected the EEA that same year and in 1995 found itself completely surrounded by the EU. Demands for the Swiss to open their highways to EU trucks and intra-EU trade increased the pressure for EU membership, but further discussion ended in March 2001 when a national referendum went heavily against EU membership.

Partly in preparation for anticipated eastern enlargement, but also to account for the progress of European integration and perhaps move the EU closer to political union, two new treaties were now signed. The Treaty of Amsterdam (signed October 1997, came into force May 1999) did little more than confirm plans for eastern enlargement and the launch of the single currency, confirm plans for the CFSP (creating a new office of High Representative for the CFSP), extend EU policy responsibilities to health and consumer protection, incorporate the Schengen Agreement into the treaties, and expand the powers of the European Parliament.

Equally modest was the Treaty of Nice (signed February 2001), which made a few more changes to the structure of the EU institutions, including increasing the size of the European Commission and the European Parliament, and redistributing the votes in the Council of Ministers. But EU leaders were taken by surprise in June 2001 when Irish voters rejected the terms of the treaty, its opponents arguing that it involved the surrender of too much national control, and being particularly concerned about the implications for Irish neutrality. A second vote was taken in Ireland in October 2002, following assurances that Ireland's neutrality on security issues would be respected, and – thanks in part to a bigger turnout – the treaty was accepted by a 63 per cent majority, and came into force in February 2003.

To Lisbon and the eurozone crisis (2003–)

More significant for the long-term development of the EU was the progress made in the 1990s on the single currency. A decision had been taken in 1995 to call it the euro, and the timetable agreed under Maastricht required participating states to fix their exchange rates in January 1999. Several 'convergence criteria' were considered essential prerequisites: these included placing limits on national budget deficits, public debt, consumer inflation, and long-term interest rates. At a special EU summit in May 1998 it was decided that all but Greece met the conditions, but public and political opinion in the member states was divided on which should or would fix their exchange rates. There was also public resistance to the idea of the single currency in several countries, notably Britain and Germany. In the event, all but Denmark, Sweden, and the UK adopted the euro when it came into being as an electronic currency in January 1999, the participating national currencies being finally abolished in March 2002.

But against the background of these developments there were concerns about the inability of the European marketplace to improve its rates of productivity or to create enough new jobs to meet demand. The term Eurosclerosis had been coined earlier by Giersch (1985) to describe the problem, and there was little sign of change in the late 1990s, prompting a decision by the European Council in March 2000 to launch the Lisbon Strategy. This set the goal of making the EU – by 2010 – the most dynamic economy in the world, which demanded the creation of more jobs, bringing more women into the workplace, liberalizing telecommunications and energy markets, improving transport, and opening up labour markets. In the event, the targets proved too ambitious, and Lisbon was superseded by the Europe 2020 Strategy, focusing on innovation, education, sustainable growth, a low-carbon economy, and job creation (see Chapter 7 for more details).

These debates took place against a background of the most serious rift in transatlantic relations in decades. Following the September 2001 terrorist attacks in the United States, the administration of George W. Bush had quickly orchestrated a multinational attack on Afghanistan, accused of being a harbour for terrorists. But then it turned its attention to Iraq, claiming that the regime of Saddam Hussein possessed weapons of mass destruction and posed a substantial security threat. European public opinion was strongly against the proposed invasion of Iraq, but EU governments were split, with France and Germany leading the opposition and Britain and Spain offering support. It seemed that all the mounting questions about American leadership of the Atlantic Alliance had now come to a head, as well as all the questions about the EU's inability to make a mark on the global stage (see Chapter 9 for more details).

In May 2004, the EU began its most significant round of enlargements when ten Eastern European and Mediterranean states joined: Cyprus, the Czech Republic, Estonia, Hungary, Latvia, Lithuania, Malta, Poland, Slovenia, and Slovakia. All their economies combined were smaller than that of the Netherlands, and they increased the population of the EU by less than 20 per cent; the real significance of the 2004 enlargement lay in the fact that the EU was no longer a club for wealthy west Europeans. The East was now included, and – for the first time – former Soviet republics (Estonia, Latvia, Lithuania) became part of the EU. As well as providing an important symbolic confirmation of the end of the cold war division of Europe, the 2004 enlargement also promised to accelerate the process of transforming the economies and democratic structures of Eastern European countries. The trends continued in January 2007 when Bulgaria and Romania joined the EU, and in July 2013 when Croatia became the 28th

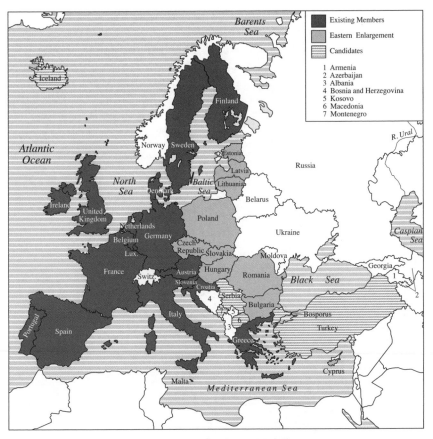

Map 3.3 *Growth of the EU, 2004–13*

member state of the EU. Iceland, Macedonia, Montenegro, Serbia and Turkey have also been accepted as 'candidate countries', meaning that they are seen to be strong contenders for future membership (see Table 3.3).

With the changes in policy and membership, the need to rewrite the rules of the EU became increasingly pressing, as did the need to make the EU more democratic and to bring it closer to its citizens. It was decided in late 2001 to establish a convention to debate the future of Europe, and to draw up a treaty containing a constitution designed to simplify and replace all the other treaties. The Convention on the Future of the European Union met between February 2002 and July 2003, bringing together 105 representatives from the 15 EU member states, 13 applicant Eastern European and Mediterranean countries, the 28 national parliaments, and the European Parliament. The convention considered numerous proposals, including an elected president

Table 3.3   *Prospective members of the EU*

	Application made	Status and challenges
Candidates		
Iceland	July 2009	Negotiations suspended by Iceland June 2013
Macedonia	March 2004	Dispute with Greece over its name
Montenegro	December 2008	Negotiations underway
Serbia	December 2009	
Turkey	April 1987	Negotiations underway
Potential candidates		
Albania	April 2009	Corruption, organized crime
Bosnia & Herzegovina		Ethnic division, political instability, corruption, organized crime
Kosovo		Unresolved legal status
Others		
Armenia		Poverty, territorial disputes
Azerbaijan		Authoritarianism, corruption, links with Russia
Belarus		Authoritarianism, links with Russia
Georgia		Civil unrest, links with Russia
Moldova		Poverty, links with Russia
Norway		Internal divisions over joining EU
Switzerland		1992 referendum rejected EU membership
Ukraine		Divided opinion on EU membership

Indicates status as of mid-2013.

of the European Council, a foreign minister for the EU, a limit on the membership of the European Commission, a common EU foreign and security policy, and a legal personality for the EU, whose laws would cancel out those of national parliaments in areas where the EU had been given competence. It took two European Council meetings (December 2003 and June 2004) to reach agreement on the draft constitutional treaty, which had then to be put to public referenda or legislative votes in every EU member state.

Lithuania became the first country to ratify with a parliamentary vote in November 2004, and Spain became the first to ratify with a national referendum in February 2005. But there were already signs of political and public resistance in several countries, notably eurosceptic Britain. But it was left to the French and the Dutch – both founding members of the EU – to stop the process in its tracks, with negative referendum votes in May and June 2005, respectively. It is questionable how much the votes were a reflection of popular opinion about integration, and how much they were approached by French and Dutch voters as an opportunity to comment on their home unpopular governments (both of which favoured the treaty). But in spite of widespread predictions of institutional collapse and loss of strategic direction, the EU survived and continued to function, while worried discussions were held about the next step.

In early 2007, EU leaders agreed to save as many elements as possible of the failed constitutional treaty, and to reformulate them into a new treaty designed mainly to adjust the institutional structure of the EU to account for enlargement. In fact the new Treaty of Lisbon was to be almost a replica of the constitution, several governments disingenuously claiming that because it was an amendment to the treaties it did not need a national referendum for approval. But Ireland was required by law to hold such a referendum, and caused consternation in June 2008 when it once again voted against a new treaty. A protocol was negotiated that addressed Irish concerns about neutrality and tax issues, and Lisbon was approved in a second Irish referendum in October 2009. As well as ending the pillar arrangement introduced by Maastricht, it made a number of key institutional changes, including the creation of a new president for the European Council and a single legal personality for the EU (see Table 3.4).

Through all the treaty changes, the identity of the EU on the global stage had undergone something of a transformation. European leaders had been embarrassed by their failure to provide leadership in responding to the violent break-up of Yugoslavia, but EU policy succeeded in Eastern Europe, where it took the lead on post-cold war reconstruction, helping former Soviet-bloc states to make the transition to democracy and free markets. Meanwhile, the role of the United States in EU affairs was declining, as reflected in the fallout from the 2003 crisis over Iraq, when US leaders were taken aback by the openness with which their policy was criticized by hostile EU governments. More was to come with the breaking in 2007 of a global financial crisis that had its origins in the United States, where too little regulation had allowed the extension of credit to consumers patently unable to service their debts, and much of that debt had been bought up by European banks and financial institutions.

The resulting problems both sparked and heralded a home-grown crisis that first captured the headlines in late 2009 with the breaking of news about debt problems in Greece. The country had been on a spending spree fuelled by lowered interest rates, manipulated statistics to exaggerate its levels of economic growth, ran a budget deficit that – at nearly 13 per cent – was far above the 3 per cent eurozone limit, and had a national (that is, sovereign) debt that was almost twice the eurozone limit of 60 per cent of GDP. Matters were made worse by widespread tax evasion, helping create a shadow economy estimated to be

Table 3.4   *The Treaty of Lisbon*

- A new president for the European Council, appointed by its members for a two-and-a-half-year term (renewable once) and approved by Parliament.
- A High Representative of the Union for Foreign Affairs and Security Policy, appointed by the European Council for five-year terms, charged with conducting the CFSP, and backed up by a new European External Action Service.
- Abolition of the pillar system introduced by Maastricht, and of the European Community.
- Equal powers for the European Parliament and the Council of the EU over proposals for almost all EU legislation.
- Recognition of the rights laid out in the Charter of Fundamental Rights, and accession to the European Convention on Human Rights.
- More powers for the EU in the areas of energy policy, public health, climate change, crime and terrorism, commercial policy, humanitarian aid, sport, tourism, research and space.
- Expansion of the use of qualified majority voting, but the national veto to be retained for foreign and defence policy and taxation.
- A single legal personality for the EU, designed to strengthen its negotiating powers on the international stage.
- Formal recognition, for the first time, of the freedom of a member state to leave the EU.

equivalent to nearly a quarter of Greek GDP. Although Greece dominated the headlines, Germany and France had also broken the eurozone rules, and there were worries about the effects of indebtedness in Portugal, Ireland, Italy and Spain.

Eurozone leaders at first avoided settling on a bail-out for Greece, and instead agreed that if Greece was unable to attract loans from the financial markets, a last-resort package of bilateral loans from inside the eurozone (mainly Germany and France) would be arranged, along with funds and technical assistance from the International Monetary Fund (IMF), assuming all eurozone states were in favour. But the initial eurozone rescue package had to be greatly increased, and was offered on condition that Greece introduce austerity measures by cutting public spending and boosting tax revenue. This sparked riots in the streets of Athens and encouraged little improvement in investor confidence. Spain, Italy, Ireland and Portugal were also asking for help, and even non-euro states such as Britain were having problems. Speculation grew of a 'Grexit' – Greece leaving the euro – and of the possible collapse of the euro, followed by the break up of the EU.

Pinning down the causes of the eurozone crisis is not easy. We must first appreciate that economic and financial experts did not fully understand how best to design the euro from the start, and when its problems began to emerge, they differed over how to explain them, and over what action to take in response. And it is almost impossible to find explanations of the crisis that are not replete with arcane jargon that can be understood only by the experts. But one of those experts, who has a skill for clarity, is the international financier George Soros. The following explanation is founded on a speech he made at an economic conference in early 2012 (Soros, 2012).

Before the introduction of the euro, poorer EU states such as Greece, Spain and Ireland had to pay more to borrow money than wealthier members, and thus were mainly obliged to live within their means. But the introduction of the euro meant that all eurozone countries could borrow at the same cheaper rate, and banks were quick to lend to the poorer states. While the German economy was doing well, exporting more, and becoming more competitive, poorer countries now lived beyond their means, using their new access to cheap credit to buy imports and build houses, while exporting less. Then came the global financial crisis, which confirmed what many had long known: that the economies of the eurozone states were quite different in terms of their structures and possibilities, and that lending to one was not the same as lending to another. Once it became clear that poorer eurozone states might have trouble repaying their debts, the interest rates on loans were raised, placing enormous pressure on the banks that had made the loans. Thus the debt problems of borrower states became intertwined with the problems faced by the banks that had made the loans, and which now faced the prospects of insolvency.

It was clearly in German interests to lead a resolution of the problem, because the collapse of the euro would have left it with uncollectable debts and surrounded by countries to which it had exported a great deal, but for which German imports were now much more expensive. The option chosen was to bail out the at-risk eurozone states while demanding austerity (cut-backs in spending) in return. But Soros believes that the authorities did not understand the nature of the euro crisis: they thought of it as a fiscal (taxing and spending) problem when it was more of a banking and competitiveness problem. And instead of trying to reduce the debt burden by shrinking economies, they should have been trying to grow their way out while working to address the design flaws in the euro. But they did not understand the nature of the problem, they could not see a clear solution, and so they sought to buy time. By early 2013, much of the earlier fuss and speculation had died down, but this did not mean that the problem had gone away.

As if these economic woes were not enough, there were signs of declining faith in the EU, as well as in national government in most EU states. Euroscepticism won new adherents, with anti-EU parties winning new support at elections in several EU states, including Austria, Denmark, Finland and Germany. Euroscepticism also became a headline issue in Britain when the Cameron government – in an attempt to address yet another squabble over the EU within the

Conservative party – promised to hold a referendum on continued British membership of the EU. It has been, in short, a deeply troubling time for the EU, raising many questions over the future of an exercise which – at least until the breaking of the eurozone crisis – had enjoyed the support of most Europeans.

Conclusions

Europe has travelled a long and winding road since the end of the Second World War. Most European states in 1945 were physically devastated, the suspicions and hostilities that had led to two world wars in the space of a generation still lingered, Western Europe found itself being pulled into a military and economic vacuum as power and influence moved outwards to the United States, and Eastern Europe came under the political and economic control of the Soviet Union. The balance of power in the west changed as an exhausted Britain and France dismantled their empires and reduced their militaries, while West Germany rebuilt and eventually became a dominant force in continental politics. Intent on avoiding future wars, and concerned about being caught in big-power rivalry, Western European leaders began considering new levels of regional cooperation, pooling the interests of their states, and helping give the region new confidence and influence.

Beginning with the limited experiment of integrating their coal and steel industries, and building on an economic foundation and security shield underwritten by the United States, six European states quickly agreed a common agricultural policy, a customs union, and the beginnings of a common market. The accession of new members in the 1970s and 1980s increased the size of the Community's population and market, pushing its borders to the edge of Russia and the Middle East. The global economic instability that followed the end of the Bretton Woods system and the energy crises of the 1970s served to emphasize the need for Western European countries to cooperate if they were to have more control over their own future rather than simply to respond to external events.

After several years of relative lethargy the European experiment was given new impetus by completion of the single market, and then by the controversial decision to stabilize exchange rates as a prelude to the abolition of national currencies and the adoption of a single European currency. At the same time, the EU showed a new face to the rest of the world, with more cooperation on foreign and trade policy (along with some embarrassing disagreements along the way). The effects of integration were felt in a growing number of policy areas, including agriculture, competition, transport, the environment, energy, telecommunications, research and development, working conditions, culture, consumer affairs, education and employment.

But ordinary Europeans have been increasingly in two minds about the merits of integration, the criticisms growing since the passage of the Maastricht treaty in the early 1990s. The 2003 controversy over Iraq drew new attention to the place of the EU in the international system, while the post-2004 eastern enlargement had an important impact on the personality of the EU, making it more truly an exercise in European integration. The failure of the European constitution proved a disappointment to many, and the less than forthright manner in which the Treaty of Lisbon was written and adopted adding to the doubts about the EU. Then came the global financial crisis of 2007–10 and the breaking in 2009 of a sovereign debt crisis, which combined to strike a devastating blow to the euro, and to spark an animated debate about the future of the EU. How this will evolve remains to be seen.

Chapter 4

The European Institutions

The EU has a complex network of institutions, but they have evolved on the basis of short-term needs and compromises, with little sense of what the 'government' of the EU might eventually become. The result has been the creation less of a structured system of government than of a fluid system of governance: decisions, laws and policies are made without the existence of formally acknowledged institutions of government. The member states are still the only formal governments, with a strong grip on the policy process, but – as we saw in Chapter 1 – the EU has gone far beyond the definition of a standard intergovernmental organization.

Briefly, the major institutions work as follows: the European Commission develops proposals for new laws and policies, on which final decisions are taken by the Council of the EU and the European Parliament. Once a decision is made, the European Commission is responsible for overseeing implementation by the member states. Meanwhile, the Court of Justice works to ensure that laws and policies meet the terms and spirit of the treaties, while the European Council brings the leaders of the member states together at summit meetings to guide the overall direction of the EU. Alongside the Big Five are a cluster of other institutions with more focused responsibilities, including the European Central Bank, the European External Action Service, the European Investment Bank, Europol and numerous specialized agencies.

Comparisons with national government institutions are only of limited value. The College of Commissioners is something like a cabinet of ministers, but not quite. The European Parliament has some of the powers of a conventional legislature, but not all. The European Commission is an executive bureaucracy, but provides more leadership than most of its national equivalents. The European Council and the Council of the EU are like nothing found in most national systems of government, although the latter can be compared in some ways to an upper chamber of a legislature. The Court of Justice is the only institution to directly parallel those found at the national level – it has most of the features of a typical constitutional court. Into this mix must be added the many subtle nuances of European decision-making, and the many informal aspects of EU government: the influence of the member states, interest groups, corporations, staff in the Commission, permanent representatives and specialized working groups in the Council of the EU, and all the muddling through and incremental change that often characterize policy making in the EU, as in national systems of government.

This chapter looks at the five major institutions of the EU, describing how they are structured and what they do, and explaining how they relate to each other and to the member states. It paints a picture of a system that is often complicated, occasionally clumsy, constantly evolving and regularly misunderstood. It argues that the EU institutions are caught in a web of competing national interests, and that the tension between intergovernmental and supranational forces has an impact on them all. But in spite of the challenges to their identity and personality, they have taken on many of the features of a distinctive supranational European political system, and they are best understood as such.

A constitution for Europe

A constitution is typically a written document that describes the structure of a system of government, outlines the powers of the different governing institutions, describes limits on those powers and lists the rights of citizens relative to government. Almost every state has one, and they are each usually supported by a constitutional court responsible for providing interpretation by measuring laws and the actions of government and citizens against the content and principles of the constitution. Most importantly, they are permanent documents, and provision is made for them to be amended, wholesale changes coming only on those rare occasions when a system of government has broken down and is in need of a thorough overhaul, as – for example – when France replaced the Fourth Republic with the Fifth Republic in 1958.

The EU has no formal constitution as such, and has instead been guided by a series of treaties which together function as something like a constitution: Paris (now expired), the two Treaties of Rome, the Single European Act, Maastricht, Amsterdam, Nice and Lisbon (see Figure 4.1). Each has amended and built upon its predecessor, resulting in a mobile constitution, or one surrounded by talk of constitution building or the 'constitutionalization' of the EU legal order (see Snyder, 2003) without achievement of a final form. For Eriksen *et al.* (2004: 4–5), the result has been a 'material constitution', meaning that the treaties are legally binding, the EU institutions amount to a political community separate from the member states, and EU law represents a constitutional legal order.

YEAR SIGNED	YEAR IN FORCE	NAME	MAIN EFFECTS
1951	1952	Treaty of Paris	Created the European Coal and Steel Community. Expired 2002
1957	1958	Treaty of Rome	Created the European Economic Community and the European Atomic Energy Community
1986	1987	Single European Act	Set goal of completing the single market within five years
1992	1993	Treaty on European Union (Maastricht)	Cleared way for economic and monetary union, created three pillars under new European Union
1997	1999	Treaty of Amsterdam	Organizational changes and expanded EU policy responsibilities
2001	2003	Treaty of Nice	Resolved institutional problems not addressed by Amsterdam
2004	Failed	Treaty on the European Constitution	Would have replaced and consolidated all existing treaties, and made significant institutional changes
2007	2009	Treaty of Lisbon	Made most of the changes intended by the constitutional treaty

Figure 4.1   *The major EU treaties*

When American leaders drew up a new federal constitution for the United States in 1787, they wrote a document that had four important features. First, it was a contract between people and government, outlining their relative roles, powers and rights. Second, it was short and succinct, meaning that it could easily be read and understood by almost anyone. Third, it was often ambiguous, allowing room for evolutionary change. Finally, there was provision for amendments to be made, but – by accident – loopholes ensured that the most important changes to the constitution were to come as a result of judicial interpretations provided by the US Supreme Court and new laws passed by the US Congress. These have changed many of the details of the structure of government, allowing the constitution more or less to keep up with the prevailing political, economic and social mood.

The EU treaties have none of these qualities. Instead of being contracts between people and government, they are contracts among governments, drawn up by their representatives meeting in intergovernmental conferences (see Box 4.1). Instead of being short,

Box 4.1   Intergovernmental conferences (IGCs)

The extent to which decision making in the EU is still intergovernmental rather than supranational is reflected in the way that many of the biggest decisions of recent years have come out of IGCs, convened outside the formal framework of the EU's institutions to allow negotiations among representatives of the governments of the member states. Even as the powers of those institutions have grown, so the IGC has become a common event on the EU calendar; there have been about a dozen IGCs since 1950, eight of which have been held since 1985. While there is nothing in the founding treaties about IGCs, they have become a normal part of the calendar of European integration.

The first opened in May 1950, was chaired by Jean Monnet, and led to the signing of the Treaty of Paris and the creation of the ECSC. The second opened at Messina in April 1955, and led to the creation of the EEC and Euratom and the signing of the Treaties of Rome. Perhaps because national leaders were focused on building the three Communities and the common market, because of the intergovernmental nature of Community decision making in the early years, and because of the fallout from the energy crises of the 1970s, it was to be another 29 years before another major IGC was convened. Concerned about the lack of progress on integration and Europe's declining economic performance in relation to the United States and Japan, an IGC launched in September 1985 had – by December – outlined the framework of what was to become the Single European Act (SEA).

Two more IGCs met during 1991 to discuss political and monetary union, their work resulting in the Treaty on European Union. Conferences in 1996 and 1997 had institutional reform and preparations for eastward enlargement at the top of their agenda, and drafted the Treaty of Amsterdam. Institutional reform was also on the agenda of the IGC that led to the 2000 Treaty of Nice, widely regarded as a disappointment. The eighth major IGC in 2003 reviewed the draft of the new European constitution, which was itself designed to 'promote new forms of European governance'. The ninth IGC in 2007 finalized the details of the Treaty of Lisbon.

they have been long and often complex, sometimes confusing even the legal experts. Instead of being ambiguous, the effort to make sure that there is minimal room for misunderstanding has produced documents that have often gone into great detail on the powers of EU institutions, the policy responsibilities of the EU and the rights of citizens. And instead of being changed only by formal amendments, by judicial interpretation or by changes in EU law, wholesale revisions have been introduced as a result of new treaties.

The European constitutional convention that met in 2002–03 might have been used as an opportunity to undertake some spring-cleaning, producing a short, readable and flexible American-style document that would replace the treaties and give Europeans a better sense of what integration meant. But where the authors of the US constitution were designing a virtually new political system from scratch, had relatively few opinions to take into account, and were dealing with just 13 largely homogeneous American states, the authors of the EU constitution were faced with the challenge of summarizing an accumulation of 50 years'-worth of treaties, and had to account not only for the views of 15 member states with often different values and priorities, but also for those of more than a dozen candidate member states from Eastern Europe. The result was a draft treaty that was long (well over 300 pages), detailed and controversial – all factors in its eventual demise at the hands of French and Dutch voters in 2005. Most of its key provisions were revived in 2007 in the form of the Treaty of Lisbon, which came into force in 2009.

The EU still does not have a formal constitution, and the fatigue generated by more than twenty years of often controversial proposals for – and votes on – new treaties has generated a widespread resistance to the idea of more treaties. But this may not matter; the Treaty of Lisbon brought the rules of the EU up to date, and for Moravcsik (2007: 23, 24, 47), the process of integration has achieved 'a stable constitutional equilibrium' that is 'likely to endure, with incremental changes, for the foreseeable future'. It is no longer necessary, he argues, for the EU to move forward to consolidate its achievements: 'When a constitutional system no longer needs to expand and deepen in order to assure its own continued existence, it is truly stable. It is a mark of constitutional maturity.'

The European Council

The European Council – which functioned on the edge of the EU system of governance until it was formally confirmed as a full institution by the Treaty of Lisbon – is best understood as a steering committee or a board of directors for the EU: it discusses broad issues and goals, leaving it to the other EU institutions to work out the details (Werts, 2008). With its headquarters in the new Europa building, due to open in 2014 across the road from the Commission in the European Quarter of Brussels, the Council consists of the heads of government of the EU member states. This group meets at least four times each year at summit meetings chaired by an appointed president, and provides strategic policy direction for the EU. The Council also has a key role in making appointments, nominating its own president, the president of the European Commission and the High Representative for foreign and security affairs.

The Council was created in 1974 in response to a feeling among some European leaders that the Community needed better leadership, and a body that could take a more long-term view of where the Community was headed. It immediately became an informal part of the Community decision-making structure, but achieved formal legal recognition only with the Single European Act. Maastricht elaborated on its role, but did not provide much clarity beyond noting that the Council would 'provide the Union with the necessary impetus for its development and shall define the general political guidelines thereof'. Lisbon noted that it should not exercise legislative functions.

The Council has been an important motor for integration, with many of the most important initiatives of recent years coming out of Council discussions, including the launch of the European Monetary System (EMS) in 1978, and the discussions that led to all the most recent European treaties. Council summits have also issued major declarations on international crises, reached key decisions on institutional changes, and given new clarity to EU foreign policy. But the Council has also had its failures, including its inability to speed up agricultural or budgetary reform, to agree common EU responses to crises in Iraq and the Balkans, or to fashion an effective response to the eurozone crisis.

Until Lisbon, the Council was chaired by the head of government of the member state holding the presidency of the Council of the EU. But in order to help provide more sustained leadership, it was decided to have an individual appointed to the job by the heads of government for a term of two and a half years, renewable once. In the lead-up to the first vote, in 2009, there was speculation that the Council would opt for a high-profile international leader such as Tony Blair, but in the end they opted for the incumbent prime minister of Belgium, Herman van Rompuy, who was all but unknown outside his native country. The leaders did not want someone in the job who would outshine them or prove too powerful, opting instead for someone with a reputation as a conciliator and consensus-builder. Van Rompuy's second and final term comes to an end in November 2014.

The European Council makes the key decisions on the overall direction of political and economic integration, internal economic issues, foreign policy issues, budget disputes, treaty revisions, new member applications and institutional reforms. It does this through a combination of brainstorming, intensive bilateral and multilateral discussions and bargaining. The results depend on a combination of the quality of organization and preparation, the leadership skills of the president and the ideological and personal agendas of individual leaders. The interpersonal dynamics of the participants is also important: for example, the political significance of the Franco-German axis was long a key part of the mechanics of decision making (although less so since east-

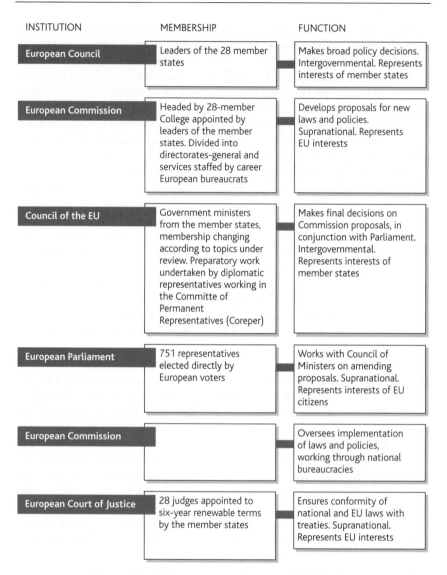

INSTITUTION	MEMBERSHIP	FUNCTION
European Council	Leaders of the 28 member states	Makes broad policy decisions. Intergovernmental. Represents interests of member states
European Commission	Headed by 28-member College appointed by leaders of the member states. Divided into directorates-general and services staffed by career European bureaucrats	Develops proposals for new laws and policies. Supranational. Represents EU interests
Council of the EU	Government ministers from the member states, membership changing according to topics under review. Preparatory work undertaken by diplomatic representatives working in the Committe of Permanent Representatives (Coreper)	Makes final decisions on Commission proposals, in conjunction with Parliament. Intergovernmental. Represents interests of member states
European Parliament	751 representatives elected directly by European voters	Works with Council of Ministers on amending proposals. Supranational. Represents interests of EU citizens
European Commission		Oversees implementation of laws and policies, working through national bureaucracies
European Court of Justice	28 judges appointed to six-year renewable terms by the member states	Ensures conformity of national and EU laws with treaties. Supranational. Represents EU interests

Figure 4.2   *The institutional structure of the EU*

ward enlargement has diluted the voting and political power of the Big Two). Leaders who have been in office a long time, who have a solid base of political support at home or who have a record of progressive positions on Europe will be in a different negotiating position from those who do not.

Regular summits of the Council are held four times each year, with additional meetings held when necessary. They once took place in the capital of the member state holding the presidency of the Council of Ministers, or in a regional city or town, but they now all take place in Brussels. The agenda is driven in part by the ongoing priorities of the EU, but also by emergencies or by unfinished business from previous meetings. Some issues (especially economic issues) are routinely discussed at every summit, while the European Commission may also promote issues it would like to see discussed. The goal is to agree a set of Conclusions, an advanced draft of which is usually awaiting the leaders at the beginning of the summit, and provides the focus for discussions.

Much symbolism is attached to the outcomes of the summits, the level of failure or success reflecting on the whole process of European integration and on the abilities of European leaders. For example, the failure of December 2003 summit intended to reach agreement on the draft constitution was seen in part as a reflection on the erratic Italian presidency and the leadership of prime minister Silvio Berlusconi. By contrast, when the German presidency was able to broker agreement at the June 2007 European Council on the treaty that would replace the failed constitution, it reflected well on the new influence of the Merkel government.

The European Commission

The European Commission is the executive-bureaucratic arm of the EU, responsible for developing proposals for new laws and policies, for overseeing the execution of those laws and policies once they are adopted, and for promoting the general interests of the EU. Its headquarters are in the Berlaymont building in Brussels, and its staff work in multiple buildings around the city, and in regional cities around the EU and national capitals around the world. It is the most supranational of the EU institutions, working to promote EU interests and acting as the driving force behind key EU policy initiatives.

While it is the best known of the major EU institutions, the Commission is also the most misunderstood. Critics charge that it is big, expensive and powerful, that it meddles in the internal affairs of member states, that its leaders are not elected, and that it has too little public accountability. But the criticism is often misguided:

- Far from being big and expensive, it has just under 40,000 staff, only two-thirds of whom work actively on policy. This makes it smaller than the administration of a medium-sized European city, and its administrative costs account for just over 2 per cent of the EU budget, or about €3.3 billion in 2011 (just under €7 per year for each resident of the EU).

- It is not particularly powerful, being less a decision-making body than a servant of the member states, charged with translating the goals of integration into specific proposals for action. Decision-making power rests with a combination of the Council of the EU, which is firmly under the control of the governments of the member states, and the European Parliament, elected by the voters of the EU.
- Although European Commissioners are not elected, they are nominated by elected national government leaders and confirmed by the elected European Parliament.
- It may sometimes appear secretive and anonymous, but its record is no worse than that of national bureaucracies, and in some ways is better. It has so few staff and resources that it must rely heavily on input from outside agencies.

The Commission is headed by a College of Commissioners with 28 members, one from each of the member states, which serves a five-year term beginning six months after elections to the European Parliament. Each commissioner has a portfolio for which he or she is responsible (ranging from competition to trade, economic and monetary affairs, the environment, transport and enlargement), and collectively they make the final decisions on which proposals for new laws and policies to send on for approval. Commissioners are nominated by their national governments, but must swear an oath of office saying that they will renounce any defence of national interests. Nominees are discussed with the Commission president, and must be acceptable to other governments and to the European Parliament (see Spence, 2006:34–8).

The dominant figure in the Commission is the president, usually the most publicly visible person in the EU hierarchy. Although no more than the chief bureaucrat of the EU, the president can influence the appointment of other commissioners, has sole power over distributing portfolios, drives the agenda for the Commission, can launch new policy initiatives, chairs meetings of the College, can reshuffle portfolios mid-term, and represents the Commission in dealings with other EU institutions and national governments. There are few formal rules regarding how the president is appointed (see Nugent, 2001:63–8), the normal procedure being for the leaders of the member states to decide the nominee at the European Council held in the June before the term of the incumbent Commission ends, settling on someone acceptable to all of them and who can win confirmation by the European Parliament. Appointed for renewable five-year terms, the president will usually be someone with a strong character and proven leadership abilities, but not so strong as to become too independent.

As with all such positions, the powers of the office depend to some extent on the personality of the office holder (see Table 4.1). Without

Table 4.1 *Presidents of the European Commission*

Term	Name	Ideology	Member state
1958–67	Walter Hallstein	Christian Democrat	West Germany
1967–70	Jean Rey	Centrist	Belgium.
1970–72	Franco Maria Malfatti	Christian Democrat	Italy
1972	Sicco Mansholt	Social Democrat	Netherlands (interim)
1973–76	François-Xavier Ortoli	Conservative	France
1977–80	Roy Jenkins	Social Democrat	UK
1981–84	Gaston Thorn	Socialist	Luxembourg
1985–94	Jacques Delors	Socialist	France
1995–99	Jacques Santer	Christian Democrat	Luxembourg
1999	Manuel Marin	Socialist	Spain (interim)
1999–2004	Romano Prodi	Centrist	Italy
2004–	José Manuel Barroso	Centrist	Portugal

question the most influential was former French economics minister Jacques Delors (1985–94), who centralized authority, had firm ideas about a strong, federal Europe asserting itself internationally, and used this vision to champion the single-market and single-currency programmes (see Ross, 1995). He was succeeded by Jacques Santer, former prime minister of Luxembourg, who avoided bold new initiatives, focusing instead on improving the implementation of existing laws and policies. The Santer College resigned en masse in January 1999 following charges of nepotism and incompetence directed against some of its members.

Santer was replaced by former Italian prime minister Romano Prodi, who witnessed the passage of the treaties of Amsterdam and Nice, the fallout over Iraq, the holding of the constitutional convention, the arrival of the euro, and the 2004 enlargement. Prodi was replaced in late 2004 by José Manuel Barroso, the incumbent prime minister of Portugal, who was faced with fighting public apathy towards the EU, improving relations with the United States, dealing with the collapse of the constitutional treaty, and responding to the breaking of the global economic crisis. He was confirmed to a second five-year term in 2009.

Below the College, the Commission is divided into 38 directorates-general (DGs) and services, the equivalent to national government ministries. Each DG is tied to a commissioner, has its own director-general and deals with a specific area of policy. The Commission also works closely with a series of several hundred advisory, management and regulatory committees made up of national government officials (in a phenomenon known as comitology), and with expert committees made up of national officials, specialists appointed by national governments, corporate interests and special interest groups.

The general task of the Commission is to ensure that EU policies are advanced in light of the treaties (for details, see Edwards and Spence, 2006: ch. 1). It does this in five ways:

- *Powers of initiation.* The Commission makes sure that the principles of the treaties are turned into laws and policies (see Box 4.2). Proposals can come from a commissioner or a staff member of one of the DGs, may be a response to a ruling by the Court of Justice, may flow out of the requirements of the treaties, or may come out of pressure exerted by member-state governments, interest groups, the European Council, the European Parliament and even private corporations. Proposals will be drafted by officials in one of the DGs and will work their way through the different levels of the DG, being discussed with other DGs and with outside parties, such as interest groups or corporations. Drafts will finally reach the College of Commissioners, which can accept or reject them, send them back for redrafting, or defer making a decision. Once accepted, proposals are sent to the European Parliament and the Council of the EU for a decision. The process can take anything from months to years, and Commission staff will be involved at every stage.
- *Powers of implementation.* Once a law or policy is accepted, the Commission must make sure that it is implemented by the member states. It has no power to do this directly, but instead works through national bureaucracies, using its power to collect information from member states, to issue written warnings, and to take to the Court of Justice any member state, corporation or individual that does not conform to the spirit of the treaties or follow subsequent EU law. The Commission adds to the pressure by publicizing progress on implementation, hoping to embarrass laggards into action.
- *Acting as the conscience of the EU.* The Commission is expected to rise above competing national interests and to represent and promote the general interest of the EU. It is also expected to help smooth the flow of decision making by mediating disagreements between or among member states and other EU institutions.
- *Management of EU finances.* The Commission makes sure that EU revenues are collected, plays a key role in drafting and guiding the EU budget through the Council of the EU and Parliament, and administers EU spending.
- *External relations.* The Commission represents the EU in dealings with international organizations such as the UN and the WTO (Smith, 2006), is a key point of contact between the EU and the rest of the world, vets applications for EU membership from aspirant states, and oversees negotiations with an applicant.

Box 4.2 European Union law

A key difference between the EU and a conventional international organization is that the EU has a body of law which is applicable in all its member states, which supersedes national law in areas where the EU has responsibility, and which is backed up by rulings from the Court of Justice. The creation of this body of law has involved the voluntary pooling of powers by the member states in a broad range of policy areas, and the development of a new level of legal authority to which the member states are subject.

The foundation of the EU legal order is provided by the treaties, which are the primary sources of EU law (Lasok , 2005: ch. 4), out of which come the secondary sources, the most important of which are the thousands of individual binding laws adopted by the EU, and which take three main forms:

• *Regulations* are the most powerful, and most like conventional acts of a national legislature. They are directly applicable in that they do not need to be turned into national law, they are binding in their entirety, and they take immediate effect on a specified date. Usually fairly narrow in intent, regulations are often designed to amend or adjust an existing law.

• *Directives* are binding in terms of goals, but it is left up to the member states to decide what action they need to take to achieve those goals. For example, a 2006 directive on equality for men and women in the workplace mandated equal access to employment, and equality in regard to pay, promotion, working conditions and social security schemes, but left it up to the member states to decide individually how to meet those targets. Directives usually include a date by which national action must be taken, and member states must tell the Commission what they are doing.

• *Decisions* are also binding, but are usually fairly specific in their intent, and aimed at one or more member states, at institutions, or even at individuals. Some are aimed at making changes in the powers of EU institutions, some are directed towards internal administrative matters, and others are issued when the Commission has to adjudicate disputes between member states or corporations.

The EU has several other administrative tools which, because they are not binding, cannot be considered laws even though they can result in policy change. *Recommendations* and *opinions* are sometimes used to test reaction to a new EU policy, but they are used mainly to persuade or to provide interpretation on the application of regulations, directives and decisions. Meanwhile, *White Papers* and *Green Papers* are documents published by the EU that test the waters by making suggestions for new policies, the latter more detailed and specific than the former.

The Commission has been at the core of European integration since the beginning, and while it is subject to the same problems as any other large organization, it has – on the whole – been a productive source of initiatives for new laws and policies, and is more accessible and open than, say, the Council of the EU. Eurosceptic media and politicians like to use the Commission as one of the key targets of their criticism, and it is usually to the Commission that they are referring when they complain about the powers and interference of 'Brussels'. But the Commission has no formally independent powers, and can do no more than it is allowed by the treaties.

The Council of the EU

The Council of the EU (also known as the Council of Ministers, or simply as 'the Council') is the key decision-making arm of the EU, sharing responsibility with the European Parliament for voting on new proposals for EU law. With its headquarters in the Justus Lipsius building in Brussels, the Council is headed by national government ministers, who meet in one of ten technical councils (or 'configurations'), the membership depending on the topic under discussion. The number of times each group of ministers meets varies according to the importance of different policy areas, so foreign and economics ministers will usually meet monthly, while other councils may meet only two or four times per year. Between meetings of ministers, national interests in the Council are protected and promoted by Permanent Representations, or national delegations of professional diplomats, which are much like embassies to the EU.

The Council is one of the least known of the major EU institutions: its meetings attract relatively little media coverage, it has been the subject of much less academic study than the Commission or Parliament, and critics of the EU often forget how much power still lies in the hands of the Council, which is one of the most intergovernmental of EU institutions. When Europeans think about the activities of the EU, they tend to first think of the Commission, forgetting that the Commission can only propose, while it is up to the Council of the EU and the European Parliament to dispose. In many ways, their powers make the Council and Parliament 'co-legislatures' of the EU.

Of the ten groups of ministers, the most important are those who meet as the General Affairs Council (GAC), which prepares – and follows up on – meetings of the European Council. The Foreign Affairs Council brings together EU foreign ministers to deal with external relations and trade issues, while economics and finance ministers meet together as the Economic and Financial Affairs Council (Ecofin), agriculture ministers as the Agriculture and Fisheries Council, and so on.

The relevant European commissioner will also attend in order to make sure that the Council does not lose sight of broader EU interests. How often each council meets depends on the importance of its policy area. Most meetings of the Council last no more than one or two days, and are held in Brussels.

Routinely overlooked in assessments of the Council is the powerful Committee of Permanent Representatives (Coreper), within which experts from the national delegations meet frequently to act as a link between Brussels and the member states, to represent the views of the national governments in decision-making, and to keep capitals in touch with developments in Brussels. Most importantly, Coreper prepares Council agendas, oversees the committees and working parties set up to sift through proposals, decides which proposals go to which council, and makes many of the decisions about which proposals will be accepted and which will be left for debate by ministers (see Hayes-Renshaw and Wallace, 2006:72–82).

Direction is given to the deliberations of the Council and Coreper by the presidency of the Council of the EU, which is held not by a person, but by a member state. Every EU member state has a turn at holding the presidency for a spell of six months, the baton being passed in January and July each year (see Table 4.2). The state holding the presidency sets the agenda for, and arranges and chairs meetings of the Council of the EU. It had more authority until Lisbon, which made two critical institutional changes: it created a new appointed president for the European Council, who took over many of the responsibilities held until then by the presidency of the Council, and it made the High Representative of the Union for Foreign Affairs and Security Policy chair of the Foreign Affairs Council.

There are both advantages and disadvantages to the rotating presidency. It allows the governments of the member states to convene

Table 4.2   *Rotation of presidencies of the Council of the EU*

	First half	*Second half*
2010	Spain	Belgium
2011	Hungary	Poland
2012	Denmark	Cyprus
2013	Ireland	Lithuania
2014	Greece	Italy
2015	Latvia	Luxembourg
2016	Netherlands	Slovakia
2017	Malta	UK
2018	Estonia	Bulgaria
2019	Austria	Romania

meetings and launch initiatives on issues of national interest, to bring those issues to the top of the EU agenda, and – if they do a good job – to earn prestige and credibility. It also helps make the process of European integration more real to the citizens of the country holding the presidency. But as the EU has grown, so has the workload of the presidency, and some of the smaller states struggle to offer the necessary leadership. As membership of the EU has expanded, so has the cycle of the presidency. With the founding six member states, each had a turn at the helm once every three years, but with 28 members the rotation has grown to 14 years.

Once the European Commission has proposed a new law, it is sent to the Council of the EU and Parliament for debate and for a final decision on adoption or rejection. The more complex proposals will usually go first to one or more specialist Council working parties, which will look them over in detail, identifying points of agreement and disagreement, and responding to suggestions for amendments made by Parliament (for more detail, see Hayes-Renshaw and Wallace, 2006). The proposal will then go to Coreper, which looks at the political implications, and tries to clear as many of the remaining problems as it can, ensuring that the meeting of ministers is as quick and as painless as possible. The proposal then moves on to the relevant Council for a final decision. Unanimity was once required, but votes are now rarely called, and where they are there are two options: a simple majority is used for procedural issues in the case of select number of specific policy issues, the balance of business (estimates suggest about 10–15 per cent of Council votes (Nugent, 2010: 156–7)) being put to a qualified majority vote (QMV).

Under QMV, each minister is given several votes roughly in proportion to the population of his or her member state (see Table 4.3), to make a total (in 2013–14) of 352. To be successful, a proposal must win at least 260 of the votes (just under 74 per cent of the total), the support of a majority of member states (if the Council is voting on a Commission proposal), and a member state can ask for a check that the votes in favour come from countries representing at least 62 per cent of the population of EU. In some policy areas, including enlargement, security and external relations, the support must be unanimous, giving every member state the power of veto. With effect from 1 November 2014, the qualified majority will be a 55 per cent majority of countries if acting on a Commission proposal (72 per cent if not), and the support of member states containing at least 62 per cent of the population of the EU.

Once a proposal has been voted on by the Council, it goes to the European Parliament, and the two institutions may pass it back and forth, with amendments, as many as three times. In the event of a failure to agree, the proposal is sent to a Conciliation Committee made

Table 4.3 *Votes in the Council of the EU*

Germany	29	Greece	12	Lithuania	7
France	29	Hungary	12	Slovakia	7
Italy	29	Portugal	12	Cyprus	4
UK	29	Austria	10	Estonia	4
Poland	27	Bulgaria	10	Latvia	4
Spain	27	Sweden	10	Luxembourg	4
Romania	14	Croatia	7	Slovenia	4
Netherlands	13	Denmark	7	Malta	3
Belgium	12	Finland	7		
Czech Republic	12	Ireland	7	Total	352

up of 28 representatives from each institution, with Commission staff also being present.

Because the Council of the EU is a meeting place for national interests, the keys to understanding how it works are terms such as *intergovernmental, compromise, bargaining* and *diplomacy*. The ministers are often leading political figures at home, so they are motivated by national political interests. Their views are also ideologically driven, and their authority will depend to some extent on the strength and stability of the governing party or coalition at home. All these factors combine to pull ministers in different directions, and to deny the Council the kind of structural regularity enjoyed by the Commission.

The European Parliament

The European Parliament (EP) is the quasi-legislative arm of the EU, and the only directly elected international legislature in the world. It has a single chamber, and the 751 Members of the European Parliament (MEPs) are elected by universal suffrage by all eligible voters in the EU for fixed, renewable five-year terms. The number of seats is divided up among the member states roughly on the basis of population, so that Germany has 96 while the four smallest countries have just six each (see Table 4.4). This formula means that bigger countries are under-represented and smaller countries over-represented, so while Germany, Britain and France each have one MEP per 830,000–860,000 citizens, the ratio for Belgium, the Czech Republic and Portugal is about 1:500,000–510,000 citizens, and for Malta and Luxembourg about 1:65,000–85,000.

Absurdly, the Parliament's buildings are divided among three cities: while the administrative headquarters are in Luxembourg, and parliamentary committees meet in Brussels for about two to three weeks every month (except August), the parliamentary chamber is situated in

Table 4.4 *Seats in the European Parliament*

Germany	96	Greece	21	Ireland	11
France	74	Hungary	21	Lithuania	11
Italy	73	Portugal	21	Latvia	8
United Kingdom	73	Sweden	20	Slovenia	8
Spain	54	Austria	18	Cyprus	6
Poland	51	Bulgaria	17	Estonia	6
Romania	32	Denmark	13	Luxembourg	6
Netherlands	26	Finland	13	Malta	6
Belgium	21	Slovakia	13		
Czech Republic	21	Croatia	11	Total	751

Strasbourg, and MEPs are expected to meet there in plenary sessions (meetings of the whole, or part-sessions) for about three or four days each month except August. Since committees are where most of the real bargaining and revising takes place, and since 'additional' plenaries can be held in Brussels, attendance at Strasbourg plenaries can sometimes be sparse. This arrangement comes courtesy of the French government, which stubbornly insists that Strasbourg must remain the site for plenary sessions, undermining the credibility of the EP while inflating its budget (see Judge and Earnshaw, 2008:148ff.)

Unlike conventional legislatures, the EP cannot introduce laws or raise revenues (powers that rest with the Commission), instead sharing the tasks of amendment and decision with the Council of the EU. Directly elected by the voters of the EU since 1979, it is the most clearly democratic of the EU institutions, and yet few EU citizens know what it does, and they have not developed the same kinds of psychological ties to the EP as they have to their national legislatures. In spite of this, the Parliament has shrewdly used its powers to play a more active role in running the EU (see Rittberger, 2005: chs 5, 6), and has been entrepreneurial in suggesting new laws and policies to the Commission. Where it once mainly reacted to Commission proposals and Council votes, it has become more assertive in launching its own initiatives and making the other institutions pay more attention to its opinions. It has also won more powers to amend laws and to check the activities of the other institutions, with the result that it now has equal standing with the Council of the EU on deciding which proposals for new laws will be enacted and which will not.

The EP is chaired by a president, elected from within the Parliament for renewable five-year terms to preside over debates during plenary sessions, decide which proposals go to which committees, and represent Parliament in relations with other institutions. The president would normally come from the majority political group, but since no group has ever won a majority of seats (see Chapter 5), an informal arrangement exists by which the job is rotated between the two major groups (conservatives and socialists) for half the life of a Parliament. To help with the task of dealing with many different political groups in Parliament, the president works with the chairs of the different groups in the Conference of Presidents, which draws up the agenda for plenary sessions and oversees the work of parliamentary committees.

Like most national legislatures, the EP has 20 standing committees and a variable number of temporary committees which meet in Brussels to consider legislation relevant to their area or to carry out parliamentary inquiries (see Judge and Earnshaw, 2008: 177–96). The committees range in size between two dozen and six dozen members, and have their own hierarchy, which reflects levels of parliamentary influence over different policy areas: among the most powerful are those dealing with the environment and the budget. Seats on committees are distributed on the basis of a mixture of the balance of party groups, the seniority of MEPs, and national interests. For example, there are more Irish and Polish MEPs on the agriculture committee than on committees dealing with foreign and defence matters.

The concern of member states with preserving their powers over decision making in the Council of the EU has resulted over the years in several changes to parliamentary rules. Parliament initially had a *consultation procedure* under which it was allowed to give a non-binding opinion to the Council of the EU before the latter adopted a new law in selected areas, but this is now rarely used. The SEA introduced a *cooperation procedure* which gave Parliament the right to a second reading for certain laws being considered by the Council of the EU, notably those relating to the single market. Maastricht created a *codecision procedure* under which Parliament was given the right to a third reading on bills, effectively giving it equal authority with the Council. With Lisbon, this became the *ordinary legislative procedure,* which is now the standard approach to law-making, giving Parliament equal powers with the Council of the EU.

In addition to these legislative powers, the Parliament also has joint powers with the Council of the EU over fixing the EU budget, so that the two institutions between them constitute the budgetary authority of the EU; they review the annual draft sent to them by the Commission, and the EP can ask for changes to the budget, ask for new appropriations for areas not covered (but cannot make decisions on how to raise money), and ultimately – with a two-thirds majority – reject the budget. Under the *consent procedure,* the support of the Parliament is needed for the accession of new members to the EU and for the conclusion of international agreements by the EU, and the Parliament also has several supervisory powers over other EU institutions, including the right to debate the annual programme of the

Box 4.3   Specialized institutions of the EU

As the EU has grown, so has the number of institutions and specialized agencies created to deal with different aspects of its work. They have been created mainly according to need, without an overall plan or template, the result being that they vary considerably in terms of their political reach, their administrative powers, their roles, their levels of independence and their internal structure. One of the best known is the European Central Bank (ECB), created in 1998 with the job of helping to manage the euro by ensuring price stability, setting interest rates, and managing the foreign reserves of the eurozone states. With the global financial crisis that broke in 2007, and the subsequent debt problems of Greece, Ireland, Portugal and Spain, the ECB became more active and the pressure to give it more powers over monetary policy grew (see Chapter 7 for more details).

New regulatory bodies were created in the wake of the global financial crisis, joining a pre-existing network of other specialized agencies, including permanent regulatory agencies with mainly technical and informational responsibilities, advisory bodies such as the Committee of the Regions, temporary executive agencies responsible for policy implementation, and agencies dealing with aspects of the Common Security and Defence Policy (CSDP) (see Appendix 3). The ad hoc nature of the way they have been created sparked a debate in 2008 over the need for a more structured approach to their management and responsibilities (European Commission, 2008), and since 2012 there have been a set of guiding principles in place that are designed to make the agencies more coherent, effective and accountable.

Commission, to put questions to the Commission, and to approve the appointment of the president of the Commission and the College of Commissioners.

The most substantial of Parliament's powers is its ability – with a two-thirds majority – to force the resignation of the College of Commissioners through a vote of censure. While this power has never been used successfully, Parliament came close in January 1999 after charges of mismanagement and nepotism were directed at two members of the College. Anticipating a vote of censure, the Santer Commission resigned just before the findings of an EP investigation were published in March. In October 2004, Parliament blocked the appointment of the new Italian Commissioner Rocco Buttiglione, who had expressed controversial views on homosexuality and women, and in 2010 Bulgarian nominee Rumiana Jeleva withdrew after Parliament raised questions about her financial declaration and her abilities to be a commissioner.

The European Court of Justice

The European Court of Justice is the supreme legal authority of the EU, and the final court of appeal on all legal questions pertaining to the EU. It consists of 28 judges appointed for renewable six-year terms, their work supported by eight advocates-general (advisers who deliver preliminary opinions on cases). It is supported by a General Court that deals with less complicated cases, and by an EU Civil Service Tribunal that deals with disputes between the EU institutions and their staff. An independent 28-member Court of Auditors (not part of the Court of Justice) is meanwhile charged with checking EU finances, and has the power to audit any person or organization receiving EU funds (with any irregularities reported to the European Anti-Fraud Office). All four institutions are based in an expanding cluster of buildings in the Centre Européen on a plateau above the city of Luxembourg.

The Court of Justice is easily the most underrated of the five major institutions of the EU, and the one that attracts the least public and political attention (or academic political analysis). While the Commission and Parliament often become embroiled in headline-making political controversies, the Court has quietly gone about its business of clarifying the meaning of the treaties and of European law. Its activities have been critical to the progress of European integration, and its role just as significant as that of the Commission or Parliament, yet few Europeans know what it does, and its decisions rarely make the news.

The job of the Court is to make sure that national and EU laws – and international agreements being considered by the EU – meet the terms and the spirit of the treaties, and that EU law is equally, fairly and consistently applied throughout the member states. It does this by ruling on the 'constitutionality' of EU law, giving opinions (preliminary rulings) to national courts in cases where there are questions about the meaning of EU law, and making judgements in disputes (direct actions) involving EU institutions, member states, individuals and corporations. In so doing, the Court makes sure that the decisions and policies of the EU are consistent and fit with the agreements inherent in the treaties. It can rule only in policy areas where the EU has competence, and so does not have powers over criminal law or family law, but has instead made most of its decisions on the kind of economic issues in which the EU has been most actively involved.

It made its most basic contribution to the process of integration in 1963 and 1964 when it declared that the Treaty of Rome was not just a treaty, but was a constitutional instrument that had direct effect on member states, and had supremacy (took precedence) over national law in policy areas where the EU has responsibility. The Court has also established important additional precedents through decisions such as the *Cassis de Dijon* case [1979], which simplified completion of the single market by establishing the principle of mutual recognition: a product made and sold legally in one member state cannot be barred from another (see Chapter 7). Other Court rulings have helped increase the powers of Parliament, strengthened individual rights, promoted the free movement of workers, reduced gender discrimination, and helped the Commission break down the barriers to competition.

Although judges serve six-year renewable terms, appointments are staggered so that about half the judges come up for renewal every three years. The judges are theoretically appointed by common agreement among the governments of the member states, so there is technically no national quota. However, because every member state has the right to make one nomination, all 28 are effectively national appointees. Apart from being acceptable to the other member states, judges must be independent, must be legally competent, and must avoid promoting the national interests of their home states. Some judges have come to the Court with experience as government ministers, some have held elective office, and others have had careers as lawyers or as academics; whatever they have done in their previous lives, they are not allowed to hold administrative or political office while they are on the Court. They can resign from the Court, but they can only be removed by the other judges (not by member states or other EU institutions), and then only by unanimous agreement that they are no longer doing their job adequately (Lasok, 2007:7–8).

The judges elect one of their own to be president by majority vote for a three-year renewable term. The president presides over Court meetings, is responsible for distributing cases among the judges and deciding the dates for hearings, and has considerable influence over the political direction of the Court. Despite his or her critical role in furthering European integration, the president – Vassilios Skouris of Greece was elected to a fourth term in 2012 – never becomes a major public figure in the same mould as the president of the Commission.

To speed up its work, the Court is divided into chambers of three, five, or thirteen judges which make the final decisions on cases. To further ease the workload, the judges are assisted by eight advocates-general, who review each of the cases as they come in, and deliver a preliminary opinion on what action should be taken and on which EU law applies. The judges are not required to agree with the opinion, or even to refer to it, but it gives them a point of reference from which to reach a decision. Although advocates-general are again appointed in theory by common accord, one is appointed by each of the Big Five member states, and the other three are appointed by the smaller states. One of the advocates-general is appointed First Advocate-General on a one-year rotation.

The Court has become busier as the reach of the EU has widened and deepened. In the 1960s it was hearing about 50 cases per year and making about 15–20 judgements, but it now hears several hundred cases each year, and makes as many as 200 judgements. As the volume of work grew during the 1970s and 1980s, it was taking as long as two years to reach a decision on more complex cases. To move matters along, a subsidiary Court of First Instance was created in 1989 (since renamed the General Court), to be the first point of decision on less complicated cases. If cases are lost at this level, the parties involved may appeal to the Court of Justice. There are 28 judges on the General Court and it uses the same basic procedures as the Court of Justice. To further ease the workload, the EU Civil Service Tribunal was created in 2004 to take over from the General Court any cases involving disputes between the EU institutions and their staff. It has seven judges appointed for six-year renewable terms.

The work of the Court comes under two main headings:

- *Preliminary rulings.* These make up the most important part of the Court's work, and account for about 40–60 per cent of the cases it considers. If a matter of EU law arises in a national court case, the national court can ask for a ruling from the Court of Justice on the interpretation or validity of that law. Members of EU institutions can also ask for preliminary rulings, but most are made on behalf of a national court, and are binding on the court in the case concerned.
- *Direct actions.* These are cases where an individual, company, member state or EU institution brings proceedings against an EU institution or a member state. For example, a member state might have failed to meet its obligations under EU law, so a case can be brought by the Commission or by another member state. Private companies can also bring actions if they think a member state is discriminating against their products. Direct actions can also be brought against the Commission or the Council to make sure that EU laws conform to the treaties, and to attempt to cancel those that do not, and against an EU institution that has failed to act in accordance with the terms of the treaties.

Unlike all the other EU institutions, where English is becoming the working language, the Court works mainly in French, although a case can be heard in any official EU language at the request of the plaintiff or defendant. Court proceedings usually begin with a written application, describing the dispute and the grounds on which the application is based. The President assigns the case to a chamber, and the defendant is given one month to lodge a statement of defence, the plaintiff a month to reply, and the defendant a further month to reply to the plaintiff. The case is then argued by the parties at a public hearing

before a chamber of judges. An advocate-general then offers a preliminary decision, which is reviewed by the judges, who in time make their
judgement.

Court decisions are supposed to be unanimous, but votes are usually
taken by a simple majority. All decisions are secret, so it is never publicly known who – if anyone – dissented. The Court has no direct
powers to enforce its judgements, so implementation is left mainly to
national courts or the governments of the member states, with the
Commission keeping a close watch (Conant, 2002). Maastricht gave
the Court of Justice new powers by allowing it to impose fines, but the
question of how the fines would be collected was left open, and the
implications of this new power are still unclear.

Conclusions

The EU has built a complex network of administrative bodies since its
inception. Among them, they are responsible for making general and
detailed policy decisions, developing and adopting laws, overseeing the
implementation of laws and policies by the member states, ensuring
that those laws and policies meet the spirit and the letter of the treaties,
and overseeing activities in a variety of areas, from environmental
management to transport, consumer protection, drug regulation and
police cooperation. In many ways they fit the standard definition of a
confederal system of administration: a general system of government
coexisting with the governments of the member states, each with
shared and independent powers, but with the balance in favour of the
member states. Except for the EP, EU citizens do not have a direct relationship with any of the EU institutions, instead relating to them
through their national governments.

Despite concerns in some of the member states about the federaliza-
tion of Europe, the institutions still lack many of the features of a conventional federal government: there is no European army or air force,
no elected European president, no European tax system, no European
foreign and defence policy and no single postal system. Furthermore,
much of the focus of decision making still rests with the European
Council and the Council of the EU, both of which are intergovernmental rather than supranational. It is here that the EU is most obviously a confederal rather than a federal arrangement. Finally, the EU is
still ultimately a voluntary arrangement, and lacks the powers to force
its member states to implement European law and policy. The withdrawal of one of its members would not be regarded as secession.

Nonetheless, while debates rage about the finer points of the decisions reached by the EU institutions, the national governments of the
member states have transferred significant responsibilities to these

institutions. Particularly since the passage of the Single European Act, the activities of the Commission, the Council of the EU, Parliament and the Court of Justice have had a more direct impact on the lives of Europeans, and government in Europe is no longer just about what happens in national capitals and regional cities, but also about what happens in Brussels, Luxembourg and Strasbourg.

The relationships among the five major institutions – and between them and the governments of the member states – change constantly as the balance of power is adjusted and fine-tuned. Out of a combination of internal convenience and external pressure is emerging a new form of governance that is winning more responsibilities as the member states cautiously transfer sovereignty from the local and national levels to the regional level. In the next chapter we will see what this has meant for the citizens of Europe.

Chapter 5

The EU and its Citizens

The Maastricht treaty famously claimed that the goal of European integration was to create 'an ever closer union among the peoples of Europe, in which decisions are taken as closely as possible to the citizen'. But critics charge the EU with being an elitist construct, offering ordinary Europeans too few opportunities directly to influence its work, and creating a problem that has been serious enough to earn its own label: the democratic deficit. It sometimes seems as though the work of the EU goes on despite public opinion, which is often confused, increasingly doubtful, and in some cases actively hostile towards integration. But how we rate the EU in terms of its democratic qualities depends on how we define it as a political entity: if it was a federal union, its democratic credentials would be weak, but if we see it as a confederal system, then its procedures are almost everything we would or could expect.

There is another kind of deficit at work about which we hear much less: the knowledge deficit. The character and personality of the EU are hard to pin down, there is no easy answer to the question 'What is the EU?', it is engaged on a journey to an unknown destination, the media often misrepresent the way it works, most academic writing on the EU makes it sound dull and legalistic, and most Europeans neither know how the EU works nor understand what difference it has made to their lives. There is a school of academic thought that Europeans can use cues provided for them on European issues by political leaders, parties, interest groups and the media, and that this allows them to make decisions on the EU as though they were informed. But this assumes that the information they receive is objective and accurate, which it often is not, and it also perpetuates the elitism for which the EU is often criticized.

It is important to remember that, as we saw in Chapter 4, the interests of citizens are represented by their national governments in the meeting rooms of the European Council and the Council of the EU, and the powers and influence of the European Parliament are growing. The European Commission is no less transparent or responsive than national bureaucracies, and is so short-staffed that it makes more use of input from ordinary citizens, interest groups and corporations than do most of its national counterparts. And in many respects the democratic and knowledge deficits in the EU are not so different from those

96

found in the member states, where citizens often complain about the lack of government transparency, and many also admit to understanding little about how government works or what it does.

This chapter asks what Europeans think about the EU, and how they participate in (or opt out of) the process of integration. It begins with an assessment of public attitudes towards integration, examining the relationship between public opinion and the decisions taken by national leaders, and discussing the dynamics of euroscepticism, the knowledge deficit and the democratic deficit. It then looks at the channels through which Europeans can express their opinions on EU policy – including elections, referenda and interest groups – and asks how effective they have been, what drives the ways in which ordinary Europeans engage with the European project, and how they make their decisions on European issues.

Public opinion and Europe

The EU has a survey research service known as Eurobarometer, which measures public opinion on topics relating to European integration. Surveys since the early 1980s have found a waxing and waning of enthusiasm: support grew to a peak in 1990, but fell in Germany after reunification, then more widely throughout the EU in the wake of the controversy over Maastricht, and even further since the breaking of the eurozone crisis in 2009. The number of people holding a positive image of the EU peaked in 2007 at 52 per cent and had fallen by 2012 to just 31 per cent, while the number of people holding negative views – which had held steady at about 15 per cent for some years – had nearly doubled by 2012 (see Figure 5.1). The highest proportion of positive views in 2012 was in countries such as Belgium, Bulgaria, Germany, Ireland and France, while the highest proportion of negative views was in Britain, Greece, Cyprus and Austria.

There has also been something of a roller-coaster in the number of people who believe that their country has benefited from membership, from 58 per cent in 1990 to 47 per cent in 2004, back up to 59 per cent in 2007, and back down to 53 per cent in 2010. Among those most convinced of the benefits are the majority of Eastern European member states, and older member states that had – at least until the 2007–10 global financial crisis – most clearly seen the economic benefits of membership, such as Ireland, Greece and Spain. Finally, while attitudes towards the euro were initially lukewarm, and in some countries actively hostile, they strengthened once it was introduced and generally remained positive even as the eurozone crisis worsened (see Figure 5.2). More than two-thirds of voters were in favour of the euro in 2012 in the Netherlands, France, Germany, Belgium, Ireland and

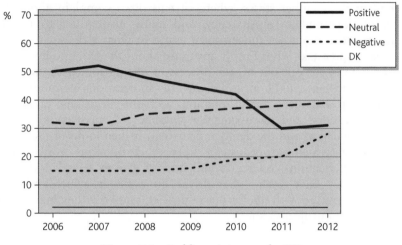

Figure 5.1 *Public opinion on the EU*

Response to the question 'Does the EU conjure up for you a very positive, fairly positive, neutral, fairly negative or very negative image?' Data from *Eurobarometer* 77, Spring 2012: 92. Data are for spring waves of *Eurobarometer* only.

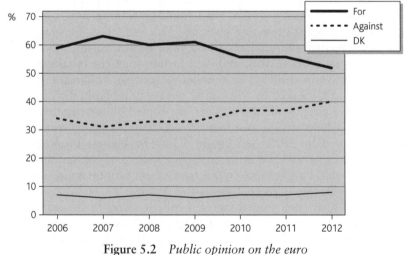

Figure 5.2 *Public opinion on the euro*

Data from *Eurobarometer* 78, Autumn 2012: 87. Data are for spring waves only.

even Greece. Opposition remained strongest (two-thirds or more) in the three countries that have long been most hostile to the euro: Denmark, Sweden and the UK (Eurobarometer 78, Autumn 2012: 88).

There are several possible explanations for these mixed opinions. First, integration is still a relatively new issue for the average European. True, the Treaty of Rome was signed back in 1957, and work was under way on the construction of the common market in the 1960s and 1970s, but it has only been since the early 1990s that the effects of integration have really begun to have much of a direct impact on the lives of Europeans, and only in the wake of the eurozone crisis that the EU has regularly been a headline issue. Most Europeans have been slow to appreciate its implications, and have not thought much about the costs and benefits of integration, or taken a European view of policy issues. Because much of the news coming out of the EU in recent years has been bad, and has spawned anti-EU political parties and movements, the reaction against integration has hardened.

Second, the actions of national and EU leaders are often at odds with the balance of public opinion. Take the issue of enlargement, for example: only 44 per cent of EU citizens supported the idea in 2000 while 35 per cent were opposed, a balance that had hardened by 2012 to 52 per cent opposed and 38 per cent in favour (Eurobarometer 54, April 2001: 82; Eurobarometer 78, Autumn 2012: 88). Undeterred, the Commission continued to negotiate with aspirant members, 13 of them joined in 2004–13, and negotiations on membership continued with several more. In a similar vein, while Eurobarometer polls have found that large majorities of Europeans do not feel that their voices count in the EU, even larger majorities feel that they are not heard by their own governments on European issues. The latter problem is reflected in the way that recent treaties – including Amsterdam, Nice and Lisbon – were agreed by the governments of the member states with little input from citizens.

Third, the effort to explain the implications, costs and benefits of integration – whether by national leaders, European institutions, the media, or academic experts – has been less than perfect. To be fair, integration is a complex process whose rules regularly change, and its implications have not always been fully understood even by policy makers; every new treaty has produced unanticipated effects and the switch to the euro was a leap into the unknown (and poorly thought out, as the eurozone crisis later revealed). But there is no constitution to which citizens can refer for clarification, the treaties confuse as much as they illuminate, the media tend to be more interested in what is wrong with the EU than what is right with it, academic scholars mainly contribute little to the public debate, and the rise of euroscepticism has been accompanied by the promotion of numerous questionable assertions about the effects of integration.

The final problem is the knowledge deficit: most ordinary Europeans admit to knowing little about how the EU functions or what it does (see Box 5.1), which places them at a disadvantage when they are asked to make decisions about EU issues or to process and contextualize the news they hear about the EU. Take, for example, the case of the May 2005 French referendum on the EU constitutional treaty: it

Box 5.1   The knowledge deficit

No matter how much the EU institutions talk about the importance of transparency and of making the EU more real to Europeans, one critical reality remains: the average European knows little about how the EU works. True, the average European also knows little about how national systems of government work, but their levels of familiarity with the EU are notably weaker. The problem is reflected in the results of Eurobarometer surveys, in which respondents since the early 1990s have been asked how much they think they know about the EU, its policies and its institutions. The results for 2000–11 showed that the number who understood it was typically less than the number who did not, but the intense media coverage of the eurozone crisis may have changed things, if only briefly (see Figure 5.3).

When tested on their objective knowledge about the EU, Europeans confirm their uncertainties. In one Eurobarometer survey in 2004, for example, 55 per cent of respondents wrongly thought that the EU was created just after the First World War, 50 per cent did not know that Members of the European Parliament were directly elected by voters, and 48 per cent incorrectly thought that the president of the European Commission was elected to that position. Meanwhile, nearly one in three Europeans had never even *heard* of the Council of the EU, and about one in five had never heard of the European Commission, the Court of Justice or the European Central Bank (Eurobarometer 61, Spring 2004.)

Many political scientists argue that voters can use information shortcuts such as party labels, elite endorsements, or cues from trusted sources to help them make political choices. Thus even where they lack much knowledge about the issues at stake, they can emulate the behavior of relatively well-informed voters (Sniderman, Brody and Tetlock, 1991; Popkin, 1994; Hobolt, 2009). But many national political parties are divided on the EU, and are often unable to send clear cues. There are also studies which question how much even the experts know, raising doubts about the quality of the cues they provide (Tetlock, 2005; Silver, 2012). Finally, if Europeans rely as much on elite cues as has been suggested, the effect has been to exacerbate the elitist nature of EU decision-making.

was rejected by 26 million voters, who constituted 5.5 per cent of the population of the EU at the time, living in a country where nearly 75 per cent of people admitted to knowing little or nothing about the content of the treaty (Eurobarometer 63, Spring 2005:138), and many of whom made their decision on the basis of their views about the incumbent Chirac administration rather than the merits of the treaty itself (Ivaldi, 2006).

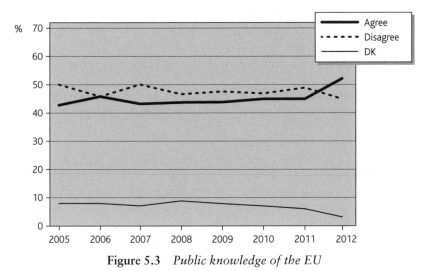

Figure 5.3   *Public knowledge of the EU*

Response to the statement 'I understand how the EU works'. Data from *Eurobarometer* 78, Autumn 2012: 82. Data are for spring waves only.

Euroscepticism

Public and political opinion on European integration and on the work of the European institutions is divided, but this is to be expected: all political activities in democratic systems have their supporters and their opponents, their champions and their critics. In the case of the EU, however, opposition and/or criticism of integration has developed a momentum that has given it an unusual standing in the debate over Europe: it has become more visible thanks in part to its growing prominence in media debates about Europe, and it has played a greater role both in domestic politics – with the rise of political parties opposed to European integration, and splits over Europe within mainstream parties – and in the broader debate about integration, where it has played a critical role in opposition to treaty reforms, enlargement and new policy initiatives.

The criticism directed at the EU is commonly labelled *euroscepticism*, but before looking at the phenomenon in more depth it is worth making two important points. First, euroscepticism is far from the monolithic and consistent philosophy that the popular use of the term implies: the views among Europe's critics range from reform of the process to the wholesale rejection of the EU. So while there are some eurosceptics who would like to see their country leave the EU altogether, there are others who seek only to make the process of integration more efficient and responsive. Second, the arguments put forward by eurosceptics vary by issue, time and member state, and in many cases are less about hostility towards European integration than about the new waves of immigration that have come in the wake of the opening of internal borders.

Eurosceptic arguments include some or all of the following:

- The European institutions are elitist, have become too powerful, and lack adequate transparency or democratic accountability.
- Integration is leading to the creation of a federal European super-state that is out of touch with citizens.
- The EU is promoting unpopular policies. For the political left, for example, this means too much of an emphasis on free markets, and for the political right it means too much power in the hands of workers.
- Too many decisions are taken by European leaders without sufficient reference to citizens.
- National sovereignty and identity are threatened by integration.
- The demands of Europe are unsustainable for more fragile economies.
- In more extreme cases, some believe that there is a conspiracy among European leaders to move ahead without reference to citizens (Booker and North, 2005).

The term *eurosceptic* is thought to have entered the political lexicon in Britain in the mid-1980s (Harmsen and Spiering, 2004: 15–16). Beginning with its early lack of interest in the EEC, and its organiza-tion in 1975 of the first and so far only national referendum on the question of whether or not to stay in the EEC, Britain developed a rep-utation as a country uncomfortable with European integration; it was often the only member state to resist critical new policy initiatives, including social policy and the Schengen agreement. At the same time, however, Britain has often been a policy leader, particularly on European foreign, trade and defence policy, and it is far from being alone in resisting some aspects of integration.

With the debate over the Maastricht treaty (signed in early 1992), more Europeans began to pay attention to the EU, whose interests were now clearly moving beyond the single market, raising troubling ques-tions about the implications for national sovereignty. Three headline events came later that year: the Danish vote against Maastricht in June, a crisis in September when Britain was obliged to withdraw from early efforts to pave the way to a single European currency, and the approval of Maastricht in France by only a small margin a few days later. Criticism of the EU began to grow, anti-EU political parties and move-ments were created, and the old assumption that initiatives on the EU could be taken by governments with minimal public input began to be questioned. Euroscepticism became particularly important in the actions and opinions of many eastern European political leaders and voters.

Euroscepticism is best understood less as a well-defined ideology than as a set of related positions based on opposition to European integration. Taggart and Szczerbiak (2004) distinguish between hard and soft forms, the former based on principled objections to the transfer of power to European institutions, being relatively easy to see, and being most obvious in the case of those who argue for the withdrawal of their home states from the EU, and in the case of political parties whose platform is opposition to the EU, such as the People's Movement in Denmark and the UK Independence Party (UKIP) in Britain. Meanwhile, soft euroscepticism is based on opposition to the direction being taken by the EU and a further expansion of its powers, and is both harder to see and more widespread. In their study of euroscepticism in east central Europe, Kopecký and Mudde (2002) make an even finer distinction between those who support and oppose European integration as a general idea, and those who support and oppose the specific work and structure of the EU.

The long-term significance of euroscepticism is hard to determine. While it has become a critical new factor since Maastricht, particularly in the domestic politics of countries such as the UK, the Netherlands, Finland and the Czech Republic, its impact will continue to depend in large part on the balance between its hard and its soft forms. The numbers of Europeans who are either strong supporters or strong opponents of the EU are relatively small, most people generally accepting the EU and only occasionally expressing strong opinions one way or the other. As we saw in Figure 5.1, the ratio of those with positive versus negative views of the EU changed between 2006 and 2012 from 3:1 to approximately 1:1, but the number of those who were neutral remained mainly unchanged. There was still majority support in 2012 for common EU monetary, defence, security and foreign policies (Eurobarometer 77, Spring 2012: 97), and the number of those who felt the EU would be stronger as a result of the eurozone crisis outnumbered the pessimists by 53 per cent to 35 per cent (Eurobarometer 78, Autumn 2012: 20).

The democratic deficit

Much of the criticism about the EU has focused on the issue of the democratic deficit, which is best understood as the gap between the powers and authority of the EU institutions and the ability of ordinary Europeans to directly influence their work and decisions. The deficit takes several forms:

- The leaders of the member states, meeting as the European Council, reach decisions on important policy matters without always referring to their electorates. Less than half the original EU-15 member states asked their citizens whether they wanted to join the European Community or the EU, for example (in contrast to the newest eastern and Mediterranean members, where referenda were held in ten of the 13 countries). The Maastricht treaty was negotiated largely behind closed doors, poorly explained to the European public and – despite the important changes it made to the structure and goals of the EU – was put to the test of a referendum in only three member states (Denmark, France and Ireland), one of which (Denmark) said no, and another of which (France) said yes only by a narrow margin.

- Despite its powers over proposing and developing new European laws, the Commission is subject to little direct or even indirect public accountability. Appointments to the College of Commissioners must be approved by Parliament, but otherwise they are made without reference to voters (much the same, it must be said, as appointments to senior positions in domestic bureaucracies). The president of the Commission is appointed by the leaders of the member states, represents the views of the EU in several international fora without a mandate from the people, and has tenure that is subject to the whims of national leaders rather than the opinions of European citizens (other than through the European Parliament).

- Most meetings of the Council of the EU and the permanent representatives in Brussels are closed to the public, despite the fact that many important decisions on the content of new laws and policies, and on their acceptance or rejection, are taken there. Ministers and representatives take the kinds of decisions that – at the national level – are taken by members of elected assemblies, who are held accountable for their actions at elections, by the media, and in the court of public opinion.

- The European Parliament – the only democratically elected institution in the EU system – cannot raise revenues or introduce new laws, and it has only a limited ability to hold the Commission accountable for its decisions. It has worked hard to win new powers for itself, but most of the important decisions on EU law and policy are still taken elsewhere.

- Europeans have no direct or indirect say in appointments to the Court of Justice, nor will they until the kind of legislative confirmation that is used for courts in many member states is adopted by the EU, and nominees to the Court of Justice and the General Court are investigated and confirmed by the European Parliament.

- The formal rights of Europeans relative to the EU institutions are modest: they can vote in European elections, petition Parliament or the European ombudsman (see below) if they feel their rights or interests have been violated, access the documents of EU institutions (within certain limits), and can request diplomatic representation outside the EU by any member state, provided their own country has no local representation.

Eurosceptics have made much of the seeming lack of democratic accountability in the EU, and yet herein lies a considerable irony: in order for the EU to become fully and directly accountable, it would need to be turned into the kind of federal system that many eurosceptics oppose. Consider, also, the opinions of ordinary Europeans about the EU. These reveal that recent levels of satisfaction and dissatisfaction with democracy in the EU and their home countries have not been all that different: in 2012, 51 per cent were satisfied with democracy at home compared to 44 per cent who were satisfied with democracy in the EU, while 39 per cent were dissatisfied with democracy at home compare to 44 per cent who were dissatisfied with democracy in the EU (Eurobarometer 77, Spring 2012: 60, 63). Nonetheless, there is a widely held perception that the EU institutions are distant and mysterious, a view that applies particularly to the European Commission, often portrayed by critics as powerful, overpaid, unaccountable and secretive.

The Commission is well aware of the problem, and made some candid admissions in a White Paper published in 2001 on the issue of governance. It argued that many people were 'losing confidence in a poorly understood and complex system to deliver the policies that they want. The Union is often seen as remote and at the same time too intrusive ... [The EU] must start adapting its institutions and establishing more coherence in its policies so that it is easier to see what it does and what it stands for.' The Paper also noted that there was a perception that the EU could not act effectively where a clear case existed (such as on unemployment, food-safety scares, and security concerns on EU borders), that even where the EU acted effectively it rarely received fair credit for its actions, that people did not see that improvements in their quality of life often came from European rather than national initiatives that 'Brussels' was 'too easily blamed by member states for difficult decisions that they themselves have agreed or even requested', and that many Europeans did not understand who took decisions that affected them and did not feel the institutions acted as an effective channel for their views and concerns (European Commission, 2001a: 3, 7).

The democratic deficit has been the topic of a scholarly debate dating back many years (see, for example, Andersen and Eliassen, 1995; Chryssochoou, 2000), but opinion is divided on whether or not it is the problem it seems. Franklin (1996:197) once described the lack of proper democratic accountability in the EU as 'a crisis of legitimacy', and this is a view still widely held. But Moravcsik (2002) argues that the EU institutions are constrained by constitutional checks and balances, including 'narrow mandates, fiscal limits, super-majoritarian and concurrent voting requirements and separation of powers'. On balance, he concludes, 'EU policy-making is, in nearly all cases, clean, transparent, effective and politically responsive to the demands of European citizens', and 'the EU redresses rather than creates biases in political representation, deliberation and output'. But much also depends upon how the EU is understood. Were it a federation, which it is not, then clearly it would performing badly. But if the EU is understood as a confederation, then the links between its institutions and its citizens are unusually strong. As we saw in Chapter 1, representation in a confederation is expected to be no more than indirect: national governments answer to their citizens, and in turn represent them in the meeting chambers of the central authority. Except in the case of the European Parliament, this is much how the EU institutions work.

The people's Europe

Reflecting the elitist qualities of the EU (or perhaps simply its evolution from an international organization into something more substantive), it took more than thirty years for political leaders to begin paying much attention to the question of how ordinary Europeans related to the process of integration. It was not until a June 1984 meeting of the EEC heads of government that the idea of a 'people's Europe' was broached, and Pietro Adonnino, a former Italian MEP, was hired to chair a committee to make suggestions on how the EEC might be brought more closely in touch with its citizens.

The committee endorsed arrangements that had already been made for a European passport: national passports were phased out after 1986 and replaced by a standardized burgundy-coloured European passport bearing the words 'European Community' (later 'European Union') in the appropriate national language, and the name and coat of arms of the holder's home state. It also endorsed arrangements for a European flag, adopting the design developed and used since 1955 by the Council of Europe: a circle of 12 gold stars on a blue background. The flag quickly became a potent symbol of Europe, visible on public buildings, shops and hotels throughout the EU, and omnipresent at meetings of EU leaders. Meanwhile the European Commission created an annual 'Europe Day' (9 May, the anniversary of the Schuman Declaration), and adopted as the official European anthem the 'Ode to Joy' by Friedrich von Schiller, sung to the final movement of Beethoven's Ninth Symphony.

The Single European Act incorporated more of the Adonnino recommendations, the most important of which was the easing of restrictions

Box 5.2   European education policy

An important element in worker mobility has been education, and while education policy still remains the preserve of the member states, efforts have been made by the EU to encourage educational exchanges and the transferability of credits and degrees (see Walkenhorst, 2008). The Lifelong Learning Programme (LLP), which in 2007 replaced an earlier programme called Socrates, helps promote cross-border education through sub-programmes called Comenius (primary and secondary school partnerships), Erasmus (higher education), Leonardo da Vinci (vocational education) and Grundtvig (adult education). Since 1999 the Bologna process (championed by the Council of Europe) has encouraged the standardization of university education, working to create a European higher-education area within which university education is compatible, comparable and transferable, and to make European higher education more attractive and internationally competitive. Bologna includes a European Credit Transfer and Accumulation System (ECTS) under which study at any university in the EU is translated into a common credit system, thus helping open up the educational options available to students in Europe. Nearly 50 countries have now signed up to the process.

The inability to speak other languages poses a practical barrier to the free movement of workers, and also stands as a potent reminder of the differences among Europeans. Almost all secondary-school pupils in the EU learn at least one foreign language, although some have had better results than others. The rise of English as the lingua franca of Europe has been notable and inexorable, helped by its use in international commerce, entertainment and sport; an estimated 85 per cent of secondary-school pupils in the EU-25 were learning English as a second language in 2004, the most active English learners being in Austria, Denmark, Finland, France, Germany, Greece, Latvia, the Netherlands, Spain and Sweden (where more than 95 per cent of students take English classes). Meanwhile, only 23 per cent of Germans are learning French, and only 18 per cent of French students are learning German (Eurostat, 2007: 91).

on the free movement of people. While the Treaty of Rome had given all Community citizens the right to 'move and reside freely' within all the member states, this was subject to 'limitations justified on grounds of public policy, public security or public health'. Since integration in the early days was economically driven, priority was given to making it easier for people who were economically active to move from one state to another. Limits were placed on migration, initially because governments wanted to protect themselves against the possibility of a shortage of skilled workers, and then because of the lack of opportunities in the target states (Barnes and Barnes, 1995:108). Changes under the SEA allowed residents of the EU-15 to move and live anywhere in the EU, provided they were covered by health insurance and had enough income to avoid being a 'burden' on the welfare system of the country to which they moved (see Chapter 7 for more discussion).

Migration has been made easier by another element of the Adonnino report that was formalized by the SEA: arrangements for the mutual recognition of professional qualifications. The Commission at first tried to work on each profession in turn, to reach agreement on the requirements, and then propose a new law. But this was time-consuming, and in 1991 a general systems directive was adopted by which the member states agreed to trust the adequacy of qualifications that required at least three years of professional training in other member states. The list of mutually recognized professions has since grown, and now includes accountants, librarians, architects, engineers and lawyers. The Commission has meanwhile published a comparative guide to national qualifications for more than 200 occupations, helping employers work out equivalencies across the member states.

While the removal of technical barriers and the promotion of language training contribute to free movement, integration will never be able to do much about the social and psychological barriers posed by differences in the routine of daily existence. Americans can readily travel from one state to another in search of jobs or to improve the quality of their lives, and will find their daily routine changing little; they will find the same chain stores, the same banking system, the same money, the same programmes on television, and so on. By contrast, Europeans not only face different languages, but must also deal with many new norms and rules, including everything from different social customs to different sets of road signs and traffic regulations, different procedures for renting or buying a home, taking out car insurance, or opening a bank account, and a new array of products on the shelves of unfamiliar local supermarket chains. An Italian moving to Denmark or a Swede moving to Hungary may eventually learn how things are done locally, but there is a limit to how much new EU laws and policies can help.

Another of the changes introduced by Maastricht was the promotion of European citizenship, although this is not what it seems. Citizenship in democracies is usually defined as full and responsible membership of a state, and has been described by some social scientists as including the right to equality before the law, the right to own property, the right to freedom of speech, and the right to a minimum standard of economic and social welfare (see Heater, 2004). But these are all rights that legal non-citizens of democracies also enjoy. What usually makes a citizen different from a non-citizen in practical terms is that a citizen can vote and run for elective office in his or her home state, can serve on a jury in that state, is eligible to serve in the armed forces of that state (although some countries allow non-citizens to serve), cannot be forcibly removed from that state to another, has the right to receive protection from the state when outside its borders, is recognized as a subject of that state by other governments, and must usually obtain the permission of other governments to travel through or live in their territory. More intangibly, citizens feel a sense of 'belonging' to their home state.

According to Lisbon, 'every person holding the nationality of a Member State shall be a citizen of the Union', but this is less substantial than it sounds, and the treaty goes on to note that 'citizenship of the Union shall be additional to and not replace national citizenship' (Article 20). For now, citizenship of the EU means that citizens of a member state finding themselves in need in a non-EU country where their home state has no diplomatic representation can receive protection from the diplomatic and consular authorities of any EU state that has a local office. It also means that citizens of one member state living in another can vote and stand for municipal and European Parliament elections (but not for national elections). But until such time as citizens of an EU member state have the right of unrestricted movement throughout the EU, and the same rights as local wherever they live, and can exchange their state passports for an EU passport, the idea of European citizenship will always be limited.

Participation and representation

The most meaningful route to the development of public interest in the EU, and of a sense of engagement, can be found in the means by which ordinary Europeans participate directly in EU decision-making and have their needs and opinions represented. These means will always be limited so long as the EU is not a full-blown system of federal government, but for now there are five channels through which Europeans can influence the outcome of EU-level policy decisions outside normal national government channels: voting in European elections, voting in national referenda, supporting the work of interest groups, using the European ombudsman, and launching a citizen initiative. Unfortunately, each has had only a limited effect on the development of a European civil society.

European elections

Held every five years since 1979, elections to the European Parliament give EU voters the opportunity to decide the make-up of the EP, which has had an increasingly effective role in making European law. Voters must be 18 years of age, must be citizens of one of the EU member states, and can vote – and even run for the Parliament – in whichever country they have legal residence. The minimum age for candidates ranges between 18 and 25, and there are also different rules on how candidates qualify; some member states do not allow independent candidates, some require candidates to pay deposits, others require them to collect signatures, and so on.

Every member state uses multi-member districts and variations on the theme of proportional representation (PR), either treating their entire territory as a single electoral district (Spain, Poland, and most of the smaller EU states) or dividing it up into several Euro-constituencies (Britain, France, Germany, Italy, Belgium and Ireland). Seats are then divided among parties according to their share of the vote. PR has the advantage of reflecting more accurately the proportion of the vote given to different parties, but it also results in many small parties being elected to Parliament. Also, PR leads to voters being represented by a group of MEPs of different parties, and constituents may never get to know or develop ties with a particular MEP.

Once elected, MEPs sit in cross-national political groups with similar goals and values. By the rules of the EP, a group must have at least 25 members from at least one-quarter of member states, with no MEP belonging to more then one group. No group has ever had enough members to form a majority, so groups must work together in order to achieve a majority. The balance of power and the order of business are also affected by frequent changes in the number and make-up of political groups. Three groups have developed a particular consistency over time – the socialists on the left, the liberals on the centre-right, and the conservative European People's Party on the right – but they have always had to share power with a cluster of smaller groups with a variety of values and opinions (see Box 5.3).

Turnout at European Parliament elections is low, compromising the credibility and political influence of Parliament. From a modest peak of 63 per cent in 1979, figures fell to just under 57 per cent in 1994, then took a relatively sharp fall to just over 49 per cent in 1999, tailing off to 43 per cent in 2009 (see Figure 5.4). Belgium and Luxembourg usually have the highest turnout (more than 90 per cent), but in most member states fewer than half of voters now cast ballots. Several countries started out on a high note upon joining the EU, only to see their voters lose enthusiasm: thus Portugal fell from 72 to 37 per cent, Austria from nearly 70 to a low of 42 per cent, and Finland from 60 to 40 per cent. Optimists expected that the figures in 2004 for new members in their first flush of membership would be high, but they turned out to be among the worst ever: less than 42 per cent turned out in most countries, and just one in five in Poland and Slovakia.

Box 5.3   Political groups in the European Parliament

European elections bring dozens of different national parties to the European Parliament, many of which consist of as few as one or two members. Since there is little that these parties can achieve alone, it is in their interests to build alliances with other parties, and thus they have habitually formed cross-European political groups. Some of these have been marriages of convenience, hut most have built more consistency and focus with time (for details, see Bardi, 2002; Corbett, Jacobs and Shackleton, 2011: ch. 5). Moving from left to right on the ideological spectrum, the groups in 2013 were as follows:

- *European United Left–Nordic Green Left (GUE–NGL)*. The main left-wing group in the EP, critical of the elitist and market-oriented policies of the EU.
- *Progressive Alliance of Socialists and Democrats (PASD)*. The second largest group in the EP, ranging from ex-communists on the left to more moderate social democrats, with members from every EU state.
- *Alliance of Liberals and Democrats for Europe (ALDE)*. Consistently the third largest group in the EP, most of its members sitting in or around the centre, and its biggest national blocs coming from Germany and the UK.
- *Greens–European Free Alliance (Greens–EFA)*. A confederation of green parties and those representing national minorities, pursuing a variety of issues related to social justice.
- *European People's Party (EPP)*. The major right-wing group in Parliament, which overtook the socialists in 1999 to become the biggest political group, with MEPs from every EU member state except the. UK.
- *European Conservatives and Reformists (ECR)*. A new group set up in 2009 to bring together parties opposed to European federalism and in favour of stronger controls on immigration. More than half its members come from the UK and Poland.
- *Europe of Freedom and Democracy (EFD)*. The most eurosceptical political group, opposing further integration and demanding that all new treaties be put to national referenda.

There are several explanations for this state of affairs: EU voters have developed relatively few psychological ties to the European Parliament, MEPs do not become well-known political figures, and there is little of the personality politics at the European level that often sparks voter interest and turnout in national elections (see discussion in Judge and Earnshaw, 2008:77–80). But perhaps the most compelling explanation is the relative significance of 'first-order' and 'second-order' elections

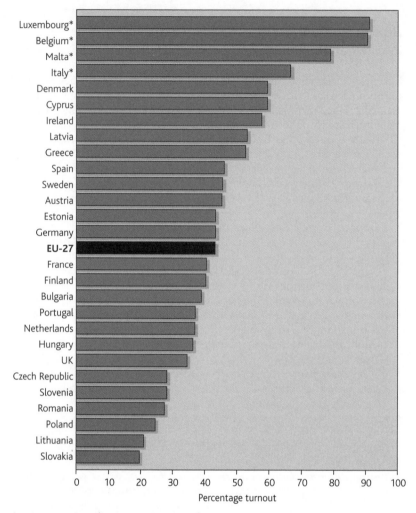

* voting compulsory (but laws rarely enforced)

Figure 5.4   *Turnout at European Parliament elections, 2009*
Data from European Parliament website, http://www.europarl.europa.eu

(Reiff and Schmitt, 1980), the rankings depending on the issues at stake. National elections are considered first-order because they determine who controls national executives and legislatures, which in turn make the decisions that are most immediate and relevant in the lives of citizens. National elections are also hard-fought and attract the most media attention. By contrast, European elections are seen as second-order because there is less at stake; there is no potential change of government involved, they draw less media attention, and most Europeans either know very little about what Parliament does, or are not well informed about European issues.

A notable quality of European elections is that they are contested by national political parties running in 28 separate sets of elections. The result is that they are not only fought more on the basis of national than of European issues, but voter turnout – and the choices made by voters – are often a reflection of how voters view their home governments and national political issues, and many will use their vote to send a message to national politicians (Heath *et al.*, 1999). Party activity at the European level has been encouraged by a growth in the number of European party organizations and confederations, which have improved coordination among like-minded national parties. The oldest of these date back to the 1970s, but it has only been since 2002 that there has been real growth in the number of European parties. They are still evolving and have not made much of a mark on the consciousness of the European voter, but they have become more adept at coordinating policy and at building links between party leaders at the national and European levels (Hix, 2005:192).

Referenda

There is no consistency to when or where they are used, but national referenda on European questions have come to play an increasingly important role in the debate over Europe. Including those held in the non-EU states of Norway and Switzerland, a total of 44 such votes have been organized to date, of which 35 have been held since 1992. Ireland has held eight, Denmark seven, and most other countries just one each, while seven countries (Belgium, Bulgaria, Cyprus, Germany, Greece, Portugal and Romania) have held none. Most referenda have fallen into one of two major categories (see Table 5.1):

- *Votes on whether or not to join the Community/EU.* The first such votes were held in Denmark, Ireland and Norway in 1972, the latter resulting in a No vote that was repeated at a second referendum in 1994. The Swiss also said No to EU membership in a referendum in 2001. All three countries that joined the EU in 1995 held referenda, as did most of the 13 countries that joined in 2004–13, the results all being positive, albeit with varied levels of enthusiasm: bare majorities of Finns, Swedes and Maltese said Yes. The only example of a territory leaving the EU came in 1982, when the 53,000 voters of Greenland – which had joined in 1973 as part of Denmark – voted to leave.
- *Votes on whether or not to accept a new treaty.* These have only been a recent phenomenon, and only in a select few countries. Denmark held a vote on the SEA in 1986, and most Danes (more

than 60 per cent) said Yes on that occasion, but in 1992 Denmark became the first member state to turn down a new treaty when a bare majority of 50.7 per cent rejected Maastricht, and 54 per cent of Irish voters turned down the Treaty of Nice in 2001. The negative votes gave Europeans pause for thought, and resulted in changes to the treaties and new referenda in both countries that went in favour of the treaties. Referenda were also held in 1998 in Denmark and Ireland on the terms of the Amsterdam treaty, and both were positive.

Some referenda have been little more than tools for political manipulation, as when Britain held a referendum in 1975 that was ostensibly about whether or not Britain should stay in the Community following renegotiation of the terms, but was actually designed to settle a division of opinion about Europe within the government (Nugent, 2010:493). Similar motives were seen by some analysts behind the promise made in early 2013 by British Prime Minister David Cameron – concerned about euroscepticism within his own party and the rise of UKIP – to hold a referendum on British membership of the UK following the next general election, due in 2015. Other referenda have had a significant impact on the course of European integration, as when the opposition of 33 million French voters (the number of eligible voters who voted No) was enough to stop the constitutional treaty dead in its tracks in 2005.

Just as important as the result of some of these referendum votes has been the symbolism often attached to the *absence* of referendums. The issue of adopting the euro was particularly controversial, and was put to a vote in just two countries, Denmark and Sweden, where the outcomes were both negative. Meanwhile, none of the 18 governments that have adopted the euro have put the decision to a referendum, often for fear of a similar result. The Blair administration in Britain promised a vote when the time was right, but never did, again mainly for fear of a negative vote; the Eurobarometer 61 poll of 2004 found 61 per cent of Britons opposed to adopting the euro. Soon after coming to office, Gordon Brown found himself in trouble over the issue of the Lisbon treaty, claiming that it was significantly different from the constitutional treaty and thus did not merit a referendum, but he failed to convince his critics.

Interest groups

While national leaders promote national agendas, NGOs – or interest groups – have cut across national frontiers to promote the shared sectional interests of groups of people in multiple member states. In addition to the EU bodies that represent these interests, such as the

Table 5.1 *National referenda on EU issues (selected)*

Year	Country	Issue	Outcome
1972	Denmark, Ireland	Join EEC	Yes
	Norway	Join EEC	No
1975	UK	Continued membership of EEC	Yes
1982	Greenland	Continued membership of EEC	No
1986	Denmark	Single European Act	Yes
1987	Ireland	Single European Act	Yes
1992	Denmark I	Maastricht treaty	No
	Ireland, France	Maastricht treaty	Yes
1993	Denmark II	Maastricht treaty	Yes
1994	Austria, Finland, Sweden	Join EU	Yes
	Norway	Join EU	No
1998	Ireland, Denmark	Treaty of Amsterdam	Yes
2000	Denmark	Adopt euro	No
2001	Ireland I	Treaty of Nice	No
2002	Ireland II	Treaty of Nice	Yes
2003	Malta, Slovenia, Hungary, Lithuania, Slovakia, Poland, Czech Republic, Estonia, Latvia	Join EU	Yes
	Sweden	Adopt euro	No
2005	Spain,	Constitutional treaty	Yes
	France, Netherlands	Constitutional treaty	No
	Luxembourg	Constitutional treaty	Yes
2008	Ireland I	Treaty of Lisbon	No
2009	Ireland II	Treaty of Lisbon	Yes

European Economic and Social Committee and the Committee of the Regions (COR), the last 20–25 years have seen the growth of hundreds of NGOs that represent the views of a large number of groups of people with a stake in EU policy and law. Many are an outgrowth of pre-existing national groups, others have been set up specifically to respond to European issues, and many have opened offices in Brussels in order to be close to the Commission and the Council of the EU. One study (Balme and Chabanet, 2008) suggests that there are more than 850 groups working to influence decisions taken at the European level, many of which date back to before 1980.

The growth in interest-group activity at the European level has paralleled the growth in the power and influence of the EU institutions, or the Europeanization of policy areas that were once the preserve of national governments (Mazey and Richardson, 1996: 200). The groups have not always simply followed the evolution of the EU, going wherever new opportunities for influence have presented themselves, but have often been actively involved in pushing the EU in new directions. Business leaders, for example, were champions of the single market, arguing that competition among European corporations was a handicap to their ability to take on the Americans and the Japanese. At the same time, the European Commission has encouraged interest group activity; it uses groups as a source of expert knowledge and to test the viability of new laws, and also uses them to monitor the compliance records of member states: most groups are only too happy to blow the whistle on their home governments if they are not implementing EU law.

Historically, business and labour groups have been the most active, mainly because the process of integration was for so long driven by economic issues (Greenwood, 2011). As the EU won new powers over competition policy, mergers and the movement of workers, so business and labour groups made greater efforts to influence the Commission and the Council of the EU. Not only are individual corporations represented either directly or through lobbying firms in Brussels, but several cross-sectoral federations have been created to represent the interests of a broader membership. These include Business Europe, which represents 41 national business federations from 35 countries, the European Round Table of Industrialists (which brings together the chief executives of major European corporations such as Vodafone, Renault, BASF, Philips, Ericsson and Nokia), and EUROCHAMBRES (the Association of European Chambers of Commerce and Industry), which represents national associations in 46 countries.

Labour is also represented in Brussels, notably through groups such as the European Trade Union Confederation (ETUC), whose membership consists of 85 European-level industry federations and national labour federations from 36 countries, including Britain's Trades Union Congress (TUC), France's Confédération Générale du Travail (CGT), and Germany's Deutscher Gewerkschaftsbund (DGB). Professional interests are represented by groups such as the Council of European Professional and Managerial Staff (EUROCADRES), and by associations representing everything from architects to dentists, journalists, opticians and vets. Several Brussels-based interest groups include member organizations from outside the EU, a reflection of how much the EU has come to matter to business and labour throughout Europe.

Groups representing public interests, such as consumer issues and the environment, have also become more active as the EU has become more involved in matters about which they care. Until the 1970s, for example, environmental groups focused their attentions on national governments, because most environmental policy in Western Europe was still made at the national level. As the Community became more active on the environment in the mid-1980s (see Chapter 8), it became a more profitable target for interest-group pressure. The new emphasis given to EU-level activities was reflected in the opening of offices in Brussels by such groups as Friends of the Earth, Greenpeace and the European Environmental Bureau, while many other groups employed full-time lobbyists. As environmental groups became more active, so did groups representing the industrial perspective on environmental issues, such as the European Chemical Industry Council (Cefic), Eurelectric (representing national electricity supply associations), and the European Crop Protection Association.

The methods that European-level groups use are similar to those used by groups at any level: promoting public awareness in support of their cause, building membership numbers in order to increase their influence and credibility, representing the views of their members, forming networks with other interest groups, providing information to the EU institutions, meeting with EU lawmakers in an attempt to influence the content of law, and monitoring the implementation of EU law at the national level. As the reach of the EU has expanded, so Brussels has witnessed another phenomenon usually associated with national capitals: the rise of the think tank. These are policy institutes set up to undertake research and to influence decision-makers through the publication of reports, the generation of public debate, and the organization of conferences and seminars. They now include among their number the Bruges Group, the Centre for a New Europe, the Centre for European Policy Studies, the European Policy Centre, Friends of Europe, the Lisbon Council and the European Enterprise Institute.

Greenwood (2011) argues that the representation of interests at the European level has become more diversified and specialized, and that European groups are becoming protagonists: they now try to influence policy rather than simply to monitor events, using increasingly sophisticated means to attract allegiance. A symbiotic relationship has developed between the Commission and interest groups, with the former actively supporting the work of many groups and giving them access to its advisory committee meetings, and the latter doing what they can to influence the content and development of policy and legislative proposals as they work their way through the Commission.

The activities of interest groups have helped offset the problem of the democratic deficit and the relative weakness of political parties working at the European level by offering Europeans channels outside the formal structure of EU institutions through which they can influence EU policy. They have also helped focus the attention of the members of interest groups on how the EU influences the policies that affect their lives, have helped draw them more actively into the process by which the EU makes its decisions, and have encouraged them to bypass their national governments and to focus their attention on European responses to shared and common problems.

Other channels

Another option for representation is offered by the office of the European ombudsman. If a legal resident of the EU feels that any of the EU institutions (other than the Court of Justice and the General Court) is guilty of 'maladministration', and can make a compelling case, the European Parliament must ask the ombudsman to review the complaint, and if necessary carry out an investigation. Appointed for a five-year term that runs concurrently with the term of Parliament, the ombudsman is expected to be both impartial and independent of any government. Since the first ombudsman was appointed in 1995, the Commission has been the target of most of the complaints, which have included charges that it has failed to carry out its responsibilities as guardian of the treaties, that it lacks sufficient transparency, and that it has abused its power. The number of complaints has grown over the years, which is probably less a sign that things are becoming worse than a sign that more people are becoming aware of the work of the ombudsman.

The most recent addition to the list of channels through which Europeans can express themselves on European issues is the citizens' initiative introduced under the terms of the Treaty of Lisbon. If at least a million EU citizens from at least seven member states can be encouraged to give their support, then the Commission can be invited to develop a new legislative proposal on a topic of interest to the organizers, so long as it is within the policy purview of the Commission. Among those launched to date have been initiatives requesting that EU citizens be allowed to vote in all elections wherever they legally reside, to set a default speed limit of 30kph (20mph) in all urban areas in the EU, and to end vivisection.

Conclusions

As we saw in earlier chapters, the EU has helped redefine the relationship among Europeans. Where they have long identified themselves in national terms, and have been tied politically, economically, legally and culturally to one nation-state or another, the reduction of the barriers to trade and to the movement of individuals over the past decade has encouraged Europeans to think of themselves as part of a larger entity with broader interests. Common policies have resulted in decision-making shifting to the EU institutions, so that an increasing number of Europeans feel the effect of decisions made at the EU level. Personal mobility has increased and, cultural barriers aside, Europeans have taken more interest in neighbours who have long been considered as 'foreign' rivals and occasionally a threat to their own national interests.

However, while this horizontal integration has been taking place, the vertical ability of Europeans directly to influence the EU has changed only slowly. Integration was long driven by the priorities and the values of the leaders of the member states, who made most of their decisions with limited reference to their citizens. The result was the creation of a European governing structure that was only indirectly accountable to the views of the people who lived within it. But much has changed since the early 1990s, with growing demands by ordinary Europeans that their opinions should be taken into account in the making of European-level policy, and new complexity being added to patterns of public opinion. Where support for integration had been growing, it began to fall in the wake of the controversy over Maastricht, and fell yet further as a result of the fallout from the euro-zone crisis. At the same time, the majority of Europeans admit that they do not really understand how the EU works, raising troubling questions about the quality of public opinion.

As European institutions struggle to make the concept of integration more real to the citizens of the member states, they are handicapped by the paucity of effective channels of accountability, and by the perpetuation of the democratic deficit. Changes made under the people's Europe programme and as a result of new treaties have brought improvements, but uniform passports, a European flag and student-exchange programmes fall short of the kinds of changes needed to make Europeans feel as though they are truly connected to the EU. For now, they are left with elections to the European Parliament, the occasional national referendum on European issues, the work of interest groups and other more limited channels for the expression of their opinions. The shift away from the elitism of the 1960s and 1970s is happening only slowly, and while the construction of a European political space is under way, most Europeans relate more directly to national politics, even using their views on what is happening in the national arena to guide their opinions on how to relate to Europe.

Chapter 6

The EU Policy Process

That the EU has the trappings of a new level of European governance is reflected in the extent to which responsibility for making policy has been transferred from the exclusive domain of national governments to their representatives working within the EU institutions. Much policy is now shaped at the EU level, many of the actions of national governments are determined by new laws and policies adopted by the EU, and in some areas – notably trade and agricultural policy – the member states now take part in the policy process as a collective. The EU institutions, and the representatives of the member states working within those institutions, have become productive policy entrepreneurs and policy shapers – certainly more so than can be said of the administrations of any conventional intergovernmental organization.

It is debatable just how much the EU member states can still do alone, and how far national interests still drive the work of the EU institutions, but there has been a clear pooling of policy responsibility by the member states. In the era of globalization, no state has true policy independence, because they are all impacted by – and must react to – international developments. This is particularly true in the spheres of economic and foreign policy. This does not mean, however, that critics of the EU do not still champion the cause of separate state identities and the protection of powers for their home governments. But others argue that the pooling of powers has been beneficial and efficient, and not a cause for concern: state identities and interests can be preserved and even promoted, they argue, in the face of common policies and joint institutions.

What is certain is that the member states of the EU relate to each other quite differently – in policy terms – from the way they did before the process of European integration began. As they have integrated their economies, agreed universal standards and regulations, and developed common policies on a wide range of issues, so the differences among them have declined and the effects of integration have become deeper and more complex. But just what this has meant for Europe poses a puzzle for Europeans and non-Europeans alike. The EU member states may still occupy individual seats in the UN and the WTO, for example, but they usually agree joint positions on important foreign policy issues, and vote as a bloc.

Chapters 4 and 5 looked at how the European institutions work and at how ordinary Europeans participate in the decision-making system.

This chapter develops that story by looking at the EU policy process: at the variable balance of policy responsibilities between the EU and the member states, at the key qualities of the EU policy process, at the underlying pressures involved in that process, and at how the policy process has changed the relationship between the parts and the whole. It then looks at the political implications of the EU budget, which plays a critical but often misunderstood role in determining policy styles and priorities. Overall, the chapter sets the scene for the impact of integration on the member states of the EU, offering a preface to the remaining chapters of the book, which look in more detail at economic, internal and external policies as they are designed and implemented at the European level.

The changing balance of authority

The way that European states relate to each other has changed dramatically in recent decades, with substantial implications for the way they design and implement policy. As late as the 1960s and 1970s, they still related to each other as sovereign entities with strong and independent national identities. They had their own bodies of law, they pursued their own distinctive sets of policies, and travellers were reminded of the differences when they crossed national borders and had to show their passports. There were controls and limits on the movement of people, money, goods and services, and citizens of one state who travelled to another felt very much that they were 'going abroad' and could not stay indefinitely without permission. The nation-state was dominant, and was both the focus of mass public loyalty and the source of primary political and administrative authority. Italians were clearly Italians, the Dutch were clearly Dutch, and Poles were clearly Poles – at least this is what most Europeans wanted to believe, or were encouraged to believe by circumstances.

The situation today is quite different, and the relationship between the EU and its member states has been transformed. There has been a shift, a pooling, or a transfer (various terms have been used) of authority from the member states to the EU, and an agreement to share the exercise of power in multiple policy areas. The member states have remained the essential building blocks in this process, but they have moved far beyond the simple cooperation normally associated with intergovernmental organizations, and have built a new layer of institutions underwritten by a common body of laws, a process driven by its own distinctive principles (see Box 6.1).

Two particular influences have come to bear on the process. On the one hand, spillover (see Chapter 1) has helped push the EU into an expanding set of policy interests, starting from a base of promoting economic integration and moving into a network of related areas, ranging from transport to communications, labour relations, judicial and police cooperation, research and development, education, financial services, the environment, and foreign and security policy. On the other hand, the brakes have been applied by the ongoing debate about subsidiarity, first raised in the European context in 1975 when the European Commission argued that the Community should be given responsibility only for those matters that the member states were no longer capable of dealing with efficiently. There was little further discussion until the mid-1980s, when member states opposed to increasing the power of the Commission began quoting the principle. It was finally brought into the mainstream of discussions about the EU by the Maastricht treaty.

Of course, it is a matter of opinion whether the member states or the EU deal better or more efficiently with any given area of policy. But whatever the answer, the gradual shift of powers to the European level has left national legislatures more marginalized in a process that has sometimes been described (pejoratively) as 'creeping federalism'. National legislatures once had almost complete authority to make laws as their members saw fit, within the limitations created by constitutions, public opinion, the powers of other government institutions, and the international community. They now find themselves limited to those policy areas in which the EU is less active, while reacting in other areas to the requirements of EU law and the pressures of regional integration. At the heart of the debate has been the troubling question of sovereignty, too much of which – argue critics of the EU – has been transferred to the EU institutions behind the backs of the ordinary European.

At first, the only powers transferred from the member states were those agreed under the terms of the Treaty of Paris that created the ECSC. But even in this limited area there was the promise of change to come: Paris gave the ECSC the power to ensure the rational use of coal resources (a precursor to environmental policy), to promote improved working conditions (a precursor to social policy) and to promote international trade (a precursor to trade and foreign policy). The logic of spillover was clearly at work from the outset, and with the near-completion of the single market and the launch of the euro, there are now few areas of economic policy in which the EU does not have at least some influence. In some, such as competition and trade policy, EU competence is now exclusive, although – at the other end of the scale – the member states still retain the bulk of control over tax policy.

On international issues, the EU still has some way to go before it can claim a common foreign policy, and the member states still have much freedom in their relationships outside Europe and in the way they define and express their security interests. But the EU is becoming a

Box 6.1 Principles of the EU policy process

The formal division of powers between the EU and its member states is summarized by four principles contained in the treaties (specifically Article 5):

- *Competence* is another term for authority, and describes the areas of policy for which the EU is responsible. For example, it has a high level of competence in the fields of competition and trade, but much less over education and taxation.
- *Conferral* is the principle that the EU can act only where it has been given authority by the member states to achieve objectives set out in the treaties, and that any areas of competence not specifically listed in the treaties default to the member states.
- *Subsidiarity* is the principle that decisions should be taken at the lowest level possible for effective action. In other words, the EU should only do what it does best.
- *Proportionality* is the principle that the EU should not go beyond taking the action needed to achieve the objectives of the treaties.

In those policy areas where the governments of the member states have agreed to provide the EU with competence, national leaders now reach most key decisions through negotiation with their counterparts in the other member states, typically in the meeting rooms of the Council of the EU and the European Council. The trend has been for national leaders to work towards multinational compromises and towards a European consensus. As this has happened, so it has become more difficult for those leaders to define and pursue the distinctive interests of their home states, assuming that state interests can always any more be clearly distinguished from European interests. At the same time, ordinary Europeans are reminded less often of their differences, and the borders that once divided the member states – and were often fought over so bitterly in one war after another – have become so porous that in some places they have become little more than a line on a map or a sign by the side of the road.

more distinctive actor on the world stage, and its effects are now felt more widely, even if sceptics still like to point to its failures and its dis-agreements (see Chapter 9). In several areas of non-economic domestic policy there has also been a clear shift towards the EU, or at least towards interstate cooperation. In many of these areas, the logic of policy integration has been clear: the building of trans-European transport and energy networks makes economic sense, environmental problems are often better dealt with by member states working together rather than in isolation, and the demands of the single market have led to cooperation on employment policy, worker mobility, education,

Table 6.1   *The division of policy authority*

Exclusive EU competence	Shared competence	Responsibility of member states
Competition	Agriculture	Broadcasting
Customs	Civil protection**	Citizenship
Fisheries conservation	Cohesion	Criminal justice
Monetary policy	Consumer protection	Defence
(eurozone)	Culture**	Education
Trade	Development cooperation	Elections
	Economic policy*	Health care
	Employment policy*	Land use
	Energy	Local transport
	External relations	Policing
	Environment	Postal services
	Fisheries	Tax policy
	Freedom, security, justice	
	Human health**	
	Humanitarian aid	
	Industry**	
	Public health	
	Research and development	
	Single market	
	Social policy	
	Space policy	
	Tourism**	
	Trans-European networks	
	Transport	
	Vocational training**	

*   EU has some powers of coordination
** EU has powers to support, coordinate or supplement actions of member states

Based on Articles 3–6 of the Treaty on the Functioning of the EU.

regional policy and justice and home affairs. In some key areas of policy, such as taxation, health care, education and policing, the balance of power still lies clearly with the member states, but the list of their policy responsibilities is becoming shorter (see Table 6.1).

The policy environment

Public policy can be defined as the deliberate action (or inaction) of government in response to the needs of society. When political parties or political leaders run for office, they do so on a platform of explanations about what they see as the most important problems and challenges facing society, and of promises about what they will do in response. The actions they take while in office, and those they opt to avoid, collectively constitute their policies. Putting it another way, if the different pressures on government – such as public opinion, economic change and external influences – are the inputs into the political process, then policies are the outputs.

Policies exist at many different levels, from the local community to towns, cities, counties, states and even at the multinational and international levels. Policies are adopted and pursued not just by governments, but by political parties, the media, lobbies and individual government institutions. Within every policy community there are multiple sub-communities with their own separate and often conflicting sets of policy interests, and this is no less true at the EU level than at the state level; European policy is influenced by international pressures and the demands of non-European states, the major EU institutions (such as the Commission, Parliament and the Council of the EU), directorates-general within the Commission, the regional policy interests of groups of member states with shared goals, the national policy interests pursued by individual member states, and the cross-national policies pursued by groups with shared interests, such as the environmental lobby, farmers, corporations, workers, labour unions, and parties within the European Parliament.

The details of EU policies can be found at three levels: primary rules consist of the broad goals outlined in the treaties, secondary rules consist of the body of several thousand laws adopted by the EU, and tertiary rules can be found in the multitude of action programmes, strategies, declarations, Green Papers and White Papers issued by EU institutions. But this implies that policy is always formal, which it is not – policy is often made up on the fly in response to crises and emergencies. Wallace (1990:54–5) offers a good working definition of the difference between formal and informal actions: formal integration involves the deliberate actions taken by policy makers to create and adjust rules, to establish and work through common institutions, to regulate, encourage or inhibit social and economic flows, and to pursue common policies, while informal integration consists of patterns of interaction that develop without the intervention of deliberate government decisions, following the dynamic of markets, technology, communications and social exchange, or the influence of mass movements. He also distinguishes between proactive and reactive integration, the former having deliberate and explicit political aims, while the latter reacts to economic and social change. The informal, in short, plays a key role in EU policy-making, as it does at the national level (see Stacey, 2010).

If all EU member states had similar political agendas, similar economic and social structures, similar levels of wealth and productivity and the same sets of standards and regulations, integration would be relatively straightforward and would lean towards the formal and the proactive. However, the member states have different structures, policies and levels of wealth, so they approach integration from different perspectives. Concerned with avoiding a multi-speed Europe, national leaders have often had to react to the unforeseen effects of integration, and so have found themselves being driven by informal pressures. For example, while the process of integration has been focused on harmonizing standards, laws and regulations, it has also obliged European leaders in some areas to agree to proceed through mutual recognition (the principle that if something is good enough for one state, it is good enough for them all).

The influences that create and impact policies at the national level are many and complex, but at the level of the EU those complexities are compounded, coming from sources that are internal and external to the EU institutions, formal and informal, predictable and unpredictable, expected and unexpected, and structured and unstructured. They include the following:

- *Treaty obligations.* The treaties outline the general goals and principles of European integration, as well as some of the more specific tasks and roles of the EU institutions. So, for example, Maastricht said that the general goals of the EU were (among others) to 'promote economic and social progress ... the strengthening of economic and social cohesion ... [and] to assert its identity on the international scene'. These are broad and ambiguous targets, but they set the foundations for policy, which must be turned into specific actions, mainly in the form of new laws.
- *Pressures to harmonize.* The need to bring national policies into alignment has been central to reducing the economic and social differences among member states, and to ensuring the smooth functioning of the single market. It accounted, for example, for most of the early initiatives on environmental policy, designed to remove the barriers to the single market created by different environmental standards.
- *Legislative pressures.* Policy is impacted by the requirements or assumptions built into EU law. This is certainly the case with laws that include an obligation for amendment or review after a specified period of time, and is particularly true of the EU's framework directives, which set general goals with the assumption that more laws – known as daughter directives – would follow, containing more detail and focus.
- *Policy evolution and spillover.* Policy is rarely static, and the principles and goals of EU policy are constantly redefined as greater understanding emerges about the causes and effects of problems, as technological developments offer new options for addressing old problems, as problems with existing policies demand adjustments

and new approaches, as the balance of interests changes within the member states, and as the political, economic and social priorities of European integration evolve.

- *Institutional pressures.* While the Commission has a monopoly over the development of new proposals for policy and law, it is subject to various formal and informal pressures, including suggestions from the European Council regarding the broad goals of EU policy, 'invitations' from the European Parliament and the Council of the EU to develop new proposals, suggestions or demands from the Parliament or the Council of the EU for changes in Commission proposals, and the impact of rulings by the Court of Justice on the content and nature of EU law.

- *International agreements.* The EU as a unit has signed numerous international treaties on behalf of the member states, most of which impose specific policy obligations on the EU. This means the development of new laws and policies to respond to those obligations, and the development of common positions taken during negotiations on the progress of implementation.

- *Political initiatives.* Individual national leaders, working alone or in combination with others, have always been at the core of important policy initiatives. Thus the early steps on building a European foreign policy came out of a decision by European leaders to organize regular meetings among the foreign ministers of the member states, much of the headway on security policy in the late 1990s was made because of initiatives taken by Tony Blair of Britain and Jacques Chirac of France (see Chapter 9), and it was agreement among EU leaders in early 2007 that led to the revival of the defunct constitutional treaty as the Treaty of Lisbon.

- *Public opinion.* Neither the EU institutions nor the leaders of the member states can ignore public opinion. It has been important, for example, in the development and agreement of new treaties, and even if voters have not always been able to express their opinions through national referenda, the unwillingness of governments to hold referenda has itself drawn attention to public opinion and has often sparked vigorous debates about Europe.

- *Internal pressures.* As integration has proceeded, so problems have presented themselves that have been internal to Europe, common to multiple member states, and potential barriers to successful integration. These have included, for example, ongoing concerns about unemployment, which have exercised EU governments for many years, or the need to monitor the movement of criminals around the EU, which has been behind an active programme of policy responses in the field of justice and home affairs.

- *External pressures.* Problems and demands have also come from outside the EU, and have often demanded the concerted and united response of all member states. In addition to the sometimes obvious and sometimes more subtle impact of pressures from the EU's major allies (such as the United States) and its competitors (such as China), policy has also responded to changes in the economic climate (at no time was this more true than during the global financial crisis of 2007–10), to trade imbalances and disputes, or to disagreements with other countries.

• *Emergencies or crises.* These have been a part of the policy calendar from the beginning, ranging from the collapse of the EDC to the empty-chair crisis, the dispute over the budget in the 1980s, the EU's failures in the Balkans in the 1990s, the 2003 fallout with the United States over Iraq, the collapse of the constitutional treaty, and the problems in the eurozone after 2009 (see Box 6.3). Each event has been followed by much hand-wringing, but has also ultimately drawn new attention to policy needs.

These multiple influences have created a complex and sometimes disorderly policy environment in which it is often difficult or impossible to be sure of the provenance of policy initiatives, or of the key actors involved in the development and implementation of policy initiatives.

The policy cycle

In an ideal world, public policy would be developed rationally, problems would be prioritized, options would be carefully researched and weighed, spending would be carefully planned, and the best solutions would be implemented, monitored and evaluated. But modern society is too complex and too full of conflicting demands to allow a meaningful cost-benefit analysis of the options available, political pressures skew the outcomes of policy, and studies of policy routinely emphasize the scarcity of real organization. The result is that policy is often driven by compromise and opportunism, and – in the words of a classic study of policy (Lindblom, 1959) – is often a matter of muddling through from one problem to another. In an attempt to impose some order on the complexity, it is common to approach policy analysis using a process model involving a cycle of actions. This implies that there is much more order to the policy process than exists in reality (see Young, 2010), but at least it offers a guide through the maze.

Problem identification and agenda-setting

Before a policy choice can be made, there must be political agreement on the existence and definition of a problem, and a decision must be

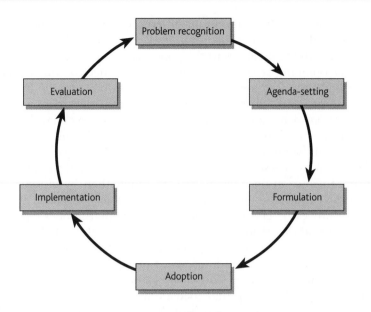

Figure 6.1 *The policy cycle*

made to add that problem to the list of policy concerns that are considered part of the remit of government. In a democracy, the development
of the policy agenda is normally driven by a combination of the individual preferences and priorities of elected officials and their advisers,
the struggles for power among political institutions (mainly the executive and the legislature), and the combined pressures of public opinion
and media attention.

To the extent that there is a European agenda (see Peters, 2001), it is
formed and driven mainly by the European Council, which outlines
broad policy goals and occasionally sparks new policy initiatives. It is
the Council, for example, that has been behind the decision to develop
every new treaty since the SEA, that has issued major declarations on
international crises, that has reached key decisions on EU institutional
changes, that has given new momentum to EU foreign policy, and that
has orchestrated the response to the eurozone crisis. But it must be
remembered that the prime ministers, chancellors and presidents who
meet as the Council are ultimately national political leaders, and that
they are torn between pursuing national and EU interests. In this they
are subject to numerous pressures: treaty obligations, recommendations from consultative committees, the initiatives of other leaders, tensions among member states, the need to harmonize laws, international
treaty requirements, discussion papers, specialist reports and changes
in the wider world.

There are at least three important differences between agenda-setting at the national and at the European level. First, elected leaders at the national level often add issues to the policy agenda in response to public and media opinion, or – more cynically – in order to win legislative votes or build support for the next national election. At the EU level, however, there is no European 'public' in the sense that there is a large body of citizens demanding change at the European level. Furthermore, there is no elected European government that is constantly looking to its standing in the polls or to the outcome of an election. Thus policy is heavily driven by pressures that are internal and external to the process of European integration, and by leaders rather than by citizens. This leads to the common – and sometimes reasonable – assertion that the EU policy process is elitist. But this is a charge that applies equally to policy making at the national level (see Dye and Zeigler, 2000).

Second, the European agenda is pulled in different directions by the often competing motives and interests of the EU institutions. So while the Commission and the Court of Justice take a supranational approach to agenda-setting that focuses on the European interest, the European Council and the Council of the EU are intergovernmental in character (and so more interested in protecting national interests), while the European Parliament's choices are driven by voter interests and the ideological leanings of MEPs, and the whole edifice is underwritten by a struggle for power and influence among the institutions.

Third, the complexity and variety of the needs and priorities of the member states make it more difficult to identify pan-European problems and to tease out the common causes of such problems, to build political support for a unified response, or to anticipate the potential effects of policy alternatives. This is particularly true in regard to policy issues on which there is less of a European consensus, such as foreign policy, where the member states bring different values and priorities to bear. It is also important to appreciate that while we may talk of the 'European agenda', it is little more than the accumulation of narrower agendas being pursued by all the actors with an interest in European policy. Each of these in their own way will limit, redirect or broaden the cumulative policy interests of the EU.

Formulation and adoption

Once a problem or a need has been recognized, a response must be formulated and adopted. In the case of the EU, this usually involves debating the options at meetings of the European Council, developing proposals for new laws and new budgetary allocations in the Commission, drafting work programmes or action programmes, publishing discussion papers, or making public announcements. Whichever response is chosen, it might be reasonable to expect that some kind of methodical analysis would be conducted in which the causes and dimensions of a problem are studied and all the options and their relative costs and benefits are considered before the most efficient policy alternative is chosen (see Dye, 2010:19). However, this rational policy model rarely works in practice, because understanding of the value preferences of Europeans is incomplete, as is the information about policy alternatives and about costs and benefits. As a result, most EU policy is designed and applied incrementally, intuitively, or in response to emergencies, crises or changes in public opinion.

In the member states, policy is usually formulated by the executive, the legislature, or government departments. In the case of the EU, however, the major focus of policy formulation is the Commission, which not only has a monopoly on the drafting of new laws and policies, but also has a pivotal position as a broker of interests and a forum for the exchange of policy ideas (Mazey and Richardson, 1997). But the Commission does not function in a policy vacuum, and its proposals are routinely amended as a result of lobbying by interest groups or national governments, as a response to internal and external emergencies and crises, and as they are discussed by consultative committees, the Council of the EU, and the European Parliament.

An approach used with increased frequency since the early 1990s has been the open method of coordination, which eschews the 'hard' setting of binding legal norms in favour of a 'soft' approach based on cooperation, reciprocal learning and the voluntary participation of member states (see Heidenreich and Bischoff, 2008). According to the Commission's own calculations, about 30 per cent of its proposals come in response to the international obligations of the EU, about 20–25 per cent come as a follow-up to resolutions or initiatives from the other European institutions, about 20 per cent involve the updating of existing EU laws, and 10–15 per cent arise out of obligations under the treaties or secondary legislation (European Commission, 2001b:6).

Once a new law or policy has been proposed by the European Commission, it must formally be adopted before it goes into effect. The final say over adoption comes out of a complex interplay involving Parliament, the Council of the EU, the Commission and the member states, with the Court of Justice providing legal interpretation when needed. As we saw in Chapter 4, changes introduced by the SEA and by the Maastricht, Amsterdam and Nice treaties have provided new powers to the European Parliament, which – in most areas – has now become a 'co-legislature' with the Council of the EU.

Implementation

Arguably the most important step in the policy cycle is implementation, the point at which the goals and objectives of government result –

or fail to result – in real change for the governed. Unfortunately, implementation has so far proved a relatively weak part of the EU policy process, and several structural problems have made it difficult always to be sure about the extent to which EU laws and policies are actually implemented in the manner in which they were intended by their authors, or make a difference in the lives of Europeans. This has been a matter of growing concern for EU institutions, within which there has been an expanding debate on how to improve implementation. The Commission itself blames nonconformity between national and EU law on the existence of two or more legal systems in several member states (notably those with a federal structure), and the difficulties that arise in amending national laws because of the effect they have on provisions in a variety of other areas, such as agriculture, transport and industry (European Commission, various years).

Within member states, implementation is normally left to bureaucrats. However, the bureaucracy of the EU – the Commission – is small and has no powers directly to enforce European law, and so must work instead to ensure implementation through national bureaucracies. The Commission occasionally convenes meetings of national representatives and experts to monitor progress, and also carries out its own investigations using its contacts in national government agencies. Most of the time, however, the Commission must rely on other sources, including the governments of member states (who will occasionally report on other governments that are failing in their obligations), whistleblowing (mainly by interest groups, the media, and private citizens), the European Parliament (which since 1983 has required that the Commission submit annual reports on the failure of member states fully to implement Community legislation) and the European ombudsman (who has the power to conduct inquiries into charges of bad administration against Community institutions, except the Court of Justice and the General Court).

In cases where implementation is slow, the Commission has three options available to it. First, it can issue a Letter of Formal Notice giving a member state time (usually about two months) to comply. Second, it can issue a Reasoned Opinion explaining why it feels there may be a violation. Finally, it can take the member state (or an individual, corporation or other institution if they are the responsible parties) to the European Court of Justice for failure to fulfil its obligations. The Commission also adds pressure by publicizing progress on implementation; the data on the number of time member states are taken to the Court of Justice for failures to fulfil their legal obligations have shown over time that Greece and Italy typically have the worst records (see Figure 6.2), a reflection of their relatively slow and inefficient bureaucracies.

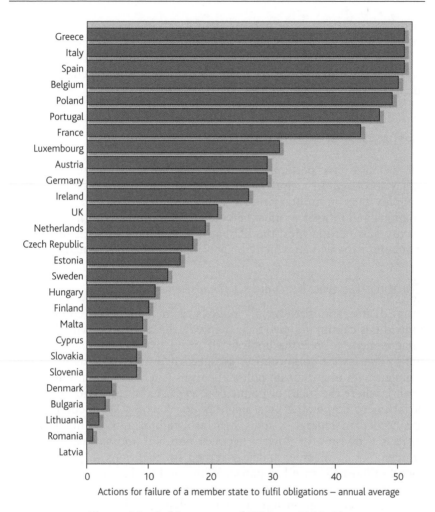

Figure 6.2 *Infringements of EU Law, 2008–12*

Source: Annual Report of European Court of Justice of the European Union: Annual Report 2012 (Luxembourg, 2013), p. 93, at http://curia.europa.eu/jcms/jcms/Jo2_7000 (retrieved April 2013).

Evaluation

The final stage in the policy cycle is to determine whether or not a law or policy has worked. This is difficult unless specific and measurable goals were set from the start and unless national bureaucrats report accurately to the Commission on the results of policies. In many cases it is almost impossible to know which actions resulted in which consequences or whether the results are being accurately reported. This is particularly true in the case of the EU, where it is difficult always to distinguish the effects of national and local government actions from those of EU law. Nonetheless, evaluation in the EU is conducted by a combination of the Commission, the Council of the EU, the European Council, the European Parliament and reports from member states, interest groups and individuals.

Features of the policy process

All societies have particular qualities that influence the nature of the policy process. In democracies, for example, the process is more complex than in authoritarian systems, simply because so many more opinions and influences must be taken into account. With its own complexity and peculiarities, the EU has a unique combination of features that colour the way in which policy is made and implemented.

Compromise and bargaining

In a democratic society, all politics is a matter of compromise. Individuals cannot all have their own way, because there will always be disagreements about the analysis of problems and the best prescriptions. The fewest compromises are needed in unitary systems of government with majoritarian political parties (such as Britain, Portugal or Spain), where the focus of political power usually rests with a national government dominated by a single political party. More compromises are needed in federal systems such as Belgium and Germany, where there is a division of powers between national and sub-national government, or in member states governed by coalitions (a phenomenon found in most EU member states). With a political arrangement such as the EU, however, where the power structure is not clearly defined, where political relationships are still evolving, and where the 'government' is effectively a coalition of the representatives of the member states, the entire policy process revolves around compromise.

Some policy initiatives, such as the single market, have been less difficult to address than others because they have enjoyed a high degree of political support. The costs to national sovereignty have been relatively low, while the potential benefits to national economies have been relatively high. But in other areas, the member states have fought hard to protect national interests, forcing sometimes unhappy compromises. The creation of the CAP, for example, was based around compromise, with France winning concessions on agriculture in return for concessions given to West German industry. Similarly, the negotiations leading up to Maastricht were riddled with compromises and package deals, notably over the timetable for the development of the single currency. The adoption of the euro was itself a compromise, with every member state given the option of either joining or not, and the rules on joining – and on managing economies once states were in the eurozone – often fudged (see Chapter 7).

Political games

A popular approach to public policy analysis is offered by game theory, which focuses on situations in which two or more actors compete against each other for influence, their positions being influenced by what they think other actors will do. In the process of seeking compromises, runs the argument, politics is typically reduced to a struggle for power and influence, with one person or group trying to win concessions from – or pressing their views on – others. Such struggles take place even in the smallest and most local of human communities, but they are magnified in the EU by its sheer size and by the extent to which member states and institutions compete with each other, unconstrained by the presence of a constitution. Peters (1992:106–7) describes three sets of interconnected games in the EU:

- A national game among member states trying to extract as much as possible from the EU while giving up as little as possible. This was the case even with the six founding members, but as the EU expanded, so the game became more complex and intense, because the stakes and the payoffs were greater, while the EU became more politically, economically and socially diverse.
- A game played out among EU institutions trying to win more power and influence relative to each other. Once just an experiment in combining coal and steel industries, European integration has spilled over into almost every area of policy, and the EU has grown to cover most of Europe. As the stakes have been raised, so the EU institutions have jockeyed with each other for a greater role.
- A bureaucratic game in which the directorates-general in the Commission have their own organizational cultures and are competing for policy space. Again, this has been driven in large part by the growing policy responsibilities of the EU, the new resources available to the Commission, and the natural inclination of bureaucracies to justify their importance and to compete for influence.

Multi-speed (or differentiated) integration

Jean Monnet was a champion of the Community method, a process by which all the member states would proceed at the same pace and would adopt and implement the same laws and policies (see Lindberg and Scheingold, 1971). But this incorrectly assumed that all the member states would agree on how to proceed, which they rarely have, an indication of this being the manner in which sub-groups of member states have occasionally moved ahead with more cooperation in a specific area within EU structures, or have opted out of different elements of European policy. This phenomenon is variously known as 'multi-speed' integration, Europe *à la carte,* varible geometry, enhanced cooperation, or differentiated integration. In contrast to formal opt-outs, the latter term is used to describe both the formal and informal arrangements for policy opt-outs as well as the discretionary elements associated with putting EU policy into practice (Sitter and Andersen, 2006). (At a more detailed level, member states can also negotiate derogations, by which they are excused from implementing a particular part of a law or treaty with which they have problems, are allowed to apply it differently, or are given a longer deadline.)

Britain was famously allowed to opt out of the Social Charter (see Chapter 8), only 18 member states have so far made the switch to the euro, not all member states have removed border controls as planned under the Schengen agreement, traditionally neutral states such as Ireland and Finland have preferred not to participate in attempts to build a common European defence policy, and several Eastern European countries were given longer to meet some of the targets on free movement or people, goods and services, and of the requirements of EU competition law. The Treaty of Amsterdam imposed conditions that limited the scope of the application of enhanced cooperation, while Nice required a minimum of eight member states to take part in any plan, removed the right of each member state to veto the plan, and provided for the possibility of enhanced cooperation in foreign policy. Lisbon provided for its extension to defence matters.

Incrementalism

Policy making in a democratic society is inevitably cautious, because neither public nor political opinion will typically tolerate radical change, and many competing views and interests have to be taken into account. Lacking the time and resources to investigate all the options available, policy makers tend to move incrementally, building on precedent, and fine-tuning what has gone before rather than bringing about wholesale change (Lindblom, 1959). This has been particularly true at the European level, driven by concerns over the loss of national sovereignty, the absence of a consensus about the wisdom of European integration, and the need for compromise. The EU has occasionally agreed relatively dramatic policy initiatives (such as the SEA, Maastricht, the launch of the euro, and eastern enlargement), but none of these changes have come without much deliberation and debate, and most EU policy-making is based on the development and elaboration of existing policies. Because there are so

Box 6.2   Europeanization

The term *public policy* is often associated with national government responses to national issues, and yet policy is made at many different levels. Of particular interest since the 1970s has been the internationalization of public policy, through which national governments have been influenced by pressures coming out of international relations, most notably out of trade and globalization. Nowhere has the process of internationalization gone as far as it has in the EU, where the harmonization of European law and policy has given rise to the phenomenon of Europeanization, which has in turn spawned a large number of analytical studies of the EU policy process.

Europeanization is usually defined as the process by which laws and policies in the member states have been brought into alignment with EU law and policy. One key set of assessments of Europeanization (Graziano and Vink, 2007:7–8) defines it as 'the domestic adaptation to European regional integration', or the process whereby administrations in the member states adapt to the requirements of EU law and policy, or the process of integration 'feeds back' into national political systems. The changes have seen differences in national laws and regulations being reduced by the agreement of European laws and regulations (see Page, 2003). But it is more than just about laws and policies; it can also be applied to understanding the meaning of 'Europe', to the new opportunities made available to interest groups by changing 'administrative structures and processes, to the general project of unifying Europe, and even to our understanding of the borders of Europe.

Opinion is divided on just how far the process of Europeanization has gone, and it is not always clear how far the pressures that have led to policy change have been clearly European, as opposed to corning out of initiatives driven by the member states or out of international pressures such as globalization. Opinion is also divided as to whether the concept is all that useful, or whether it has simply become fashionable to employ it. Part of the problem is that there is no universally accepted definition, and it is routinely reinterpreted to fit with the arguments made by individual scholars and analysts. But this is a problem common to most concepts in the social sciences. For now, at least, Europeanization is an important tool for understanding the EU policy world.

many counterweights and counterbalances in the policy process, member states and EU institutions can rarely take the initiative without conferring first with other member states or EU institutions. For the most ardent supporters of integration, the process has sometimes slowed to a crawl; for eurosceptics, meanwhile, it has usually been moving too quickly.

Spillover

Critics of the EU charge that it has become involved in too many policy areas, and that institutions such as the Commission have become too powerful and even somewhat imperious. What they often fail to realize, though, is that the EU institutions have often been driven by forces beyond their control: functionalists argue that an 'invisible hand' of integration has been at work, the launch of new initiatives often revealing or creating new problems or opportunities, which in turn can lead to pressures for additional supporting initiatives. This process of policy spillover has been one of the enduring features of policy making in the EU, the prime example coming from efforts to complete the single market. The task of removing barriers to the free movement of people, money, goods and services could not be achieved either easily or quickly, and involved making many of the adjustments – anticipated or not – that were needed to open up the European market. This meant moving into new areas of policy that were never anticipated by the founding treaties, including social issues, working conditions, and the environment.

This combination of features has created a policy process that is complex, constantly changing, and still not yet fully understood. New attention has been paid by scholars and commentators since the late 1990s to trying to better understand the different institutions of the EU, and the EU's activities in specific areas of policy. (Interestingly, there has been something of an inverse relationship between the attention paid to a policy area and its achievements on the ground; thus there have been more studies of foreign and security policy, where the EU record has been mixed, than of agricultural and trade policy, where the impact of the EU has been more substantial.) But there are still few studies of the broader policy process and of the ways in which policy making at the European level has changed the relationship among member states, and between member states and Europe as a whole (for one notable exception, see Richardson, 2006). At least part of the fault lies in the dominating influence of international relations (IR) theory in attempts to understand the EU. Scholars of IR focus less on public policy than on alliances and the balance of power. As the methods, models and approaches coming out of comparative politics and public policy play a greater role in attempts to understand the EU, so will our understanding of the European policy process.

The EU budget

The budget is one of the primary influences on policy at any level of government, because the choices that governments or political institu-

Box 6.3   Crises and European integration

When once asked by a journalist what would most likely blow a government off course, British prime minister Harold Macmillan was reputed to have answered, 'Events, dear boy, events.' The unexpected is always a factor in political life, and political leaders find themselves regularly having to respond to crises and developments that they might not have anticipated. The EU has been no different, and policies have often had to be designed or changed on the fly in response to problems that were either unexpected or had not been adequately planned for. The eurozone crisis is the latest and by far the most serious, and yet it was certainly not the first. Consider the following:

- The 1954 collapse of the European Defence Community.
- De Gaulle's unilateral veto of UK membership in 1963 and 1967.
- The 1965–66 empty-chair crisis when France withdrew from meetings of the EEC institutions.
- The failure of early efforts to build a single currency in the 1970s and again in the early 1990s.
- Efforts by the Thatcher government in the early 1980s to renegotiate the terms of the EEC budget.
- The shock Danish rejection of the Maastricht treaty in 1992, followed by EU embarrassments in addressing the crisis in the Balkans.
- The Irish rejection of the Treaty of Nice in 1999 and of the Treaty of Lisbon in 2008.
- The collapse of the constitutional treaty following rejection in France and the Netherlands in 2005. (This led not only to speculation of the immediate organizational collapse of the EU (which did not happen), but also prompted national leaders to push the constitutional treaty through as the slightly redesigned Treaty of Lisbon, sparking more protests.)

Designing policy on the basis of crisis management is not the best way to proceed, but it is often unavoidable. No government can ever anticipate all the problems it is likely to face, and given that the EU has always been made up on the fly with only a general idea about its ultimate destination, it has been particularly prone to having to deal with the unexpected.

tions make regarding how and where to raise and spend money affect both their policy options and the effectiveness of the policies they pursue. It is typically less a question of how *much* is raised and spent than of *how* and *where* that money is raised and spent. The revenue and spending of the EU is no exception, and its budget has frequently set off controversies that have resulted in member states being at odds with one another and with the EU institutions, and substantial myths being circulated about the size of the budget. The level of controversy is surprising considering the numbers involved: the EU budget in 2013 was just under €151 billion ($197 billion), or 1.13 per cent of the combined gross national income (GNI) of the member states. This worked out at 82 euro cents per day for each person in the EU. Furthermore, the budget must be balanced – unlike the case with many of the member states, there is no EU debt and no deficit. Given recent debt and deficit problems in several member states, they could perhaps stand to learn something from the rules they themselves agreed for the EU budget.

In spite of this, the EU budget has been the source of often heated political battles over the years, most centred on the relative amounts given and received by each member state, and on the balance between national contributions and the EU's own resources (independent sources of revenue) (see Laffan and Lindner, 2010: 214ff.). Changes in the early 1970s led to an increase in the proportion of revenues derived from the Community's own resources: customs duties, levies on agricultural imports, and a small proportion of value-added tax (VAT). But there were two problems with this formula: it took little account of the relative size of the economies of member states, and the amounts raised were insufficient to meet the needs of the Community. By the early 1980s, the Community was nearly bankrupt, and it was obvious that either revenue had to be increased or spending had to be restructured or cut.

Matters came to a head over the insistence by the then new British prime minister, Margaret Thatcher, that Britain's contributions be recalculated. Arguing that Britain bore an unfair share of the Community budget, and received an inadequate amount in return, she generated alarm at her first European Council appearance in 1979 by bluntly telling her Community partners that she wanted a reformation of the budget (expressed colourfully but inaccurately as 'I want my money back'). Her campaign continued through the early 1980s, tied to her demands for a reform of the CAP. After much acrimonious debate, a complex deal was reached in 1984 by which Britain's contributions were cut, its rebates were increased, and the overall budget was recalculated in preparation for the accession of Spain and Portugal.

The long-term effect of the changes has been to make the richer states the biggest net contributors, and poorer states the biggest net recipients. When the Commission published its Agenda 2000 proposals in 1997, aimed at preparing for eastward enlargement and reform of the CAP and the regional funds, it stirred up a new hornets' nest of debate: several countries that were net contributors – including Austria, Germany, the Netherlands and Sweden – began pressing for a re-examination of the budget, suggesting that contributions be capped at 0.3 per cent of national income. This caused partiular nervousness among net recipients such as Greece and Spain, which were concerned that they would have to take on a greater burden of funding rebates.

The accumulation of reforms to the budget has resulted in the structure we find today:

- The budget cannot be greater than 1.24 per cent of the combined GNI of the member states, and cannot be in deficit.
- Just over 70 per cent of revenues come from the member states as a fixed percentage of their GNI with each member state paying a set amount in proportion to its GNI.
- Just over 13 per cent come from so-called 'traditional' own resources, mainly customs duties on imports from non-member states and agricultural levies.
- Just under 12 per cent come from VAT.
- The balance comes from other sources, including taxes on EU staff salaries, contributions to EU programmes from non-EU countries, and fines on companies for breaching EU competition law.
- The biggest contributors to the budget in 2011 (in order) were Germany, France, Italy, the UK and Spain, and the biggest recipients were Poland, Spain, France, Germany, Italy, Belgium, the UK and Greece.
- Since 2006, the EU has replaced annual budgets with seven-year Multi-annual Financial Frameworks (MFFs). The first ran from 2007 to 2013, and the second from 2014 to 2020, and the use of this tool has greatly decreased the amount of time and stress devoted to budgetary planning.

In terms of spending, the EU budget has raised a separate set of political problems. Like almost every budget, EU expenses consist of a combination of mandatory payments over which it has little or no choice (such as agricultural price supports) and discretionary payments (such as spending on regional or energy policy) regarding which there is more flexibility. EU spending is about equally divided between the two:

- In 2013, about 36 per cent of spending went on cohesion policy: development spending on poorer regions of the EU, including spending under the European Social Fund aimed at helping offset the effects of unemployment, and investments in agriculture. The proportion of EU expenditures in this area has almost tripled since the mid-1970s.
- About 29 per cent of spending went to agricultural subsidies, and a further 10 per cent to rural development, supports to fisheries, and the environment. Thanks to reforms in agricultural policy (see

Chapter 7), the proportion of EU spending that goes to agriculture has fallen substantially from its peak during the 1970s, when it accounted for nearly 75 per cent of the budget.

• Just under 6 per cent went to administrative costs for the EU institutions. Critics of the EU routinely and misguidedly argue that the EU institutions spend far more than they actually do, and this has become one of the great myths of euroscepticism. Recent Eurobarometer polls have found that between one-quarter and one-third of Europeans think that administrative overheads are the single biggest item on the EU budget.

• Most of the balance (about €12 billion, or 7.8 per cent of the total) went to all the other policy areas in which the EU was active, including external policies, transport, energy, consumer policy, research and development and education.

The EU budget is only partly a reflection of the policy areas in which the member states have agreed to transfer competence to the EU institutions. Looking at the figures, one could easily conclude that Europe was not much more than an exercise in social, agricultural and regional development. But it must be remembered that much of the work of the EU involves little operational cost; for example, the entire single-market programme has been based largely on the development of new laws and policies. The same is true of competition policy, trade matters and fiscal policy. It must also be remembered that the member states have their own domestic budgets to invest in agriculture and in the kind of development supported by EU cohesion policy. So, in this sense, the EU budget is little more than a complement to the work of the member states.

Conclusions

While debates rage about the powers and nature of the EU, with both support for and resistance to the expansion of its powers and responsibilities (as well as much misunderstanding about precisely how the EU works), there is no question that its member states have pooled authority in the meeting rooms of the EU institutions, and now have less policy independence than they did even twenty years ago. Integration has changed the relationship among EU member states at several levels: there has been a reduction in social differences, a harmonization of standards, laws and regulations, and a removal of the physical and fiscal barriers that have differentiated the member states from one another.

There is also an emerging consensus that cooperation in a variety of other areas makes better sense than independent action, which can lead

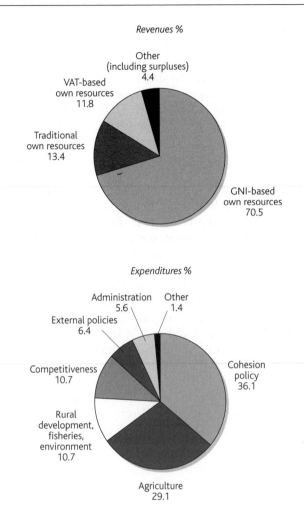

Figure 6.3   *The EU budget*

Data for 2011 from European Commission at http://ec.europa.eu/budget (retrieved May 2013).

to unnecessary competition and duplication of effort. It is still too early to talk about a federal relationship among the member states, and between them and the EU institutions, but the trend is undoubtedly in that direction – to the alarm of eurosceptics. Several levels of governance are being created, all with independent powers. How far European cooperation will go depends on how we choose to define subsidiarity, but while this is moving higher up the agenda of EU negotiations, the definition of which issues are best dealt with at the level of the member state and which at the level of Europe remains fluid.

The member states still have a large measure of control over domestic policy, in a wide variety of important areas, from tax policy to education, criminal justice and health care. Compared, for example, to the American case, where the states now have only residual responsibilities in a modest selection of areas, and whose independence from national government in Washington DC is largely symbolic, the member states of the EU are still powerful, independent actors that work together in a confederal arrangement. But how long this will last is debatable. Internal political and economic pressures have meant a gradual shift of powers by the member states, a steady accumulation of responsibilities by the EU institutions, and – increasingly – the sense that Europe is governed both from Brussels and from 28 national capitals. But it is critical to appreciate that 'Brussels' has few independent powers, and that EU decision-making is still very much driven by the representatives of the member states meeting in those Brussels-based institutions.

External pressures are also bound to continue to tighten the definition of Europe. Most of the rest of the world has not yet woken up to the implications of European integration, and to the idea that the 28 member states of the EU can and should be seen as a political and economic unit, that is exerting its global influence ever more effectively. Non-Europeans still treat Europeans mainly as citizens of individual member states, but this is slowly changing. As it does, it will give Europeans themselves a greater sense that they can be both European *and* British or Italian or Greek or Czech or Lithuanian. This in turn will give a tighter definition to the concept of Europe.

Chapter 7

Economic Policy

Economic matters have long dominated the life and work of the EU, at few times more intensely than since the breaking in 2009 of the crisis in the eurozone. The causes and effects of that crisis are deep and complex, involving a mix of design problems inherent in the euro, fallout from the global financial crisis of 2007–10, poor policy decisions by several eurozone states, and a failure by leaders of key EU member states to take decisive action. But so wrenching have been its effects – leading to speculation that the euro might be at risk, and indeed that the entire exercise of European integration might collapse – that economic matters have recently crowded out most others on the EU agenda.

The priority given to economic integration dates back to the initial experiment in pooling coal and steel production, and continued with efforts to agree a customs union, early attempts to achieve exchange-rate stability and address the economic decline of the European Community, and the building of the single market. There is now much freer movement of people, money, goods and services within the EU, a change that has had revolutionary consequences for business and consumers. New jobs and opportunities for trade have been created, standards have been harmonized, consumer choice has broadened and prices have come down. European corporations have engaged in cross-border mergers and acquisitions, the Commission keeping a close eye on attempts to circumvent policies on competition. And the EU has built a system of trans-European networks aimed at integrating the transport, energy supply and telecommunications sectors of the member states.

But much remains to be done. The EU may be the world's wealthiest marketplace and its biggest trading power, but efforts to make it the most dynamic and competitive knowledge-based economy in the world have fallen short. Unemployment rates remain stubbornly high in many places (only becoming worse in the wake of the financial and eurozone crises), there are still too many barriers to free trade in services, there are still many limitations on the free movement of labour, and not enough has been done to open up the digital marketplace. The double blow of the global financial crisis and the eurozone crisis knocked European integration off track, obliging EU leaders to rethink their approaches to monetary and fiscal policy. The effects of the crises

– many of which are still not fully understood – will be felt for many years to come.

This chapter begins with a survey of the goals and effects of the single market, which has long been the backbone of the European project; even most eurosceptics would acknowledge that promoting free trade within Europe has always been a worthwhile objective. It reviews the steps taken to build the single market, and offers examples of some of the consequences, also making the point that there are still significant limits on the movement of people, money, goods and (particularly) services. The chapter then looks at the implications of the single market for European business, and at the dynamics of EU competition policy. It ends with a discussion of the euro: how and why it was created, why the eurozone went into crisis, what was done to address the crisis, and what the future might hold for the European single currency.

The single market

One of the core goals of the Treaty of Rome was the establishment of a single (or internal or common) market in which there would be no barriers to the free movement of people, services and capital. So central was this goal to the early identity and purpose of the European Economic Community that the EEC was long known interchangeably as the Common Market. Rome also called for the establishment of a customs union in which all obstacles to trade among EEC members would be removed and a common external tariff agreed for all goods coming into the EEC. While the customs union was completed without much fanfare in 1968, non-tariff barriers to trade among the member states persisted, including variations in technical standards and quality controls, different health and safety standards, and different rates of indirect taxation.

Prospects for the single market seemed to wane in the mid-1970s as recession encouraged member states to protect their national markets and corporations, and worked independently on problems such as high unemployment, low investment and slow growth. National monopolies in transport and communications more often bought services and products from local sources rather than seeking more competitive options outside their borders. Technical standards varied across the Community, adding a potent block to trade in merchandise. Member states had laws requiring foreign firms active within their borders to buy goods with local content, and a host of border and customs controls persisted, along with varying rates of value-added tax (VAT) (see Neal, 2007:129). By the 1980s it had become clear that urgent action was needed to reverse the EC's relative economic decline, and a boost

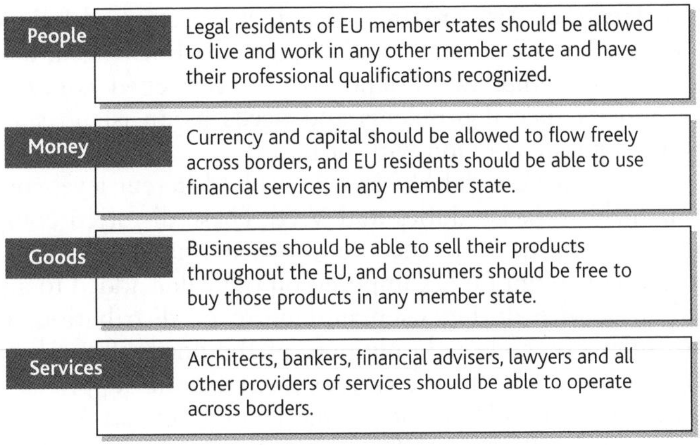

People	Legal residents of EU member states should be allowed to live and work in any other member state and have their professional qualifications recognized.
Money	Currency and capital should be allowed to flow freely across borders, and EU residents should be able to use financial services in any member state.
Goods	Businesses should be able to sell their products throughout the EU, and consumers should be free to buy those products in any member state.
Services	Architects, bankers, financial advisers, lawyers and all other providers of services should be able to operate across borders.

Figure 7.1 *The four freedoms of the single market*

had to be given to the single market programme in order to respond to foreign competition. At its February 1985 meeting, the European Council agreed that it was time to refocus on the single market, particularly on the achievement of the 'four freedoms' (see Figure 7.1).

Progress on the single market was at the top of the agenda for Jacques Delors, the new president of the Commission, and he charged trade and industry commissioner Lord Cockfield with drawing up a White Paper outlining the necessary changes (European Commission, 1985). These in turn became the basis of the Single European Act (SEA), which was signed in February 1986 and came into force in July 1987. The first new treaty since Rome in 1957, the SEA not only accelerated completion of the single market, but also made economic integration more real to millions of people who might until then have been only vaguely aware of the work of the Community. And compared to later treaties, the SEA was both relatively non-controversial and widely welcomed. Its core goal was the removal, by the end of 1992, of the remaining non-tariff barriers to the single market, which took three main forms.

First, there were physical barriers, the most obvious of which were customs and immigration checks. These were not only expensive, inconsistent and time-consuming, but interfered with the free flow of people, goods and services. They also posed a psychological barrier to integration, reminding Europeans that they still lived in a region of independent states. A critical step in the removal of border controls came in June 1985 with the Schengen Agreement, signed in the Luxembourg town of that name by France, West Germany and the Benelux countries. Providing for the fast-track removal of controls, it came into force in 1995 and was incorporated into the EU treaties by the 1997 Treaty of Amsterdam. Other than Britain and Ireland, every member state has since signed and implemented Schengen, along with Iceland, Norway and Switzerland. Britain has cited concerns about security and its special problems and needs as an island state, while Ireland has a passport union with Britain.

Second, there were fiscal barriers, notably different levels of indirect taxation, such as excise duties and VAT. These distorted competition, created artificial price differences, and posed a handicap to trade. VAT is a form of consumption tax imposed on the value added to a product, material or service during its manufacture or distribution. Unlike a standard sales tax, collected only once at the point of purchase by the consumer, VAT is collected at various stages in the supply chain. (It is used throughout the EU but not in the United States.) Agreement was reached in the 1990s on an EU-wide VAT system, and since 2006 the minimum rate has been set at 15 per cent, but less progress has been made towards harmonizing corporation tax or the setting of minimum withholding tax on savings. Matters are complicated by the near-complete lack of competence that the EU institutions have in the field of tax policy.

Finally, technical barriers came in the form mainly of thousands of different regulations and safety, health, environmental and consumer protection standards (Neal, 2007:131). Early attempts to develop Community-wide standards proved time-consuming and tedious, three breakthroughs eventually helping clear many bureaucratic and political hurdles: a 1979 decision by the Court of Justice established the principle of mutual recognition (if a product met local standards in one country, it could not be barred from another); a 1983 mutual information directive required member states to tell the Commission and the other member states if they planned to develop new domestic technical regulations; and a 'new approach' to technical regulation was introduced by the Cockfield report, whereby instead of agreements being reached on every rule and regulation, laws would be passed setting general objectives, the details of which could then be drawn up by private standards institutes, such as the European Standardization Committee (CEN) and the European Confederation of Posts and Telecommunications Administrations (ETSI).

The most direct and practical effect of the single market on ordinary Europeans has been freedom of movement. Travelling through Europe in the 1960s involved producing passports and sometimes visas, processing through customs and immigration, and often stringent limitations on long stays in other countries or the movement of funds. Today, with some conditions, almost any citizen or legal resident of an EU member state can live and work in any other EU member state, open a bank account, take out a mortgage, transfer capital, get an education, and both vote and run in local and European elections. For

Box 7.1 Trans-European networks

Until 1987, harmonization of the transport sector was one of the great failures of the single market: little of substance had been done to deal with problems such as time-consuming cross-border checks on trucks, national systems of motorways that did not connect with each other, air-traffic control systems using 20 different operating systems and 70 computer programming languages, and telephone lines incapable of carrying advanced electronic communications. In response, efforts have been made at the EU level to develop trans-European networks (TENs) aimed at integrating the different transport, energy supply and telecommunications systems of the member states.

Pressure to develop energy-supply networks has grown out of a combination of plans for a better integrated and interconnected single market for gas and electricity supply, for greater liberalization of that market, and for addressing the problems associated with the EU's dependence on Russia for more than a third of its oil and natural gas needs. Much of the Russian gas comes via pipelines that run through Ukraine, which has twice in recent years been in payment disputes with Russia, and has tapped some of the gas supply destined for the EU. When Russia cut the supply in retaliation in 2008, it was also cut off to more than a dozen other European countries. The construction of the Nord Stream supply pipeline direct from Russia to Germany via the Baltic Sea is under way, along with the South Stream pipeline from Russia to the Balkans via the Black Sea.

Priority has also been given to improving rail, road and water transport links within the EU, with new or improved railway track and new roads. The programme has helped link major cities, better connecting wealthier and poorer parts of the EU, helping revitalize rail transport, supporting high-speed rail systems, expanding shipping lanes around the coasts of the EU, improving the ability of producers to convey their goods to market, and contributing to the reduction of oil dependency and greenhouse emissions. But the connections are still incomplete: railways are disjointed as a result of different track gauges and signalling systems, rules protecting favoured operators, and variable track quality. Little progress has also been made with the Single European Sky project, launched in 2002 with the goal of creating a single European airspace that would triple capacity, improve safety, cut air traffic management costs in half, modernize sometimes archaic technology, and reduce the environmental impact of flying.

stays of up to three months, the most that they will usually be asked to do is to present a valid identity card or passport. For stays of more than six months, they must either have a job, have sufficient resources and health insurance to ensure that they do not become a burden on local social services, be a student engaged in a formal course of education, or be a family member of someone who meets one of these three criteria. After five years of legal residence, citizens of other EU member states can apply for permanent residence in the new country. Rights of entry and residence can only be limited or denied on the grounds of public policy, public security or public health, and not for economic reasons. There are greater restrictions on residents of Eastern Europe, because of concerns about migration, but these have eased with time.

With the internal barriers having loosened considerably, businesses are able to sell their products more widely, competition and choice have grown, prices have come down as consumers have had more options from which to choose, and regulations on health and safety have been harmonized in the interests of removing barriers to the single market. Take, for example, the changes that have come to air travel. Because most European states are too small to support a significant domestic industry, most flights in Europe are international. Until the 1980s, most European countries had state-owned national carriers that were fiercely protected by their governments, even if they made losses. Air transport was so highly regulated and expensive that it was sometimes cheaper to fly from one European city to another via the United States rather than direct. Thanks to privatization and liberalization (much of it sparked by the Single European Act), loss-making airlines have fallen by the wayside, there have been new pressures for airlines to merge, there has been a growth in the number of cut-price operators such as easyJet and Ryanair, and ticket prices have fallen. Passenger rights have been strengthened, and common standards have been set for air transport security, including rules on the screening of passengers and baggage.

There have also been positive developments in the communications market. With the break-up of telephone monopolies, the creation of new service providers and regulations on charges, the costs of using phones has been falling steadily across the EU since the late 1990s. Additionally, EU law in 2013 put an end to the practice by service providers of raising roaming costs for consumers outside their home states. As well as placing a cap on the cost of calls, texting and data transfer, the law also allows consumers to choose a different operator abroad than the one they use at home. The European Commission has also persuaded mobile phone manufacturers (without the passage of new laws) to replace multiple mobile phone chargers with a single micro-USB plug, reducing costs and inconvenience to customers and reducing electrical waste.

The EU has run into problems with its plans to develop independence of the US-operated Global Positioning System (GPS) by setting up an alternative global navigation satellite system known as Galileo. GPS was developed by the United States mainly for military purposes, and because the United States reserves the right to limit its signal strength, or to close public access during times of conflict, there are clear incentives for the EU to develop an alternative. Galileo is designed for civilian use and is intended to be compatible with GPS, while being capable of operating autonomously. Several non-EU countries have joined the project, including China and India, and there has been talk of several others joining in the future, including Australia, Brazil, Canada, Japan, Mexico and Russia. Hopes of having it operational by 2010 proved overly optimistic, however: delays arose out of a failure to agree a public-private funding partnership, only four test satellites were in orbit by 2012, and completion is currently scheduled for 2019.

In spite of all the achievements of the single market, much still remains to be done. Many legal and technical barriers remain in place, there are still limits on the movement of people (particularly from east to west), tax rates vary, multiple standards and regulations often still apply to goods produced in different countries, and language differences remain a potent barrier to the free flow of workers. In the European energy sector, there is still much state intervention and fragmentation, and little coordination. In the case of financial services (banking, insurance, and investment services), handicaps persist in the form of different tax systems, bureaucratic hurdles, and a lack of price transparency. And when it comes to e-commerce, high-speed broadband access remains limited, companies must deal with different tax systems, and consumers are sometimes discouraged from using the internet for cross-border purchases because of concerns about speed, cost, safety of delivery and security of payments (Mettler and Stępień, 2012).

A new set of challenges to the single market has been introduced with eastern enlargement, which brought greater social and economic diversity to the EU, but also widened the income gap (see Chapter 8 for details). The rural populations of Eastern European member states are typically bigger than those of the western EU-15, unemployment rates are higher, there has been less investment in infrastructure and communications, and the labour force is less educated. In the years leading up to accession, eastern states made so many changes to their trade and investment policies that they had already felt most of the economic effects of enlargement before joining, they were already competing in the single market, and there was already free movement of money, goods and services (but not labour) (Grabbe, 2004). However, improvements in competitiveness are still needed, as well as investments in infrastructure and worker education.

Meanwhile, there has been the bigger question of the place of the EU in the global marketplace. As a result of calls in the late 1990s for a new focus on modernizing the European economy, the European Council meeting in Lisbon in March 2000 set the ambitious goal of making the changes needed to finally complete the single market and to create 'the most competitive and dynamic knowledge-based economy on the planet within ten years', bringing the EU up to the levels of competitiveness and dynamism that are (or, at least, were) features of the US economy. The Lisbon Strategy called on EU governments to make a wide range of changes, including integration and liberalization of the telecommunications market, liberalization of the gas and electricity markets, rationalized road tax and air traffic-control systems, lower unemployment, movement towards harmonization of EU corporate tax, and more progress towards making the EU a digital, knowledge-based economy (Wallace, 2004).

An interim report prepared in 2004 by a committee chaired by former Dutch prime minister Wim Kok argued that the Lisbon Strategy was not working: there was still too much regulation, too much protection for workers against dismissal, and not enough market liberalization or entrepreneurial freedom. The EU had also fallen behind in research and development, with expenditure as a percentage of GNI stagnating since the mid-1990s, contrasting with the much higher levels in the United States (much of it generated by the vast US defence industry), and with the high growth in Japan, China and South Korea. As a result of its problems, the Lisbon Strategy was transformed into the Europe 2020 Strategy, which moved the deadline to 2020 and focused on innovation, education, research and development, sustainable growth, a low-carbon economy and job creation. But meeting these targets was made all the more difficult by the effects of the global financial and eurozone crises.

European business and the single market

European business has been deeply impacted by integration, which has given it access to a far bigger market, and has allowed it to play to its strengths, to employ economies of scale, to make greater profits, and to compete more effectively with non-European corporations. The harmonization of laws has also meant a reduction in the number and complexity of national standards and regulations and their replacement with Europe-wide systems, decreasing the bureaucratic burdens on business, removing the need for sometimes expensive and time-consuming testing in multiple countries, and cutting delivery times and costs. As a result, it is harder today to find members of the business community who complain about the single market than to find those who argue that it has not gone far enough and that there are still too many remaining barriers to free trade.

After the Second World War, European companies lost markets at home and abroad to competition, first from the United States and then from Japan. US and Japanese corporations were more dynamic,

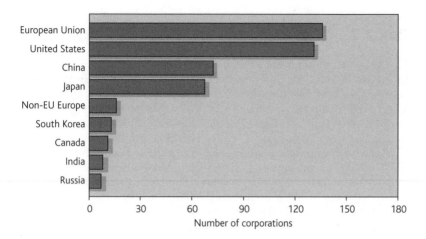

Figure 7.2   *The world's biggest corporations, by region, 2012*

Data from *Fortune* magazine at http://money.cnn.com/magazines/fortune/global500/2012
(retrieved May 2013).

invested more in research and development, and had access to large home markets. Meanwhile, European business was handicapped in its attempts to move across borders into neighbouring states, facing merger and capital gains taxes, double taxation on profits, different legal systems, different regulations and standards, and limits on the movement of goods and services. Hence the bulk of merger and takeover activity until the 1960s was either within individual countries or between European and non-European companies (Layton, 1971: 3).

With competitiveness pushed to the top of the European agenda by the single market, by the late 1980s the Community was addressing market fragmentation and the promotion by national governments of often state-owned 'national champions'. It also launched new programmes aimed at encouraging research in information technology, advanced communications, industrial technologies, and weapons manufacture (Tsoukalis, 1997:49–51). The single market increased the number of consumers that companies could reach, the later advent of the euro made it easier for companies in search of acquisitions to borrow money and buy other companies, and the general trend towards globalization greatly increased the number of acquisition opportunities, joint ventures and corporate mergers. One of the results was a growth in the number, size and reach of European multinationals, reflected in their rising presence on the *Fortune* magazine Global 500 list of the world's biggest companies (by revenue) (see Figure 7.2). They include (in 2012) Royal Dutch Shell, BP, Volkswagen, E.ON, ING, AXA, Allianz, BNP Paribas, GDF Suez, Carrefour, Banco Santander, Assicurazioni Generali, HSBC, Tesco and BASF.

Box 7.2   Europe and the aerospace industry

Few areas of multinational business have seen quite so many changes in recent decades as the aerospace industry, where rationalization, competition and other economic pressures have cut the number of large civilian aircraft producers in the world from dozens to just two: Airbus and Boeing. Famous names of Western European aviation – from Vickers to Hawker Siddeley, Supermarine, Dornier, Messerschmitt and Sud Aviation – have all gone, while in Britain alone the 19 aircraft producers of the 1940s had been whittled down by the mid-1980s to just one, BAE Systems. Similar pressures have led to similar changes in the United States, where Lockheed now focuses on military aircraft and McDonnell Douglas was taken over in 1997 by Boeing, now the only remaining American manufacturer of large civilian aircraft.

Much of the responsibility for the changes on both sides of the Atlantic lies with the success of Airbus, a European consortium founded in 1970, and whose share of the new civil aircraft market has grown since 1975 from 10 per cent to more than 50 per cent. Airbus civilian airliners are made by the Airbus Group, a consortium known until 2014 as the European Aeronautic Defence and Space company (EADS), created in 2000 by a merger between Aérospatiale Matra of France, DaimlerChrysler Aerospace of Germany and Construcciones Aeronáuticas (CASA) of Spain (BAE had a 20 per cent share until 2006, when it decided to sell out and focus on the US defence market; its efforts to merge with EADS in 2012 failed thanks mainly to the inability of the three national governments to agree terms). Airbus produces a line of 12 different airliners, including the double-decker A380, the world's largest passenger aircraft, capable of carrying 500–800 passengers, which took its first commercial flight in October 2007.

The creation of both Airbus and EADS was prompted by the argument that economies of scale were giving American manufacturers an advantage over their European competitors, whose national markets were too small to sustain them. Similar arguments have encouraged transnational cooperation in Western Europe on military aircraft and missiles. Individual member states still make competitive products, but are finding that it makes better commercial sense to pool resources. Successful collaborations include production of the Tornado fighter-bomber and the Eurofighter Typhoon, both made by British-German–Italian consortiums. In April 2001, BAE, EADS, and Finmeccanica of Italy joined forces to create MBDA, the world's second largest producer of missiles after Raytheon of the United States.

Probably the most famous European joint venture has been Airbus –
see Box 7.2. Others have included those between Thompson of France
and Philips of the Netherlands on high-definition television, Pirelli of
Italy and Dunlop of Britain on tyres, BMW and Rolls-Royce on aero-
engines, and among the members of the European Space Agency (ESA).
Set up in 1973 in an attempt to promote European cooperation in
space research, the ESA now has 20 members: the Czech Republic,
Norway, Poland, Romania, Switzerland and all the western EU-15
states. Europe has also offered competition to the Americans in the
field of satellite launching, with ten European countries working
together in Arianespace, a space-launch consortium owned by governments and state-owned companies (France has a stake of just over 60
per cent). Following the launch of the first in its series of Ariane
rockets in 1979 from Kourou in French Guiana, Arianespace grew to
take over more than half the global market for commercial satellite
launches, but now faces new competition from the United States,
China and Russia.

The growth of new pan-European businesses seeking to profit from the
opportunities offered by the single market, and looking to create 'world-
size' companies to compete more effectively with the United States and
Japan, has led to a surge in merger and acquisition activities, notably in
the chemicals, pharmaceuticals and telecommunications industries.
Notable recent examples include the mergers since 1989 among a
number of British, Canadian and American pharmaceuticals companies
to create GlaxoSmithKline, a string of takeovers by the French insurance
company AXA (by 2012 the second biggest insurer in the world), the
$203 billion acquisition in 2000 of Mannesmann of Germany by
Vodafone Air Touch of the UK (the second largest acquisition in history),
several mergers and cooperative ventures in the energy market revolving
around EDF and GDF Suez in France and E.ON and RWE in Germany,
the 2009 merger between British Airways and Iberia of Spain, and the
2012 merger between Porsche and Volkswagen (the latter hopes to
become the world's largest vehicle manufacturer by 2018).

The new opportunities offered at home have been accompanied by
growth in the flows of foreign direct investment (FDI) both into the
EU, and from the EU into other countries. In the period 2006–11,
more than $4.3 trillion was invested in the EU-27, or more than twice
the amount that was invested over the same period in the United
States, nearly nine times the amount invested in Japan, and 18 times
the amount invested in China. Britain, France, Belgium, Germany and
Italy were the main targets in 2011, drawing in two-thirds of the EU
total among them. In terms of outflows, the EU in that period invested
nearly $3.1 trillion, or more than twice the amount invested by the
United States. In 2011, the biggest EU investors – in order – were
Britain, France, Germany, Spain, Italy and Luxembourg, which

together spent $210 billion, or nearly as much as the United States (OECD website, 2013). The cumulative levels of investment are reflected in FDI stocks, where once again the EU dominates, in terms both of inward and outward investment – see Figure 7.3. High levels of FDI are helpful for economic growth and job creation, are an important source of external finance and are reflective of faith in – and the openness of – the markets that are the targets of that investment.

The more notable examples of European companies reaching outside the EU to create large new corporations include the 1998 takeover by British Petroleum of Amoco in the United States, and the subsequent merger between BP Amoco and Atlantic Richfield; the 1999 takeover by Germany's Daimler of the US automobile manufacturer Chrysler (which came to an unhappy end in 2007, but in 2009 Fiat took a 20 per cent stake in Chrysler, with plans to exert more control as the company was reprivatized in 2011), the 2000 takeover by Germany's Deutsche Telekom of Voicestream in the United States, the 2003 merger between Britain's P&O Princess and the United States' Carnival to create the world's largest holiday cruise group, and the 2013 purchase for $20 billion by Belgium's Anheuser-Busch InBev (the world's largest brewer of beer) of its remaining stake in Mexico's Grupo Modelo.

Bigger is not necessarily better in the corporate world, because takeovers can reduce competition and consumer choice by creating industries that dominate or monopolize a particular sector of the economy. The success of the single market ultimately relies on an effective competition policy, ensuring that companies do not become too big in concentrated markets, or that national governments do not give domestic companies unfair advantages through subsidies and tax breaks. Out of these concerns has come what has been described as one of the flagship policies of the EU (Cini and McGowan, 2009:1), and one in which the EU has intervened in the economic life not just of member states, but also of non-member countries. EU competition policy has four key objectives:

- Watching for restrictive practices, including conflicts of interest and the abuse of dominant positions through price-fixing, charging significantly different prices in different markets, or the existence of domestic laws that interfere with competition; thus, for example, the Commission ordered Germany in 2003–04 to cancel a law adopted in the 1960s that prevented Volkswagen from being taken over by another company.
- Controlling mergers in order to prevent the development of companies with too great a share of their particular markets, which would allow them to squeeze out smaller competitors. So, for example, the Commission blocked (for the third time) the proposed takeover in 2013 by low-cost carrier Ryanair of the Irish national airline Aer

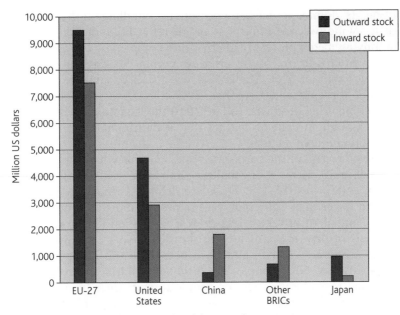

Figure 7.3 *Levels of foreign direct investment*

FDI stock refers to the total value of investments in or by a country or group of countries at a specific point in time. Figures shown are for 2011. Source: Organization for Economic Cooperation and Development at http://www.oecd.org/statistics (retrieved June 2013).

Lingus on the grounds that the new company would have a near-monopoly on flights into and out of Dublin.

- Monitoring state aid. The Commission monitors the provision of subsidies, loans, grants and tax breaks to companies so as to ensure that they are not given an unfair advantage over competitors (Allen, 1996). Temporary aid is permissible in times of real need, as is aid for research and development and for regional development, but state aid must generally be in the interest of the EU as a whole.

- Promoting the competitiveness of European companies by protecting intellectual and industrial property, reducing the bureaucratic burden, providing help with research and development, and providing aid to small and medium enterprises.

Reflecting the new economic influence of the EU at the global level, recent targets of Commission investigations into mergers have even included American corporations. Thus it blocked a proposed merger in 1997 between Boeing and McDonnell Douglas, prompting then Vice-President Al Gore to threaten a transatlantic trade war (the merger went ahead after compromises were reached). It made world headlines in March 2004 by imposing a record fine of €479 million (then $622 million) on the software-manufacturer Microsoft, which it accused of abusing its dominant market position by bundling its Media Player with its Windows operating system, thereby discouraging consumers from buying media players made by other companies. The Commission ordered Microsoft to begin offering within 90 days a version of Windows without the Media Player installed, and to reveal its Windows software codes so that rival companies could more easily design compatible products. In late 2010 the Commission began investigating Google in light of charges that it discriminated on its website against other search engines.

At the other end of the corporate scale, EU policy has not overlooked the needs and interests of smaller companies, known as small and medium enterprises (SMEs). These are defined as independent companies with fewer than 250 employees (although most are much smaller) and an annual turnover of less than €50 million. They account for two-thirds of private-sector jobs in the EU, have a critical role in the region's economic growth, and have been high on the agenda of EU economic policy. For example, the 2008 Small Business Act for Europe is designed to make it easier for people to start their own businesses, and to access contracts, loans and research funding. EU law on late payments has also been a particular boon to SMEs; when someone provides a service and the client is late paying the fee, the cost is passed on to the provider, a problem that interferes with the functioning of the single market, distorts competition, and can be a crippling burden to small companies. A 2011 EU directive reduces late payments by setting common standards and requirements for all the member states. Work is also under way on a programme designed to make it easier for entrepreneurs to access venture capital across borders.

One area of economic activity in which the EU has lagged has been in encouraging new business start-ups. While large new European multinationals have been competing head-to-head with their American rivals, there has been what critics regard as a clear failure to encourage ambitious entrepreneurs in the EU. Big companies tend not to like dealing with small ones, entrepreneurs often leave Europe for more open pastures in the United States, bankruptcies can take years to discharge (contributing to a culture of risk aversion), and venture capital is often hard to attract (*The Economist*, 'Briefing: European entrepreneurs', 28 July 2012).The result is that while the United States has become famous for producing new and innovative companies like Apple, Google and Amazon, the EU has lagged far behind; while the United States generated 51 new big companies in the period 1950–2000, and emerging markets generated 46, Europe generated just 12 over the same period (Philippon and Véron, 2008). As former Spanish prime minister Felipe González put it, 'We stifle innovation [and] this is why Europe has failed to produce a Bill Gates' (*Financial Times*, 'Rebel seeks innovators to shake up Europe', 15 January 2008).

Inside the eurozone

In March 2002, after years of false-starts and often difficult economic adjustment, 12 EU member states took one of the most far-reaching steps in the history of integration: they abolished their separate national currencies and replaced them with the new European currency, the euro. It was a move that was a long time coming, meeting considerable political resistance along the way and causing economic difficulties for several member states, and yet it was driven by the belief that few barriers to the single market were as fundamental as the existence of multiple different currencies with fluctuating exchange rates. At the same time, the surrender of national currencies raised many questions about sovereignty and independence: by giving up their national currencies, the governments of eurozone states were agreeing to give up control over important domestic economic policy choices, such as the ability to adjust interest rates and to devalue their currencies. Critics also saw the adoption of the euro as another step towards the creation of a unified system of European government. There were also concerns that not all eurozone states were sufficiently prepared to adopt the euro, a problem that has since come home to roost.

It was understood as early as the 1950s that stable exchange rates would be an important part of the effective functioning of a single market. That stability was provided by the postwar system of fixed exchange rates, but the system began to crumble in the late 1960s, and finally collapsed with the US decision in 1971 to end the link between gold and the US dollar (see Chapter 3). A plan was agreed to work towards adopting a single currency in stages by 1980, but was derailed by international currency turbulence in the wake of the energy crises of the 1970s. A second attempt was made in March 1979 with the launch of the European Monetary System (EMS), based on an Exchange Rate Mechanism (ERM) intended to encourage exchange rate stability. An artificial currency called the European Currency Unit (ecu) was created as an anchor, exchange rates between member states were set in ecus, and countries in the ERM undertook to make sure that those rates fluctuated by no more than 2.25 per cent either way. Although several member states found it difficult to keep their currencies stable relative to the ecu, the EMS contributed to exchange-rate stability in the 1980s, and helped accustom Europeans to the idea of a single currency.

In 1989 a plan developed under the leadership of Commission president Jacques Delors proposed a staged move towards a single currency: all member states would join the ERM, the band of exchange rate fluctuations would be narrowed before being fixed irrevocably, and then the single currency would be introduced. Despite the near-collapse of the ERM in 1992–93 – when Britain and Italy pulled out, several other countries had to devalue their currencies, and the bands of exchange-rate fluctuation had to be widened – the Maastricht treaty affirmed the basic principles behind the Delors plan. EU member states wanting to adopt the single currency had to meet several so-called convergence criteria that were considered essential prerequisites:

- A national budget deficit of less than 3 per cent of GDP.
- A public debt of less than 60 per cent of GDP.
- A consumer inflation rate within 1.5 per cent of the average in the three countries with the lowest rates.
- A long-term interest rate within 2 per cent of the average in the three countries with the lowest rates.
- A record of keeping exchange rates within ERM fluctuation margins for two years.

At the Madrid European Council in December 1995, EU leaders decided to call the new currency the euro, and agreed to introduce it in three stages. The first came in May 1998 when it was determined which countries were ready: all member states had met the budget deficit goal, but only seven had met the debt target, Germany and Ireland had not met the inflation reduction target, and Greece had not been able to reduce its interest rates sufficiently. Maastricht, however, included a fudge clause that allowed countries to qualify if their debt-to-GDP ratio was 'sufficiently diminishing and approaching the reference value at a satisfactory pace'. In the event, despite the fact that the national debts of Belgium and Italy were nearly twice the target, all but Britain, Denmark (both of which met all the criteria), Greece and Sweden announced their intention to adopt the euro.

The second stage came on 1 January 1999 when the euro was officially launched as an electronic currency, participating countries fixed their exchange rates, and the new European Central Bank began overseeing the single monetary policy. All its dealings with commercial banks and all its foreign exchange activities were now transacted in euros, and the euro was quoted against the yen and the dollar. Pause for thought was provided in September 2000 when, in a national referendum, Danes voted against adoption (they were followed three years later by the Swedes). Polls also found opponents outnumbering supporters in Germany (although the balance later reversed), and opposition in Britain running at five to three in 2002, hardening to two to one by 2009. More concerns were sparked when the value of the euro against other currencies fell from an opening level of $1.18 to a low of 83 cents in October 2000 (it was back up to nearly $1.60 in July 2008, down again to $1.19 in June 2010, and back up to $1.30 in July 2013). Nonetheless, plans for the transition proceeded, with the printing of 14.5 billion euro-banknotes and the minting of 56 billion

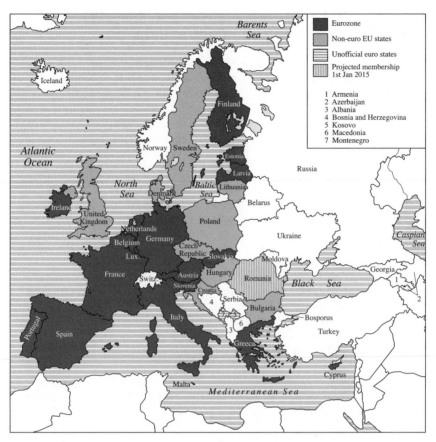

Map 7.1   *The eurozone*

coins. In January 2001 Greece became the twelfth member state to join the eurozone, having met the targets for reduced inflation and (so it claimed) budget deficits.

The final stage began on 1 January 2002, when euro coins and notes replaced those of participating states. The original plan had been for the euro and national currencies to be in concurrent circulation for six months, but it was subsequently decided that Europeans were to be given just two months to make the final transition from national currencies to the euro, and national currencies ceased to be legal tender in the eurozone on 1 March 2002. After (for some of them) centuries of fiscal independence, the 12 members of the eurozone were making the final irrevocable step to abolish their national currencies, and Deutschmarks, drachmas, escudos, francs, guilders, lire, marks, pesetas, punts and schillings faded into history. In January 2007 Slovenia became the first Eastern European member state to adopt the

Box 7.3   The European Central Bank

Since its creation in 1998, the European Central Bank (ECB) has played an increasingly important role not just in the lives of Europeans (particularly those living in the eurozone) but has also become a key actor in the world of international monetary policy. Its role and influence (as well as some of its structural weaknesses) has been most clearly on display during the crisis that broke in the eurozone in 2009.

First proposed in 1988, it was founded in 1994 as the European Monetary Institute (EMI) and finally established in June 1998 as the European Central Bank. Based in Frankfurt, its main job is to work with the national banks of eurozone states, within what is called the Eurosystem, to ensure monetary stability in the eurozone, to encourage financial integration, and to manage the foreign reserves of the eurozone. It has a Governing Council consisting of the central bank governors from each participating state, and a six-member full-time Executive Board. Board members serve non-renewable terms of eight years and can only be removed by their peers or by an order from the European Court of Justice. The Bank also has links to non-euro EU states through a General Council composed of the central bank governors of all EU member states. A new exchange-rate mechanism (ERM II) links the euro with the national currencies of non-participating countries, and the ECB is allowed to take action to support non-participating countries so long as this does not conflict with its primary task of maintaining monetary stability among participating countries.

The structure of the ECB is an almost direct copy of the famously independent German Bundesbank. In fact, it makes the Bundesbank seem quite restricted by comparison, and the ECB was already being described in 1998 as 'the most powerful single monetary authority in the world' (*European Voice*, April 1998). But Howarth and Loedel (2005: xi) may be going too far when they describe it as 'the most important institutional creation in Europe since the institutionalization of the nation state in the seventeenth century'. Neither national nor EU leaders are allowed to try to influence the Bank, its board, or its constituent national central banks, and the only body that can play any kind of watchdog role over the Bank is the monetary subcommittee of the European Parliament, but it so far lacks the resources to be able to hold the Bank or its president particularly accountable. This makes the ECB quite different from the US Federal Reserve, whose chair is regularly brought to account for its policies before the banking committee of the US Senate.

euro, and it was followed by Cyprus and Malta in 2008, by Slovakia in 2009, by Estonia in 2011 and by Latvia in 2014.

Opinion was mixed on the benefits and costs of the euro, and it is probably safe to say that no one chapter in the history of European integration was approached with so much trepidation, and – after some initial optimism – has gone on to cause so much public consternation and so many political headaches. Among the projected benefits were:

1. *Monetary stability.* The devaluations and revaluations of national currencies that were a feature of national monetary policy in eurozone countries in the 1970s and 1980s were initially replaced with greater stability, reducing the planning problems that once came with changes in the value of currencies.
2. *Greater convenience for travellers.* Instead of having to change currencies when they cross borders, and paying for goods and services with unfamiliar banknotes and coins, travellers now use the same currency wherever they go in the eurozone.
3. *Psychological benefits.* The euro was expected to make Europeans more aware of being part of the common enterprise of integration (although the euro crisis has given them cause to wonder), and also to make foreign visitors more aware of the EU; they may not always understand the latter, but they cannot ignore the effect of the euro in their pocket.
4. *Greater price transparency*, allowing consumers to more easily compare prices across borders. This also promotes competition thanks to pressure on businesses to make their products available at similar prices throughout the eurozone.
5. *Fewer bureaucratic barriers* to the transfer of large sums of money across borders, and businesses must no longer spend time and money changing currency, thus saving them transaction costs.
6. *Global economic and political influence.* The euro is a world-class currency in the same league as the US dollar and the Japanese yen, providing the eurozone with a political tool that allows it to have greater international influence, rather than having to react to developments in the United States and Japan. Prior to the eurozone crisis, a growing number of analysts saw it as a substantial threat to the global dominance of the US dollar. Given domestic economic problems in the United States and the possibility of a recovery in the eurozone, such speculation may one day return.

At the same time, the adoption of the euro has been a gamble. Never before has a similar group of large sovereign states with a long history of independence combined their currencies on a similar scale, and the risks were significantly greater than those involved in completing the single market. Furthermore, all the key preparatory decisions about the euro were taken by national leaders with little or no regard for public opinion, which was often hostile to the idea, and uncertain about the implications. The costs of the euro have included the following:

1. *Loss of sovereignty and national identity.* States joining the euro have given up critical tools for economic management, taking another and substantial step towards the surrender of control over domestic economic policy.
2. *Loss of policy independence.* States have different economic cycles, and separate currencies allow them to devalue, borrow, adjust interest rates, and take other measures in response to changed economic circumstances. Such flexibility is no longer available to eurozone states; they no longer have national banks that can make independent judgements on interest rates, and they are more exposed than before to economic problems and mismanagement in other eurozone states. In short, the members of the eurozone must rise or fall together.
3. Some economists were concerned about the *underlying weaknesses in EU economies* in 1997–98, and raised questions about the extent to which figures relating to the convergence criteria were being fudged to allow countries that had not met those criteria to take part. Some feared that these weaknesses could result in a high-credibility Deutschmark being replaced with a low-credibility euro, undermining economic health throughout the EU.
4. *The perpetuation of pockets of wealth and poverty.* Unless Europeans learn each other's languages and are able to move freely in search of jobs, the danger of the euro is that it will perpetuate the pockets of wealth and poverty that exist across the EU, thereby interfering with the development of the single market. Having a common currency in a country as big as the United States works mainly because people can move freely; this is not true of the EU, where there are still psychological and social barriers to movement.

Some of the problems inherent in the euro became clear even before it was finally adopted, with the signing in 1997 – at the insistence of Germany – of a stability and growth pact. Generated by concerns that governments in the eurozone might try to circumvent ECB monetary policies by increasing spending and running large budget deficits, the pact required that eurozone members keep their budget deficits to less than 3 per cent of GDP, and placed a 60 per cent limit on government borrowing (Hosli, 2005:67–9). Unfortunately, recession came to most industrialized countries in 2002–03, and France, Germany, Italy and Portugal quickly found themselves either in breach of the deficit limit or running the danger of crossing the 3 per cent barrier; they were later joined by Greece and the Netherlands. While there was general agreement on the principle of the pact, there was criticism that it was too inflexible (in that it made no distinctions among countries with different economic bases) and that its focus on curbing inflation left it poorly equipped to deal with slow economic growth.

By the second half of 2003 the European Central Bank was warning that most eurozone countries were in danger of failing to meet the target on budget deficits, thereby damaging the prospects for economic growth. In November 2003, the two biggest eurozone economies – France and Germany – both broke the limits and prevented other EU finance ministers from imposing large fines on the two countries (a decision that was annulled by the European Court of Justice in July 2004). Its ministers, along with their British counterpart, argued that the rules of the pact were too rigid and needed to be applied more flexibly if they were to work. By December the pact had all but collapsed and new rules were being explored to promote fiscal stability in the eurozone, including the granting of permission to selected countries in difficulties to temporarily carry larger deficits.

Then came the global financial crisis of 2007–10, set off in the United States by a combination of lax financial regulation and the extension of too much credit to consumers unable to manage debt. Many of the so-called 'toxic assets' of US banks and financial institutions were bought by their European counterparts, such that when the crisis broke in 2007, its effects reached around the world. After some initial indecision, EU governments bailed out banks and other financial institutions whose collapse might have posed systemic risks to the EU financial system, and supported a stimulus package proposed by the European Commission. The ECB meanwhile cut interest rates, and calls were made for a complete overhaul of the EU financial system.

But the downturn exposed problems in several eurozone states, notably in Greece. It had been allowed to join the euro in 2001 in spite of its failure to meet all the terms of membership (notably control of its budget deficit), it then went on a spending spree fuelled by cheaper borrowing, and its government manipulated statistics to exaggerate economic health while failing to collect enough revenue because of widespread tax evasion. When the global financial crisis found the Greek economy weak and exposed, and when the EU and the International Monetary Fund (IMF) agreed a financial bailout for Greece, it was on condition that the government implement drastic (and politically unpopular) spending cuts. But the Greek economy accounted for just two per cent of that of the eurozone area; of far greater concern was the prospect that Greece's problems might be contagious, leading to problems in other eurozone countries facing budgetary pressures, such as Portugal, Ireland, Italy and Spain (generating the acronym PIIGS).

Those problems duly emerged, but the causes were not all the same. In the case of Ireland, for example, which had enjoyed double-digit annual economic growth and record low unemployment in the 1990s, the problem was the bursting of a housing bubble in 2008, when Ireland declared itself in a recession, government revenues fell, unemployment levels rose, bankruptcies grew, and bad debts brought problems for Irish banks. In the case of Spain, a combination of inflation, a large trade deficit, the bursting of a property bubble and loss of competitiveness brought economic weakness even before the breaking of the eurozone crisis. Italy was cause for some of the greatest worries because it is the third largest economy in the eurozone, and the economic downturn was signalled by a large decline in industrial production, bankruptcies and failures in the corporate sector, and widespread corruption.

When it became too expensive for the more troubled euro states to borrow on the open market (rates for lending went up and some speculators even bet on the possibility of a default), an EU–IMF–ECB rescue package was offered on condition that Greece cut public spending and boost tax revenue. But austerity caused problems for the most indebted countries and also for the larger economies, such as Germany and France. The end result was a two-pronged approach based on safeguarding the financial stability of the eurozone and strengthening its institutional architecture. A legislative package on improved economic governance was adopted at the end of 2011; known as the 'six-pack', it included a stronger growth and stability pact which moved beyond budget deficits to include public debts, and required that member states focus more on long-term economic sustainability. New arrangements were also made to detect underlying structural weaknesses.

In an effort to improve the coordination of economic policies, in 2012 all 27 EU countries – with the exception of Britain and the Czech Republic – adopted a new fiscal compact formally titled the Treaty on Stability, Coordination and Governance in the Economic and Monetary Union. Entering into force in January 2013, it formalized fiscal rules into national law, including provisions of balanced budgets. Meanwhile, several new institutions were created: a temporary European Financial Stability Facility is being gradually replaced by a permanent European Stability Mechanism designed to offer economic crisis resolution (it has the capacity to raise capital by issuing bonds and other debt instruments and to lend up to €500 billion), several supervisory authorities were set up in 2011 to keep an eye on the banking, insurance and securities industries, and in 2012 it was decided to set up a single supervisory mechanism for banks as a first step towards a future European banking union.

Conclusions

Although the work of the EU has been driven most obviously by economic factors – and particularly by the goal of free trade in a single market – European leaders have found, through neofunctionalist logic, that economic integration has had a spillover effect on many other policy areas. Most notably, they have found that completion of the single market was a more complex notion than originally expected. The primary objective of the single market was the removal of tariffs and non-tariff barriers to trade; while tariff barriers were relatively easy to identify, the seeming innocuousness of the term 'non-tariff barriers' hid a multitude of problems, handicaps and obstacles.

Among other things, economic integration has meant removing cross-border checks on people and goods, controlling the movement of drugs and terrorists, agreeing standard levels of indirect taxation, harmonizing technical standards on thousands of goods and services, agreeing regulations in the interests of consumer safety, reaching agreement on professional qualifications, allowing Europeans to take capital and pensions with them when they move to another EU state, opening up (but also keeping a close eye on) the European market for joint ventures and corporate mergers, developing trans-European transport and energy supply networks, opening up the cross-border digital market, developing common approaches to working conditions, establishing common environmental standards, developing poorer rural and urban areas in order to avoid trade distortions, and creating an equitable and efficient agricultural sector.

In a sense, however, everything that was agreed prior to the 1990s – the thousands of decisions taken by prime ministers, chancellors, presidents, ministers and European bureaucrats, and the thousands of EU directives, regulations and decisions developed and agreed by the member states – was but a prelude to the biggest economic project of all, the conversion to a single currency. In March 2002, 12 of the 15 member states abolished their national currencies and adopted the euro, and six more later followed. Many questions were raised about the wisdom of the positions taken both by the champions and the opponents. Were the former too hasty in their decision to press on, regardless of their domestic economic problems? Would the adoption of the euro prove to be a disruptive step too far, or one of the most farsighted and creative decisions ever taken by Europe's leaders? What impact would it have, directly or indirectly, on economic development in Eastern Europe?

The global financial crisis that broke in 2007 exposed many of the weaknesses in European and American economic policy, and had a knock-on effect in the eurozone. It revealed a combination of bad design and bad decisions, and while many argue that it reflected far more poorly on the behaviour of national governments than on the principle of a single currency, others argued that it was indicative of the costs of a process of integration that had moved too far and too quickly. As to whether the glass is half full or half empty, however, the jury remains out. The most strident warnings of collapse in the eurozone, followed by the collapse of the EU, have not come to pass, but it will be many years before the implications of the eurozone crisis become clear.

Chapter 8

Internal Policies

The logic of policy spillover suggested from the outset that effective economic integration in Europe was never going to be possible without integration in a range of related policy areas. It was clear early on, for example, that economic differences within and among the member states would need to be evened out by investing in economic development and job creation, the free movement of labour, improved living and working conditions, and the rights and benefits of workers. And as long as there were economic and social differences among the member states, there would always be barriers to free trade.

The Treaty of Rome listed only agriculture, trade, transport and competition as specific policy interests of the EEC. It also noted that the EEC should promote 'a harmonious development of economic activities, a continuous and balanced expansion, an increase in stability, an accelerated raising of the standard of living and closer relations between the [member states]', but these were all general goals rather than the basis for specific policies. It was only when the member states started taking the steps to achieve these goals that they learned what the job meant in practice, and found themselves being pushed in surprising directions by the pressures of spillover.

With the six founding states being approximately equivalent in terms of their levels of wealth, and of their economic and social structures, there was little early focus on qualitative issues. But internal differences grew with the first enlargement in 1973, and the pressures for change grew with the international economic turbulence of the 1970s; by the 1980s there was new evidence that the Community was falling behind the United States and Japan on several fronts. With this in mind, there was a new focus on transferring resources and opportunities to those parts of the Community suffering the greatest handicaps, and working on removing the functional barriers to the single market. This in turn meant removing the regulatory imbalances that interfered with free trade and free movement, an effort that pushed integration into policy areas never envisioned by the authors of the Treaty of Rome, including the environment, education, culture, asylum and immigration.

This chapter looks at the internal policies of the EU. It is based on the premise that Europeans today – particularly those living in the western EU, and even in spite of the fallout from the global financial and eurozone crises – are among the most affluent and privileged people on earth, living longer and healthier lives, and having better access to jobs, education, housing, nutrition and consumer goods than the citizens of almost every other part of the world. But it also notes that Europeans do not have to look far to find decaying industrial areas, underdeveloped rural areas, pockets of poverty and high unemployment, and social dysfunction. EU policies have helped address some of these problems, but the effective management of resources – and the creation of a more even playing field – remain critical priorities. The challenges have deepened in recent years with burgeoning unemployment and the expanded economic and social differences brought on by enlargement to relatively poor eastern states.

Regional policy

Regional policy is one of the biggest items on the EU budget, accounting for more than one-third of spending (or nearly €350 billion in the 2007–13 budget cycle). Its goal is to reduce the disparities in wealth, income and opportunity that exist between Europe's regions and which interfere with broad economic development. It focuses on helping bring the poorer member states closer to the level of their wealthier partners by making investments in decaying industrial areas and poorer rural areas, promoting balanced economic development, addressing the handicaps posed by geographic remoteness or underdeveloped links between urban and rural areas, and dealing with the causes of social deprivation and poor education.

Even within its wealthier member states there are regional disparities, but as the EU has expanded in area, and brought in poorer parts of Europe, so the differences have increased in both size and effect, in many cases worsened by the fallout from the financial and eurozone crises. Expressing the average per capita GDP for the EU as 100, levels in 2011 ranged from a high in Luxembourg of 271 to lows in Romania and Bulgaria of less than half the EU average (see Figure 8.1). (Greece took a particularly notable tumble from 94 in 2009 to 79 in 2011.)

Even before the recent economic troubles, the poorest parts of the EU were mainly on the eastern, southern and western margins: Eastern Europe, eastern Germany, Greece, southern Italy, Spain, Portugal, western Ireland and western Scotland. The relative poverty of these regions had different causes: some were depressed agricultural areas with little industry and high unemployment, some were declining industrial areas with outdated factories and machinery, some (notably islands) are sparsely populated or geographically isolated from the opportunities offered by bigger markets, the eastern member states of the EU suffered the effects of Soviet-style central planning, and most

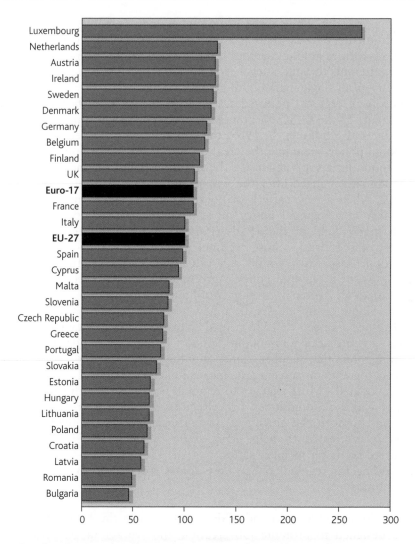

Data from Eurostat at http://epp.eurostat.ec.europa.eu (retrieved May 2013). Figures are for 2011, and indicate per capita GDP adjusted for purchasing power relative to the average for the EU-27, which is expressed as 100. For comparison, the figure for the United States was 148.

Figure 8.1 *Per capita GDP in the EU*

suffered lower levels of education and health care and had underdeveloped infrastructure, especially roads and utilities.

The wealthier EU member states have long had their own domestic programmes of economic and social development, aimed at encouraging new investment in poorer areas, at offsetting the effects of rural decline, and at trying to revive old industrial areas and the centres of large cities. But while these programmes may help offset disparities within member states, there is a limit to how much they can deal with such disparities among member states. And as long as those differences exist, attempts to build a level economic and social playing field within the European single market will be undermined.

European regional policy dates back to the 1950s, when provision was made by the ECSC for grants to depressed areas for industrial conversion and retraining. In 1969, the Commission proposed a common regional policy, including the creation of a regional development fund, but found little support among the governments of the member states. The climate changed after the first round of enlargement in the early 1970s, when a new pattern of political and economic interests made the idea of a regional policy more palatable. Most importantly, the 'rich man's club' of the 1950s (Italy excepted) had been joined by Britain and Ireland, whose regional problems not only widened the economic disparities within the EEC, but also strengthened Italy's demands for a regional policy. Agreement was thus reached to create the European Regional Development Fund (ERDF).

The Single European Act drew new attention to regional disparities, and reforms agreed in 1988 helped improve the efficiency of regional policy by setting up Community Support Frameworks under which the Commission, the member states and the regions would work more closely together on agreeing the means to achieve regional development planning goals. More changes to regional policy came with Maastricht, under which a Committee of the Regions (COR) was created to give regional authorities a greater say in European policy, and the Cohesion Fund was created to help offset some of the costs of integration incurred by newer member states.

Funding for regional policy now comes from three so-called structural funds:

- The European Social Fund (ESF), created under the Treaty of Rome, is designed to promote job creation and worker mobility, and to combat long-term unemployment and help workers adapt to technological change. Particular attention is paid to the needs of migrant workers, women and the disabled.
- The ERDF, created in 1975, supports underdeveloped areas (particularly those affected by the decline of traditional industries such as coal, steel and textiles) and inner cities with investments in infrastructure.
- The Cohesion Fund compensates poorer states (those with a per capita gross national income less than 90 per cent of the EU average) for the costs incurred by the tightening of environmental regulations, and provides financial assistance for transport and renewable energy projects. All funding goes to the 12 newest members of the EU, along with Greece.

Additional funds have more focused goals: the EU Solidarity Fund (created in 2002 in response to serious floods in several countries) is designed to help the EU respond more quickly to natural disasters, the European Agricultural Fund for Rural Development was set up in 2006 under the Common Agricultural Policy to help modernize farming and forestry, the Instrument for Pre-Accession Assistance makes investments in potential future member states (most of the spending going to Turkey and the Balkans), and the Globalization Adjustment Fund was set up in 2007 to help workers who have lost their jobs as a result of trade liberalization.

Spending on regional policy is driven by three main objectives:

- The Convergence Objective targets regions with a per capita GDP of less than 75 per cent of the EU average, the goal being to encourage more investment, new jobs and improved infrastructure. It accounts for more than 80 per cent of EU regional spending, the biggest recipients being Poland, Spain, the Czech Republic, Hungary and Italy.
- The Regional Competitiveness and Employment Objective covers parts of the EU not addressed by the Convergence Objective, the goal being to make these areas more competitive and more attractive for investment, and to create a knock-on effect throughout the EU. Funds come from the ERDF and the ESF, and the biggest recipients in 2007–13 were France, Germany, the UK and Italy.
- The Territorial Cooperation Objective focuses on encouraging cooperation between European regions, and the development of common solutions to the challenges of urban, rural and coastal development. Financed out of the ERDF, it accounted for less than three per cent of structural fund spending in 2007–13.

The jury is still out on the effectiveness of EU regional policy. Armstrong (1993) suggested quite early on that there were several benefits to a joint EU approach: it ensured that spending was concentrated in the areas of greatest need, it ensured coordination of the spending of the different member states, and it encouraged the member states to work together on one of the most critical barriers to integration. A common policy also meant that the member states had a vested interest in the welfare of their EU partners, helped member states deal with some of the potentially damaging effects of integration (such as loss of jobs and greater economic competition), and introduced an important psychological element: citizens of poorer regions receiving EU assistance were made more aware of the benefits of EU membership, while citizens of the wealthier states that were net contributors had a vested interest in ensuring that such spending was effective.

But an independent report commissioned by the European Commission and published in 2004 concluded that there was little hard evidence either that regional differences had been closed, or that they had not (Sapir *et al.*, 2004). There is still a substantial gap in per capita GDP between the richest and poorest member states, a problem that has been exacerbated by the fallout from the global financial and eurozone crises. Clearly much more needs to be done to reduce regional disparities, but this will be hard as long as most EU member states continue to suffer the effects of the economic downturn.

Employment and social policy

One of the most abject failures of European integration has been its inability to ease unemployment, the persistence of which (in Europe) was once described as equivalent to the persistence of poverty in the United States (Dahrendorf, 1988:149). The single market has not been able to generate enough jobs for Europeans, for reasons which are unclear. Part of the problem has been the large number of unskilled workers in the EU, and another part of the problem is that while millions of new jobs were created before the economic downturn in 2007–10, nearly half were temporary or part-time jobs, many of them in the service sector, and because most were being filled by men and women new to the job market, they did little to help ease long-term unemployment.

The fallout from the global financial crisis has only made matters worse: in early 2013, unemployment rates varied from lows of 4–6 per cent in Austria, Germany and the Netherlands to highs of more than 25 per cent in Spain and Greece (see Figure 8.2). The overall average for the EU-27 was nearly 11 per cent, and for the eurozone, 12 per cent, but these numbers hide one of the most worrying problems relating to employment: the large number of younger Europeans who lack jobs. Unemployment rates among those in the 15–25 age group were more than twice the overall EU figure in mid-2013, with more than half of younger Greeks and Spaniards out of work, more than 40 per cent out of work in Italy, and more than one in four out of work in France and Portugal. The absence of opportunities and hope for so many Europeans may be the biggest economic and social challenge that the EU faces, with worries that it will feed into stifled ambition, political restlessness, anti-EU sentiment and resentment towards immigrants.

The EU's employment and social policies have attempted to address these problems by focusing on job creation, the free movement of labour, improved living and working conditions, and protecting the rights and benefits of workers. A truly open single market demands equal pay, equal working conditions, comparable standards on workers' rights and women's rights and an expansion of the skilled workforce. Without these qualities, poorer European states will suffer the effects of competition from their wealthier partners in the EU,

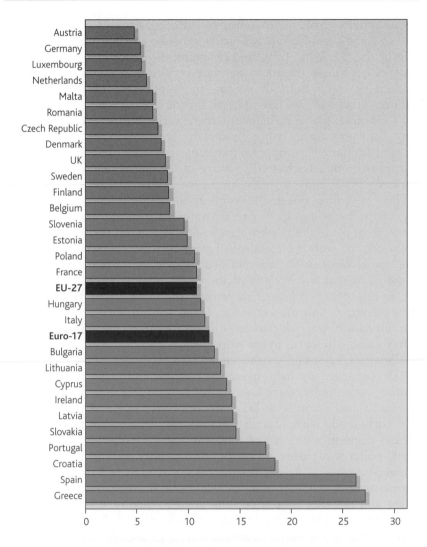

Data from Eurostat at http://epp.eurostat.ec.europa.eu (retrieved May 2013). Figures are for January 2013. For comparison, the figure for the United States was 7.9.

Figure 8.2 *Unemployment in the EU*

while those with less progressive employment laws will lose jobs to those that offer better working conditions. These concerns, combined with the long history of welfare promotion in individual Western European states, have helped make social policy an important part of the EU agenda.

The matter of the rights, opportunities and benefits provided to potential, actual or former workers has proved controversial, because social policy treads on sensitive ideological and cultural toes. Conservatives and liberals will never agree on the best way of building a level social playing field, and programmes that may be regarded as progressive by one member state may be seen as a threat to economic welfare or even cultural identity by another. Generally speaking, national labour unions have been in favour of EU social policy, as have the Commission and Parliament (where social democratic parties have long been prominent), while business interests and conservative political parties have been opposed, arguing that social policy could make European companies less competitive in the global market (Geyer and Springer, 1998: 208).

There was little direct discussion about social questions during the negotiations leading up to the Treaty of Rome, and while the treaty made it the Community's business to deal with such matters as the free movement of workers, equal pay for equal work, working conditions, and social security for migrant workers, it was based on the naive assumption that the benefits of the single market would improve life for all European workers. This proved true to the extent that it helped increase wages, but market forces failed to deal with gender and age discrimination, wage disparities, different levels of unemployment, and safety and health needs in the workplace.

When restrictions on the movement of workers were eased in the late 1960s in order to help overcome labour shortages in the larger northern economies, there was an influx of immigrants from southern Europe, mostly from non-EC states such as Greece, Portugal, Spain and Turkey, and what was then Yugoslavia. With enlargement creating greater disparities in levels of economic wealth within the Community, social policy was pushed up the political agenda and the first in a series of four-year Social Action Programmes was launched in 1974. While aimed at developing a plan to achieve full employment, improved living and working conditions, and gender equality, a combination of recession and ideological resistance from several European leaders ensured that many of the words failed to be translated into practical change.

Because a core goal of the Single European Act (SEA) was the freedom of Europeans to live and work wherever they liked in the EC, social policy came to the fore again as questions were raised about the mobility of workers and about 'social dumping': money, services and businesses moving to those parts of the Community with the lowest wages and social security costs. The Commission tried to focus the attention of national governments on the 'social dimension' of the single market, but economic recession made sure that the SEA initially lacked such a dimension. This encouraged the then Commission president Jacques Delors to launch an attempt in 1988 to draw more attention to the social consequences of the single market.

Sparked by Belgium's adoption of a national charter of basic social rights, the idea of a European charter was broached in 1987, and the Community Charter of Fundamental Social Rights of Workers (known generally as the Social Charter) was adopted at the 1989 Strasbourg summit. Plans to incorporate the charter into Maastricht were blocked by Britain, and it was only following the 1997 election of Tony Blair that Britain changed its position and the charter was incorporated by the Treaty of Amsterdam. Among other things, it notes the right to freedom of movement, to fair remuneration for employment, to social protection (including a minimum income for those unable to find employment), to freedom of association and collective bargaining, to equal treatment, to health, safety and protection in the workplace, and to a retirement income that allows a reasonable standard of living.

Workers' rights in the EU have been tightened and have become among the most generous in the world. For example, the 1993 Working Time Directive sets a maximum of 48 hours of work per week (including overtime), a minimum daily rest period of 11 hours in every 24, and a minimum of four weeks paid leave per year. France went further by setting a 35-hour working week, while Britain has railed against the limit. One of the effects is that the average number of hours an employee worked in a year in 2012 was significantly lower in most European countries (as low as 1400 in the Netherlands and Germany, but still more than 2000 in Greece) compared to 1800 in the United States and 2000 in Russia and South Korea (OECD web site, 2013). Other EU laws set a minimum of four months' leave for new parents, guarantee the right of return to the same job after the parental leave is taken, and established (as long ago as 1975) the principle of equal pay for comparable work. In spite of this, there is still a gender pay-gap in the EU, with women on average in 2008 earning 17.5 per cent less than men (which still compares well with the 38 per cent gap in South Korea, and 33 per cent in Japan and the United States) (OECD website, 2013).

Another of the changes that came with Amsterdam was the introduction of an employment chapter that called on member states to 'work towards developing a coordinated strategy for employment'. However, it only required the Commission and the member states to report to each other, and most of the responsibility for employment policy remained with the member states. Geyer and Springer (1998: 210) argue that EU employment policy had 'high visibility but little focus', and that the search for solutions was hampered by a lack of support in the member states, and by the problem of trying to create jobs through increased competitiveness while preserving the traditional rights of employees. Employment is a key part of the Europe 2020 strategy, aimed at addressing problems in the EU growth model and replacing it with one that is both more sustainable and inclusive. The European

Box 8.1   Is there a European dream?

With all the bad economic news that has been coming out of Europe of late, it can sometimes be forgotten that Europeans are among the most privileged people in the world. They have access to an advanced system of education and health care, an extensive and generous welfare system, a vibrant consumer society, and a sophisticated transport and communications system. They enjoy almost universal literacy, employed Europeans enjoy more paid holiday leave and leisure time than anyone else, and the provision of shelter and nutrition is more than adequate. One American observer, Jeremy Rifkin, has been so impressed that he sees the quality of life of Europeans as a whole eclipsing that of Americans, long thought of as living in the world's most socially privileged country (Rifkin, 2004). Another, Steven Hill, suggests that 'most of the world is recognizing the advantages of the European way', with its steady-state economy and emphasis on sustainable development (Hill, 2010).

Much of the European story can be traced back to the philosophy adopted by most Western European governments after the Second World War that the state should provide a wide range of basic social services, creating a safety net through which even the poorest and the most underprivileged would not be allowed to slip. Hence every European state has some form of state education and national health care, and provisions for children and the aged have increased as the number of lone-parent families and retirees has grown. Most wealthier European states even do well in comparison with the United States, which has the most technologically advanced health care in the world but lacks a comprehensive national health service, and is one of the richest economies in the world yet still has 15 per cent of its people living m poverty.

But not all of Europe's welfare policies have succeeded, and it is one of the great ironies of life in modern industrialized democracies that considerable want continues to exist in the midst of plenty. Poverty has not gone away and in several places has worsened, creating considerable differences across Europe. This is particularly true of the number of children living in poverty, which stands at less than 10 per cent in Germany, the Netherlands and Sweden, but is almost twice as high in Britain and Italy. There have also been many troubling questions asked of late about how long Europe can continue to sustain this way of life, given its declining and ageing population. But in the debate about Europe's future, it is important to look at the achievements as well as the failures, and also to consider the European record in comparison to developments in other parts of the world.

Employment Strategy is central to this, with its efforts to encourage EU member states to share information and coordinate their national employment programmes.

- The
  with
  tionis
- Diffe
  temp
  1997

With
clear. E
amalga
mently
reform
budget
nationa
to repla
fell bel
and to
aside'
1998 a
tion, v
prices
direct
devote
  Easte
of the
Europe
econo
farmin
Poles
Swedi
(Riege
states
also n
made
allow
€22 k
Acces
(SAPA
and it
startin
5 per
  Tod
paym
rural
safety

At the core of EU activities (CAP), which was long based on motion of a single market in agr ence (a system of protectionism produce over imported produce), of the CAP had to be shared eq What this meant in practical po was that Community farmers price for their produce, regardle world prices, or of the levels of EU's internal market was prote member states shared the financi

In many ways this policy w markets stabilized, supplies wer were protected from fluctuati wealthier, and their livelihoods The EU today is by far the accounting in 2011 for 41 per c four times as much as the United (World Trade Organization webs prices, European farmers have land, so that production has go EU is now self-sufficient in al produce in its climate (including and dairy products). The CAP a successes, because farmers have mechanization and the increased tainly been at the core of agricult

Unfortunately, the CAP also cre

- EU-15 farmers produced more stockpiles of surplus produce, olive oil, raisins, figs and even
- The CAP created economic d would have gone out of busine land, and failed to close the farmers, which grew with easte
- The CAP caused environme increased use of chemical fert hedges and trees and the 'recla making farms bigger and more
- The CAP made food more exp pluses.
- Because so much of the EU bu agriculture, there was less avail

soured EU relations the idea of a protec-
posed an irresistible ulent claims (Grant,
rm of the CAP was ave the land, and to it units, were vehe-rmany. Pressures for nize the Community amunity during inter-reement was reached ct payments if prices ain, beef, and butter, production (the 'set-rms agreed between ubsidies and produc-ayment. Guaranteed ts were all reduced, re of the EU budget to the issue, because ity of most Eastern has greater political, en its relatively large ns and 15 per cent of per cent of Danish, per cent of Britons) y to the new member t special efforts were an farmers were not romise agreed was to gricultural payments, 06 under the Special Rural Development prepare for the CAP, sed in over ten years, annual increments of its early days. Direct ave been available for ow seen mainly as a k too low. Where the

Box 8.2　The Common Fisheries Policy

The fishing industry employs barely 400,000 people in the EU, or a fraction of the workforce, but the state of the industry has important implications for coastal communities all around the EU; especially important given that 23 of the 28 member states have coasts, and there are heavy concentrations of population in coastal areas. Disputes over fishing grounds in European waters once led to bitter confrontations, such as the infamous 'cod wars' of the 1960s between Britain and Iceland over access to fisheries in the north Atlantic, and to political battles such as the opposition from many in Britain in the 1990s to the presence of Spanish trawlers in traditional British fishing waters.

Although it has attracted much less controversy (or spending) than the CAP, the EU's Common Fisheries Policy (CFP) has occasionally attracted sustained political attention (see Lequesne, 2004). Tracing its origins to the 1976 changes in international law by which access to marine resources was expanded from 19km (12 miles) to 322km (200 miles) from the coastline, it was adopted in 1983. Aimed at supporting a competitive and sustainable fishing industry, it has focused on imposing national quotas (Total Allowable Catches, or TACs), setting rules on fishing gear and mesh sizes for fishing nets, requiring accurate reporting of catches and landings, setting rules on the protection of marine wildlife and vulnerable species of fish, requiring licensing for all EU fishing boats, operating a management policy that limits the size of EU fishing fleets, managing the market in order to monitor prices, quality and competition, and reaching agreements with third countries on access to their fishing grounds.

The results have been mixed. Overfishing is a global problem, with estimates that as much as one-fifth of the worldwide fish catch is unregulated and illegal, fears that overfishing has left major fish stocks depleted, and concerns that – combined with the effects of pollution – the sustainability and future of marine ecosystems are threatened (see Clover, 2005). Fisheries are a classic example of a common-pool resource, or one that does not come under the jurisdiction of a single state or authority, and so is open to unregulated exploitation. Rational self-interest encourages all those who have access to the resource to extract as much of it as possible, maximizing their benefits at the cost of the whole. For this reason, the CFP cannot function in isolation, but must be part of a global regime to manage fisheries.

CAP was once about ensuring regular food supplies, today it is more about helping European farmers to survive and to compete in global markets. There is more of a focus on quality rather than quantity, driven mainly by changing consumer demands and concerns about the state of the environment. CAP payments have conditions attached, linked to food safety, animal health and welfare, sustainable development and the management of rural landscapes. And where once agricultural subsidies had swallowed up as much as 70 per cent of the EU budget, today they account for about one-third of spending.

Justice and home affairs

With the opportunities created by the single market, it was perhaps inevitable that the EU would sooner or later turn its attention to the management of asylum, immigration, crime and terrorism, developing common internal policies while also keeping an eye on the management of external borders. These are areas of policy known collectively as justice and home affairs (JHA) and are a prime example of the phenomenon of spillover at work; the governments of EU member states discovered and developed them more by accident than by intention. The Council of Europe was more active initially, addressing issues related to criminal matters and human rights. As controls on cross-border movement in Europe began to ease, more attention was paid to cross-border crime and terrorism, and more efforts were made to encourage police and judicial cooperation. The loss by several member states of their land borders with non-Community states following completion of the single market led to new demands for cooperation and burden-sharing. This was followed by an increase in the number of visa applications in the wake of the Balkan civil wars, and then by the need for a more structured approach to international terrorism following the September 2001 attacks in the United States. As the movement of people inside the EU became easier, so the need to strengthen external borders became more obvious (see Wolff et al, 2009).

The goal now is to create an 'area of freedom, security and justice', meaning one in which security, rights and free movement are assured. But there is still no single policy on JHA, the focus having been more on cooperation than on harmonization, resulting in a pattern of shared competences involving European, state and sub-state levels of governance (Lavenex, 2010: 458). Nonetheless, these cooperative efforts were incorporated by Lisbon into the mainstream of EU policy concerns, and there has been much institutional, legal and procedural change:

- Europol (the European Police Office) is a criminal intelligence agency that became fully operational in 1998, encouraging cross-border police cooperation and becoming one of the more prominent of the EU's specialized agencies.
- Also in 1998, a new European judicial network was charged with improving judicial cooperation by linking contact points in the

member states. In 2002 it was strengthened with the creation of a new Judicial Cooperation Unit (Eurojust) set up to improve investigations and prosecutions involving two or more member states.

- In 2004 the Hague Programme listed ten priorities for EU policy, including a comprehensive response to terrorism, the integrated management of the EU's external borders, and the creation of a common asylum procedure.
- In 2004, the European Agency for the Management of Operational Cooperation at the External Borders of the Member States of the EU (better known as Frontex) was created to coordinate external border management for the EU as a whole. It encourages cooperation among national border agencies, developing common training standards, collating and analysing intelligence, and providing a rapid response ability through European Border Guard Teams trained to respond to crises.
- The European Arrest Warrant was introduced in 2004, allowing member states to request the arrest of a criminal in another state and his/her transfer to the issuing state within 90 days. It was joined in 2008 by a European evidence warrant designed to standardize methods for obtaining documents, data and other evidence in cross-border cases.
- In 2009 the EU Blue Card (modelled on the US Green Card) was established as a single work and residence permit for skilled migrants.
- The EU Internal Security Strategy was adopted in 2010 to provide the principles and guidelines for EU policy, identifying such priorities as disrupting international criminal networks, preventing terrorism, addressing cyber-security, and increasing resilience to crises and disasters.

Migration is at the heart of the policy coordination. While there has long been movement across borders within Europe, such movement has become easier, the motives for migration have changed, and a new dimension has been added by the arrival of large numbers of newcomers of different ethnicities and religions from outside Europe – see Box 8.3. The number of migrants is difficult to calculate because of the problem of record-keeping in an era of open borders; according to Eurostat, there are nearly 32 million people living legally in EU member states of which they were not nationals, of which nearly two-thirds are citizens of non-EU states (Vasileva, 2010). More than one-third of the population of Luxembourg is foreign-born, while Ireland, Austria, Spain, Sweden and Germany also have large immigrant populations (United Nations, 2009).

And while legal immigration can be managed in terms of the source countries, the numbers allowed in, and the jobs they fill, illegal immi-

Box 8.3 Immigration and Europe

Migration is nothing new to Europe; the region, after all, has a long history of waves of invaders moving out from their homelands and altering the cultural, political and linguistic landscape of newly colonized regions. Hence the famous quip by the historian H.A.L. Fisher that 'Europe is a continent of energetic mongrels.' It is also difficult – in the era of passports, visas and long queues at airport security – to remember that until the early twentieth century it was relatively easy for those with the financial means to travel wherever they wanted in Europe. But migration has taken on an entirely new meaning in the wake of the single market, and as political and economic pressures have increased, so have the number of people seeking to come to Europe from outside the region. Where once Europeans focused on what was happening at home, cross-border issues have moved up the agenda, resulting in what Parsons and Smeeding (2006: 1) describe as an 'historic transformation'. Race, religion and culture have entered the public debate as never before.

The changes are not unique to Europe, of course, because wherever there is economic opportunity there will be people from other countries seeking to access it, and all the most prosperous parts of the world have become magnets for immigrants. While it is difficult to be sure about the dimensions of the phenomenon, UN data suggest that the number of international migrants grew worldwide between 1990 and 2010 by more than 37 per cent, reaching a total of 214 million. Of those, about 70 million (or one-third) were in Europe (United Nations, 2009). By 2008, the EU-25 had become the second most popular target for legal immigration after the United States, accounting for nearly 2.5 million immigrants (compared to the 2.7 million who entered the United States). The most popular destinations were Spain, Germany, the UK, France and the Netherlands (OECD web site, 2013).

With acceleration of the single-market programme in the 1980s there was a move away from national policies on immigration and towards a more coordinated European approach. But rhetoric has often outweighed substance, and the waters of the debate have been muddied by the often emotive injection of myths, stereotypes and discrimination. There has been rising support for anti-immigration political parties in multiple EU member states, whose policies often overlap with hostility to European integration. But there is still no common EU immigration policy, mainly thanks to widespread support for the idea that member states should have the right to decide how many immigrants they will accept, and a belief that Europe already has enough people, and that the EU should be tightening rather than loosening its borders.

gration poses an entirely different set of challenges: illegal immigrants are usually unskilled, they will often risk much to move to a new country, and their presence overlaps with concerns about human trafficking, drug trafficking and terrorism. The related matter of asylum has moved up the agenda as the number of people seeking protection in the wake of war and ethnic conflict in Asia and Africa has increased: the EU received about 75 per cent of the applications lodged with industrialized countries in 2007–09, most coming from Iraq, Russia, Somalia and Afghanistan (United Nations High Commissioner for Refugees web site, 2013). And finally there is the problem of cross-border crime; if business and consumers have exploited the new opportunities made available by the single market, so have criminals, and new policies and cooperative procedures have had to be developed in response.

There is also the challenge of controlling terrorism, which has been a headline problem in Europe since the activities of separatist and anarchist groups picked up speed in the 1970s. It has achieved new prominence with the added threat of Islamic extremism in the wake of the 2001 attacks in the United States, which resulted in the European Council adopting a rushed Action Plan on Combating Terrorism, which was revised after the London bombings in 2004 and the Madrid bombings in 2005, and has been revised several more times since. In 2005 a Counter-Terrorism Strategy was agreed, based on the four Ps: *protecting* Europeans by reducing Europe's vulnerability to attacks, *preventing* people from turning to terrorism by addressing the root causes of radicalization, *pursuing* terrorists across borders and globally, and better *preparing* European authorities to respond to attacks. In spite of the publicity generated by Islamic extremism, Europol data show that nationalist, separatist and anarchist movements have been involved in far more successful or attempted attacks in recent years (Europol, 2013).

Environmental policy

When the Treaty of Rome was drafted and signed, environmental concerns barely registered on the radars of government or of public opinion. It would not be until the 1960s that broader awareness began to emerge of the need to manage natural resources and to limit the damaging effects of human activity, but even then the response of most governments was to create new institutions rather than develop substantive policies to pass new laws; the environmental implications of economic development were little appreciated or understood, and industry resisted efforts to develop new regulations. The few pieces of environmental law that were agreed by the Community in the 1960s were prompted less by concern about environmental quality than by worries over the extent to which different national environmental standards were distorting competition and complicating progress on the common market.

By the early 1970s thinking had begun to change. There was a public reaction against what was seen as uncaring affluence, generated by a combination of improved scientific understanding, worsening air and water quality, several headline-making environmental disasters, and new affluence among the western middle classes (see McCormick, 1995, Chapter 3). Just as the governments of the member states could not avoid being caught up in the growing demand for a response, so the improvement of environmental quality had to be pushed up the agenda of European integration. The 1972 UN Conference on the Human Environment, held in Stockholm, proved to be a landmark, and the Community responded in 1973 with the publication of its first Environmental Action Programme. More programmes followed (the most recent covering the period 2012–20), at first emphasizing preventive action but then emphasizing sustainable development, or the need to ensure that development does not result in permanent environmental change or natural resource depletion. In 1986 the Single European Act gave the environment legal status as a Community policy concern, while later institutional changes gave the European Parliament a greater role in environmental policy making, and introduced qualified majority voting on most issues related to environmental law and policy.

A multinational response to environmental problems makes sense at several levels:

- Many problems – such as air and water pollution – are not limited by national frontiers, and are best addressed by several governments working together. Thus the air pollution created in Britain and Germany and blown by the wind to Scandinavia can only effectively be addressed by producers and recipients working together, and the management of rivers that run through several countries – such as the Rhine and the Danube – can only work if designed and implemented by all these countries.
- Individual countries working alone may not want to take action for fear of saddling themselves with costs that would undermine their economic competitiveness; they have fewer such fears when several countries are working towards the same goals at the same time. As states become more dependent on trade and foreign investment, and the barriers to trade come down, so parochial worries about loss of comparative economic advantage become less important.
- The economic benefits of removing barriers to free trade (including different environmental standards) help offset some of the costs of taking action.

- Rich countries can help poor countries address environmental problems through funding assistance and a sharing of technical knowledge, and over the long term will see fewer factories closing and being moved to countries with lower environmental standards.

EU activities on the environment today have widespread public and political support. Eurobarometer polls find that most Europeans rank environmental protection above finance, defence or employment as an issue of EU concern, that most feel pollution is an 'urgent and immediate problem', and that most agree that environmental protection is a policy area better addressed jointly by EU states than by member states alone. Underpinning these opinions has been the growth in support for Green political parties, which since the late 1980s have won seats in the national legislatures of most EU member states, and have been members of coalition governments in Belgium, Finland, France, Germany, Ireland, Italy and Latvia. In 2013 there were Green members from more than a dozen (mainly western) member states in the European Parliament.

A substantial body of environmental law has been agreed by the EU, with most of the activity focusing on improving water and air quality; controlling the production and disposal of waste from agriculture, industry and domestic households; monitoring the production and use of chemicals; encouraging the protection of wildlife and natural habitats; making the EU a quieter place by placing limits on the noise pollution allowed by everything from road vehicles to aircraft, compressors, tower cranes, welding generators, power generators and concrete breakers; and controlling the use of genetically modified organisms (GMOs). The goals of EU policy have meanwhile been given better definition by the work of the European Environment Agency, a data-gathering agency that provides information to the other EU institutions and publishes assessments of the state of the European environment. The story those assessments tell is mixed:

- Europe's water and air are cleaner, there is more public awareness of the threats posed by chemicals to food and water, and differences in environmental standards pose less of a handicap than before to trade among the member states.
- Levels of sulphur dioxide, lead and particulates have fallen in the EU, but many European cities still have dirty air, mainly because of heavy (and growing) concentrations of road traffic, a problem worsened by the often dirtier and relatively poorly maintained vehicles found in Eastern Europe.
- Intensive agriculture continues to exert pressure on natural habitats, helping threaten 45 per cent of Europe's reptiles and 42 per cent of its mammals with extinction, introducing nitrogen and phosphorus

into surface waters, and emitting acidifying ammonia into the atmosphere. Meanwhile, groundwater concentrations of some pesticides frequently exceed maximum admissible levels.

- There has been little progress in the development of waste-disposal policies, and total waste production continues to grow, although the proportion going into landfill has fallen as the use of incinerators has grown.
- Freshwater is overexploited and is polluted by sewage, pesticides and industrial waste, and overfishing and pollution continue to be problems in many coastal zones and marine waters.

Environmental management is now one of the most important areas of policy activity for the EU, ranking only behind foreign policy cooperation, economic issues and agriculture in terms of the level of political activity involved. Environmental policy in the EU is now made more as a result of joint European initiatives than as a result of activities at the level of the member states. In the cases of countries such as Portugal and Spain, and of most Eastern European states, which had taken little action on the environment before joining the EU, their national laws are now almost entirely driven by the requirements of EU law. At the same time, this rather glowing assessment of the results of EU initiatives needs to be tempered with some qualifications, and when it comes to the place of the EU in the international system, the contrasting cases of chemicals and climate-change policies giving some insight into the problems and prospects.

On the chemicals front, the EU has agreed a body of laws designed to control the release of new chemicals on to the market, to prevent accidents at chemical plants, to control the use of pesticides and to regulate trade in dangerous chemicals. The focus switched over time from efforts to remove obstacles to the common market posed by different sets of national regulations, to a desire to protect consumers with measures to ban or limit the commercialization of dangerous substances and preparations, to an effort to minimize the impact of chemicals on the environment. Capping this story was the entering into force in 2007 of the REACH regulation (Registration, Evaluation, Authorization and Restriction of Chemical Substances).

Prompted by concerns about how many new chemical compounds were being placed on the market every year with little information about their potential threats to human health and the environment, REACH requires that manufacturers and importers gather information on the properties of chemicals and report to the European Chemicals Agency. That information is made available to consumers and industry so that they know of any associated risks, providing an inbuilt motive for manufacturers to develop safer alternatives. The United States has traditionally taken a laxer approach to the regulation of chemicals, giving manufacturers more latitude over releasing information, and the US government initially lobbied hard against REACH. It ultimately had to concede not only to its passage, however, but to the new reality that US chemical manufacturers would have to follow the EU lead or else lose access to the lucrative European market for many of their products (Layton, 2008).

On climate change, the role of the EU as a leader is more questionable. It is – along with the United States, China and India – one of the world's four major players, and as such has been at the heart of efforts to achieve international agreement (see Jordan *et al.*, 2010 and Wurzel and Connelly, 2010). But the story has not gone the way that many would have hoped. The Community championed the signature of the 1992 UN Framework Convention on Climate Change, as well as a protocol signed in Kyoto, Japan, in 1997, that was designed to give the convention some substance. In 2000 the Commission launched the European Climate Change Programme, which identified measures that could be taken to reduce emissions, and in 2002 the EU-15 ratified Kyoto, committing them to cutting carbon dioxide (CO_2) emissions by 8 per cent by 2008–12 on 1990 levels. At the heart of EU efforts is the EU Emissions Trading Scheme, launched in 2005, under which member states set a national cap on CO_2 emissions from industries, which are issued with emission allowances. Those that use less than their allotted number of allowances can sell them to companies that are having trouble meeting the limits.

The results have been mixed. By 2004, the EU-25 had reduced its CO_2 emissions by 7.3 per cent, compared to a rise in US emissions of 15.8 per cent (United Nations Framework Convention on Climate Change website, 2007). But three years later emissions were down only 4.3 per cent, and the EU was not down far enough to meet the Kyoto targets. In 2007, the EU announced its 20-20-20 strategy, aimed at cutting CO_2 emissions by 2020 (over 1990 levels) and generating at least 20 per cent of its energy from renewable sources. It went to a meeting of signatories of the climate-change convention held in Copenhagen in 2009 with something of a sense of moral superiority, but was criticized for not taking enough of a leadership position, contributing to an embarrassing failure to achieve agreement there. By 2010 its emissions were down overall more than 15 per cent over 1990 levels, but the story with individual EU states varied substantially – see Figure 8.3. But whatever the EU is able to contribute to addressing climate change, little will be achieved without a dramatic change of direction in the world's three biggest producers of greenhouse gases: China, the United States and India.

Regional cooperation among countries promises a quicker and more effective resolution of transnational environmental problems than any other approach, at least among countries with similar political

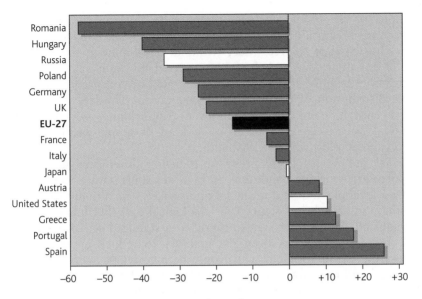

Data from UN Framework Convention on Climate Change at
http://unfccc.int/ghg_data/ghg_data_unfccc/items/4146.php (retrieved July 2013).
Figures are for signatories of Annex I of the UNFCCC only. By comparison, Chinese
emissions grew over the same period by an estimated 230 per cent and Indian
emissions by 200 per cent (International Energy Agency data at http://www.iea.org).

Figure 8.3   *Changes in EU greenhouse gas emissions, 1990–2010*

systems and similar levels of economic development. The eastern enlargement muddied the waters in the EU because of the significantly different environmental standards inherited by Eastern Europe from the Soviet era. But free-market forces of the kind brought by the EU are likely to have a more efficient and effective result than the imposition of regulations that give developing countries little incentive to think about environmental planning. Given the extent to which the causes and effects of environmental problems do not respect national frontiers, and the extent to which shared responses are more effective than unilateral responses, the EU model may provide the only adequate response to such problems, mainly because it encourages different states to cooperate rather than to adopt potentially conflicting objectives.

Conclusions

The EU approaches to regional, employment, social, agricultural, agricultural, asylum, immigration and environmental policy provide illustrations of the kinds of forces that are at work in the process of European integration, and that involve encouraging cooperation and removing barriers to free trade. Regional development, for example, has meant an attempt to help the poorer parts of the EU catch up with their richer neighbours, with the utopian goal of encouraging an equitable distribution of the benefits of integration. The free market can never entirely eliminate inequalities of opportunity, which is why regional policy has been based on a kind of grand welfare system involving the redistribution of wealth.

Social policy has been aimed at reducing differences in income, opportunity, working conditions and worker skills with a view to creating a level playing field in the labour market. The attempt to build a common approach has stepped on ideological toes, but has ultimately brought all the member states around to a standard set of objectives. The biggest failure has been the inability to reduce unemployment across the EU, a problem which only became worse with the global financial and the eurozone crises, and which will continue to compromise some of the achievements of the single market until it can be turned around.

The case of agricultural policy has been something of an aberration, the result of a political pact between two of the founding member states. In practice it has been interventionist, starting out as an attempt to offer equal opportunities to farmers across the EU, and to invest in rural economies that might otherwise have been left behind. It became almost too successful, encouraging European farmers to produce as much as the land would sustain, rather than being driven by what the market would bear. But this has now changed.

The policy areas that have been collectively addressed as justice and home affairs – including asylum, immigration, cross-border crime, terrorism and border control – were all mainly unanticipated but inevitable consequences of the need to manage some of the effects of the single market. JHA deals with a combination of matters that are both internal and external to the EU, including free movement of people within the EU and control of the EU's external borders. With time, these efforts have developed more consistency, moving from a loose collection of intergovernmental initiatives to a more coordinated supranational approach, but there is still much more to be done.

In the case of the environment, there is little question that international cooperation is desirable and even inevitable. Problems such as air and water pollution ignore national boundaries, and there are repeated examples from around the world of one state being a producer and downwind or downstream states being recipients. As the global economy expands, the barriers posed to trade by different environmental standards add a new dimension. There will always be ideological disagreement about the extent to which the state should manage natural resources and regulate industry, but there is an emerging consensus that the EU has been a positive force in environmental protection, and that European environmental problems are better dealt with at the EU level than at the national or local level.

Chapter 9

External Policies

Much as there is little agreement on how best to understand the EU as an organization, so there is little agreement on its place in the global system. In many respects the EU member states continue to function independently, but in others they are better regarded as a single bloc. On foreign and security policy, for example, the EU has developed many common positions, but member states still have their own more particular interests, and the EU is still not regarded as a global actor in the same league as the United States, China or Russia. But when trade issues are on the agenda, or third parties seek access to the European marketplace, the EU can be thought of as a unit. Meanwhile, there are sub-groups of member states working on their own projects, as in the case of the 18 members of the eurozone.

The long-time lack of focus, consistency and policy leadership, and the resulting confusion felt by other countries, was neatly summed up in a (sadly, apocryphal) question credited to former US Secretary of State Henry Kissinger: 'When I want to speak to Europe, whom do I call?' Some clarity was provided in 1999 when four external relations portfolios in the Commission were replaced with one, and a new position of High Representative was appointed to be the first point of contact on foreign and security policy matters. The office was confirmed under Lisbon, and given new powers, including a seat in both the European Commission and the Council of the EU, and management of a new European diplomatic service. But the EU is still represented in most high-level meetings by the president of the Commission, as well as – since the passage of the Treaty of Lisbon – the president of the European Council. Small wonder, then, that President George W. Bush is reputed to have commented during a visit to Strasbourg, 'You guys sure have a lot of presidents.'

While the steps taken by the EU to build a common foreign and security policy have been halting, there are few remaining doubts about its global economic status. It is the world's richest marketplace, accounting for 25 per cent of global GDP, 16 per cent of merchandise trade and 23 per cent of trade in commercial services. It is a dominating actor in global trade negotiations, the biggest market in the world for mergers and acquisitions, and the biggest source of (and target for) foreign direct investment. In spite of recent problems with the euro, its global economic profile is substantial, and much is

194

expected of the EU on the world stage, both by its own members and by other countries. Whether it has been able to deliver, though, is another matter.

The first half of this chapter surveys EU activities in the fields of foreign, security and trade policy, and the second half looks in turn at its collective relations with key parts of the world. The latter begins with an assessment of EU–US relations, then of relations with neighbouring states in eastern Europe, the Middle East and North Africa, then at the dynamics of the evolving EU–China relationship, and finishes with a review of EU development policy. The chapter argues that while there has been much progress in giving more clarity to the shape of the EU as a global actor, much remains to be done in the face of changes in the nature of the international system.

Foreign policy

In their attempts to build a common European foreign policy, EU leaders have found themselves pulled in multiple directions. On the one hand it has been clear that the EU will punch below its weight unless its member states work as a group. On the other hand there has been the fear that coordination will interfere with state sovereignty and the freedom of member states to pursue matters of national interest. Complicating the picture, there are legal and constitutional difficulties regarding policy responsibility, and the leaders of EU states are divided over how far they should continue to follow the lead of the United States and how far they should (or could) build more policy independence for the EU. And then there is the practical and philosophical problem of just how far the EU can expect to make itself heard on the global stage so long as it lacks a unified military and a single defence policy (see discussion later in this chapter).

But whatever the leaders of EU states think, many ordinary Europeans appear to have made up their minds:

- In polls taken between 1999 and 2011, about 70–75 per cent supported a common EU defence and security policy, with only about 15–20 per cent opposed (Eurobarometer 77, Spring 2012:97).
- In the same period, about 60–65 per cent favoured a common EU foreign policy, with only about 20–25 per cent opposed (Eurobarometer 77, Spring 2012:97).
- About two-thirds of those surveyed in 2010 felt that the EU had influence as an international player, although only 39 per cent felt that the interests of their home country were taken into account, while 50 per cent did not (Eurobarometer 75, Spring 2011:36).

The Treaties of Rome made no mention of foreign policy, and the EEC long focused on domestic economic policy. But the logic of spillover implied that the development of the single market would make it difficult to avoid the agreement of common external policies. Early moves in that direction included the failed European Defence and Political Communities (see Chapter 3), and Charles de Gaulle's plans for regular meetings among the leaders of the Six to coordinate foreign policy. It was only at their summit in The Hague in 1969 that leaders looked more closely at foreign policy, paving the way for the 1970 launch of European Political Cooperation (EPC), a process by which the foreign ministers met to discuss and coordinate policy positions. EPC remained a loose and voluntary arrangement outside the Community, but consultation became habit-forming, and led to the creation in 1974 of the European Council.

The EPC was given formal recognition with the Single European Act, which confirmed that the member states would 'endeavour jointly to formulate and implement a European foreign policy'. But the Gulf War of 1990–91 – set off by the Iraqi invasion of Kuwait in August 1990 – found the Community both divided and unprepared. The United States orchestrated a multinational response, but while the Community was quick to ban Iraqi oil imports, suspend trade agreements, freeze Iraqi assets and give emergency aid to frontline states (Ginsberg, 2001:193), in terms of hard military action, its member states were divided: Britain and France made major commitments of troops, combat air-craft and naval vessels; Germany was limited by a postwar tradition of pacifism and constitutional limits on military deployments; Belgium, Portugal and Spain made minimal military contributions; and Ireland remained neutral (van Eekelen, 1990; Anderson, 1992). The response, charged Luxembourg foreign minister Jacques Poos, underlined 'the political insignificance of Europe', while for Belgian foreign minister Mark Eyskens it showed that the EC was 'an economic giant, a political dwarf, and a military worm' (*New York Times*, 25 January 1991).

Under the terms of Maastricht, the EU adopted a Common Foreign and Security Policy (CFSP). Its goals were only loosely defined, with vague talk about the need to safeguard 'common values' and 'fundamental interests', 'to preserve peace and strengthen international security', and to 'promote international cooperation', but it encouraged a convergence of positions among the member states on key international issues. Their UN ambassadors met frequently to coordinate policy, the EU agreed several common strategies, such as those on Russia and Ukraine, joint actions such as transporting humanitarian aid to Bosnia and sending observers to elections in Russia and South Africa, and common positions on EU relations with other countries, including the Balkans, the Middle East, Burma and Zimbabwe. The EU also coordinated western aid to Eastern Europe, Russia and the former

Soviet republics during the 1990s, and became the major supplier of aid to developing countries.

But the examples of weakness and division remained, nowhere more so than in the Balkans in the 1990s (see Peterson, 2003). When the ethnic, religious and nationalist tensions that had long been kept in check by the Tito regime (1944–80) broke into the open, and Croatia and Slovenia seceded from Yugoslavia in June 1991, the Yugoslav federal army responded with force. The EU organized a peace conference, but then lost its credibility when it recognized Croatia and Slovenia in January 1992, and it was left to the United States to broker the Dayton peace accords in 1995. Then there was the EU's feeble response to the 1998 crisis in the Yugoslav province of Kosovo: when ethnic Albanians in Kosovo began agitating for independence from Serb-dominated Yugoslavia, the government of Slobodan Milošević responded with force, leading to a massive refugee problem and reports of massacres of both Kosovars and Muslims. When the military response eventually came, in March 1999, it was led not by the EU but by the United States under the auspices of NATO.

Some of the structural weaknesses in the CFSP were addressed by the Treaty of Amsterdam: a Policy Planning and Early Warning Unit was created in Brussels to help the EU anticipate foreign crises, and the four different regional external affairs portfolios in the European Commission were replaced with a single foreign-policy post and the appointment of a High Representative for the CFSP; the first office-holder was Javier Solana, former secretary-general of NATO. But these institutional changes were not enough to prevent the most open and famous of all recent foreign policy disputes: the split over the 2003 invasion of Iraq. While there was transatlantic political unity on the US-led invasion of Afghanistan in 2002, there was a dramatic parting of the ways over Iraq, with questions over the rationale behind the invasion: charges that Iraqi leader Saddam Hussein possessed weapons of mass destruction, aspired to build nuclear weapons, and posed a threat to neighbouring states.

EU governments fell into three camps: supporters of US policy included Britain, Denmark, Italy, the Netherlands, Spain and many in Eastern Europe; opponents included Austria, Belgium, France, Germany and Greece; those that took no position included Finland, Ireland, Portugal and Sweden. But often overlooked, and yet far more significant, was the uniformity of public opposition to the war in the EU: 70–90 per cent were opposed in every EU member state, including those whose governments supported the invasion. Several of the latter found themselves in trouble with their electorates, and massive public demonstrations were held in most major European capitals, including Berlin, London and Rome. A June 2003 opinion poll found reduced faith in American global leadership, and even in Germany – long a staunch US ally – 81 per cent felt that the EU was more important than the United States to their vital interests, up from 55 per cent in 2002 (Asmus *et al.*, 2003). Most remarkably, another survey found that 53 per cent of Europeans viewed the United States as a threat to world peace on a par with North Korea and Iran (Eurobarometer poll, October 2003).

The disagreement had three major effects. First, it shook EU–US relations to their core, raising new questions in the minds of Europeans about the extent to which the EU should continue to rely on US foreign- and security-policy leadership, and generating an angry response among American politicians (some of whom, in a fit of pique, arranged to have the French fries served in the cafeteria of the US Congress renamed 'freedom fries'). Second, when the weapons of mass destruction were not found, and questions were asked about the extent to which the United States and Britain had manufactured the case for going to war, a major blow was dealt to the credibility of US policy leadership. Finally, the dispute reminded the EU once again just how poorly developed were its foreign policy structures, decades after the first attempts had been made to build common European positions.

Lisbon brought the most recent round of institutional changes, not only confirming the revamped post of High Representative (HR), but making the office-holder a vice-president of the Commission, chair of the Foreign Affairs Council in the Council of the EU, and director of the new European External Action Service (EEAS) (see Box 9.1). Some consternation was created when the European Council opted to give the job to Baroness Catherine Ashton, a relatively unknown British politician then serving as commissioner for trade. But at least the EU had made a clear move towards providing the metaphorical telephone number for which Kissinger had asked. The president of the Commission and the president of the European Council are also part of the mix, but in the combination of the HR and the EEAS, the EU today has something more like a European department of foreign affairs.

Security policy

Dealing with the foreign element of the CFSP – while not easy – has been less politically troubling than dealing with the security element. Together the EU member states have formidable military power at their disposal, with nuclear weapons (in Britain and France), nearly 1.9 million active personnel, nearly 3500 combat aircraft, and more non-nuclear submarines and surface naval combat vessels than the United States (aircraft carriers excepted) (see International Institute for Strategic Studies, 2013). Were it to agree a common defence policy and shared command structures, it might transform itself into a military

Box 9.1 The European External Action Service

The creation of a large new bureaucracy is not by itself the solution to a policy problem, and the development of new procedures and hierarchies can sometimes generate new problems. However, the EU long lacked an institutional focus for its interests in external relations, and the creation of the EEAS helped address that deficiency. First proposed as one of the initiatives of the failed constitutional treaty, the EEAS reappeared in the Treaty of Lisbon, and was formally launched on 1 December 2010. It is a combination foreign ministry and diplomatic service for the EU, designed to work with the diplomatic services of the member states to manage EU foreign and security policies, and to support the work of the High Representative. It is unique in the EU institutional system, combining the external relations departments of the Commission and the Council of the EU into an independent body with its own budget. It cannot make policy, but instead acts on decisions reached by the Council and Parliament, its job made easier by the fact that the HR has seats in both the Commission and the Council.

When Lisbon also created the new position of president of the European Council, there was speculation that this would cause confusion, and there was some debate about which of the two positions was potentially the more powerful. Given that the president of the European Council is expected to be a facilitator and consensus-builder rather than a leader, and that the HR has leadership of the EEAS, there was initial speculation that the latter was actually the more powerful of the two positions.

There was a struggle for power in 2010 between the Commission (hoping to give up as few of its former responsibilities as possible) and Parliament (hoping to win as many oversight responsibilities as possible). With the final creation of the EEAS, departments and staff were transferred from the Council of the EU (including those dealing with military matters, intelligence and crisis management) and from the Commission, including the directorates-general for external relations and development. The overseas delegations that until then had been managed by the Commission were also transferred and renamed European Union delegations. The jury still remains out on the effects of the EEAS, but as part of the ongoing pooling of responsibility for external relations, and efforts to give the EU a clearer presence on the world stage, its creation was an important step forward.

superpower. But EU governments have independent opinions and priorities when it comes to committing their forces, there is still only limited coordination on policy, and progress on setting up a European defence force has been slow. There has also been an ongoing division of opinion within the EU about how to relate to NATO and the United

Box 9.2   What future for NATO?

During the cold war (roughly 1949 to 1989), the mission of NATO (the North Atlantic Treaty Organization) was relatively clear: it was a defensive organization dominated by the United States that led the way in protecting western Europe (and, ultimately, US interests) against the possibility of a Soviet attack. It was countered by the creation in 1955 of the Warsaw Pact, a mutual defence agreement between the Soviet Union and seven eastern European states. As far as most Western Europeans were concerned, the security alliance with the United States was critical, and their governments were loath to do anything publicly that might undermine the alliance.

But with the end of the cold war there was a change of mission: the Soviet threat disappeared, most of the Eastern European countries once under Soviet control moved quickly into the democratic and capitalist orbit, and NATO was transformed into an alliance with both defensive and offensive capacities. Where its operations had once been limited to the territory of its member states, and it was defensive in nature, it both moved out of area and took an offensive posture in 1995 with a two-week bombing campaign in Bosnia and Herzegovina. In 2001 it invoked Article 5 of its founding charter for the first time ('an armed attack against one or more of them ... shall be considered an attack against them all') to justify the invasion of Afghanistan in the wake of the September 2001 terrorist attacks in the United States. And with its membership growing (it has added 12 new members since the end of the cold war, mainly from Eastern Europe), both its personality and its purpose have clearly changed.

Questions are asked about the political willingness and economic ability of NATO's European members to contribute significantly to the financial and military costs of future NATO operations, while Europeans worry over recent signs that the United States is looking more towards China as a source of future threats. The nature of warfare has also been changing, with suggestions that wars are increasingly fought within rather than between states (Human Security Report Project, 2011), and hence that security is more a matter of helping countries sort out their internal problems rather than preparing for invasion from those countries. Meanwhile, Slaughter (2011) suggests that the era of large-scale multi-year conflicts involving ground invasions of one country by another may be over, and that future conflict is more likely to be fought on the digital frontier, conducted by special forces, and targeted at individuals rather than states or large groups. The future of NATO is, in short, uncertain.

States (see Box 9.2), and – as we saw in Chapter 2 – Europeans generally have a preference for using civilian rather than military means for the resolution of conflict. In short, the EU as a security actor is – in the opinion of Howorth (2007:3) – still in its 'early infancy'.

Maastricht stated that one of the goals of the EU should be 'to assert its identity on the international scene, in particular through the implementation of a common foreign and security policy including the eventual framing of a common defence policy'. But while the CFSP moved defence more squarely onto the EU agenda, Maastricht provided a loophole by committing member states to a common policy that would 'include all questions related to the security of the Union, including the *eventual* framing of a common defence policy, *which might in time* lead to a common defence' (emphasis added).

In June 1992, EU foreign and defence ministers meeting at Petersberg, near Bonn, Germany, issued a declaration in which they agreed that military units from member states could be used to promote the Petersberg tasks: humanitarian, rescue, peacekeeping and other crisis-management jobs (including peacemaking). Early indications of how this might work came when EU personnel worked with NATO in monitoring the UN embargo on Serbia and Montenegro, helped set up a unified Croat–Muslim police force to support the administration of the city of Mostar in Bosnia in 1994–96, and helped restructure and train the Albanian police force in 1997. The Treaty of Amsterdam incorporated the Petersberg tasks into the EU treaties, and at a meeting in Saint-Malo in France in December 1998, British prime minister Tony Blair and French president Jacques Chirac declared that the EU should be in a position to play a full role in international affairs, 'must have the capacity for autonomous action, backed up by credible military forces, the means to decide to use them, and the readiness to do so', and suggested the creation of a European rapid-reaction force. This was later endorsed by German chancellor Gerhard Schröder.

The result was the launch in 1999 of the European Security and Defence Policy (ESDP) (see Howorth, 2003). An integral part of the CFSP, this was initially to consist of two key components: the Petersberg tasks, and a 60,000-member Rapid Reaction Force (RRF) that could be deployed at 60 days' notice, could be sustained for at least one year and could carry out these tasks. The Force was not intended to be a standing army, was designed to complement rather than compete with NATO, and could only act when NATO had decided not to be involved in a crisis. The plan was to have it ready by the end of 2003, but it proved more of a challenge than expected, and by 2004 the EU was talking of the more modest goal of creating 'battle groups' that could be deployed more quickly and for shorter periods than the RRF. The groups would consist of 1500 troops each that could be committed within 15 days, and could be sustainable for between 30 and 120 days. That same year, the European Defence Agency was created within which national defence ministers could meet to promote planning and research in the interests of the ESDP.

The terrorist attacks on the World Trade Center in New York and on the Pentagon in Washington DC in September 2001 brought new issues into the equation. The meaning of 'war' and 'defence' had already changed with the end of the cold war, but the attacks – and the response to them – forced a review of defence-policy priorities on both sides of the Atlantic: terrorism (especially when it involved suicide attacks) could not be met with conventional military responses. Many European leaders hoped for a new era in transatlantic relations, with a new US emphasis on multilateralism and diplomacy, but these hopes were dashed in the fallout from the dispute over Iraq, which emphasized to many that the EU needed to more forcefully outline and pursue its distinctive position on security issues.

In 2003, the European Council adopted the European Security Strategy, the first ever declaration by EU member states of their strategic goals. It argued that the EU was 'inevitably a global player', and 'should be ready to share in the responsibility for global security', listing the key threats facing the EU as terrorism, weapons of mass destruction, regional conflicts, failing states and organized crime. Against the background of a changing transatlantic relationship, the draft EU constitution included the stipulation that the EU should take a more active role in its own defence, talking of the 'progressive framing of a common Union defence policy' leading to a common defence 'when the European Council, acting unanimously, so decides'.

But even if they are to be guided by the Petersberg tasks, the question still remains as to how European defence forces should be organized. Europeanists such as France continue to want to develop an independent EU capability. The United States is content to see the Europeans taking responsibility for those tasks from which NATO should best keep its distance, but insists that there should be no overlap or rivalry in the event of the creation of a separate European institution. Meanwhile, Atlanticists such as Britain continue to feel nervous about undermining the US commitment to Europe.

And the problems do not end there. While there is no questioning the American superiority in the field of military power (the United States currently spends almost as much on defence every year as the rest of the world combined), an issue often overlooked in the debate about the global role of the EU is the question of soft power. This is defined by Joseph Nye (2004:x) as 'the ability to get what you want through attraction rather than coercion', and is centred on culture, political ideals and policies rather than on the threat of violence. Critics of the United States often argue that it relies too much on hard power rather than soft power, and that this has been one of the causes of the decline

Table 9.1   *EU peacekeeping and police missions (selected)*

Name	Country	Launch	Character	Purpose
CONCORDIA	Macedonia	2003	Military	Support for peace agreement
EUFOR ALTHEA	Bosnia	2004	Military	Capacity-building/training for military
EUJUST LEX	Iraq	2005	Civilian	To help strengthen criminal justice system
EUSEC RD	DR Congo	2005	Military	Training and reorganization of armed forces
EU BAM	Palestine	2005	Civilian	Border assistance mission at Rafah crossing point
EUPOL	Afghanistan	2007	Civilian	To establish and train police force
EULEX	Kosovo	2008	Civilian	To help strengthen judicial system
EUMM	Georgia	2008	Civilian	Monitoring and stabilization project
EUCAP NESTOR	Horn of Africa	2011	Civilian	To strengthen maritime capacities and combat piracy
EUFOR	Libya	2011	Military	Humanitarian assistance support
EUBAM	Libya	2013	Civilian	To help Libya secure its borders
EUTM	Mali	2013	Military	Training and reorganization of armed forces
EUCAP SAHEL	Niger	2013	Military	To help Niger address armed terrorism and organized crime
EUAVSEC	South Sudan	2013	Civilian	Training of airport staff

in the credibility of US foreign policy. By contrast, the EU – making a virtue of necessity, argue some, while pursuing a deliberate policy, argue others (see discussion in Chapter 2) – has become adept at using soft power in its dealings with other countries, developing a record for peacekeeping instead of peacemaking (see Table 9.1). In a world in which violence is increasingly rejected as a tool of statecraft (at least among wealthy liberal democracies), the use of diplomacy, political influence and the pressures of economic competition may be giving the EU a strategic advantage that reduces the need to develop a significant common military capacity.

This is not to suggest that the EU is either unwilling or unable to use hard power. In spite of its internal political disagreements, the EU has achieved more on security cooperation than most people think, driven by a desire to decrease its reliance on the United States (Jones, 2007). It is also both willing and able to use hard power when needed (Giegerich and Wallace, 2004). By 2006, the EU was contributing 60 per cent of the forces in Afghanistan, while 12 EU states had 19,000 troops in Iraq. National military interventions have also continued, including Britain's operation in Sierra Leone in 2001 (establishing order after a UN force had failed) and France's operations in Côte d'Ivoire in 2002 and in Mali in 2012. The EU has also imposed sanctions against more than two dozen countries, including trade and travel bans on Belarus; arms embargoes on Côte d'Ivoire, Eritrea, Iraq, Lebanon and Myanmar; the freezing of funds of leaders in the Democratic Republic of Congo, Egypt, Guinea-Bissau, Iraq, Sudan and Zimbabwe; restrictions on travel from Iran and Liberia; and wide-ranging bans on trade with North Korea, Somalia and Syria.

Another of the changes that came with Lisbon was the renaming of the ESDP as the Common Security and Defence Policy (CSDP). It continues with the Petersberg tasks, to which are added three new tasks: joint disarmament operations, military advice and assistance, and support for post-conflict stabilization. Lisbon also introduced a mutual defence clause, obliging member states to come to the aid of any other member state that was attacked, so long as the traditional neutrality of some of those states was not threatened, and so long as the help given did not affect NATO commitments. The European Defence Agency now has strengthened abilities to improve the military capacities of EU member states, and the overall goal of the CSDP is to help the EU respond proactively to international crises using a mix of civilian and military tools, and eventually to establish a common EU defence system.

Trade policy

While there is little evidence to suggest that the EU could (or even wants to) become a major military actor, there are no doubts at all about its status as an economic superpower. The single market is all but complete, the euro has been adopted by 18 member states, the Commission has the authority to speak on behalf of the EU in global trade negotiations, and it is now well understood that the EU is the most powerful actor in those negotiations. The statistics paint a clear and incontestable picture:

- With just over 7 per cent of the world's population, the EU accounts for 25 per cent of the world's GDP and for bigger shares of trade in merchandise and commercial services than either the United States

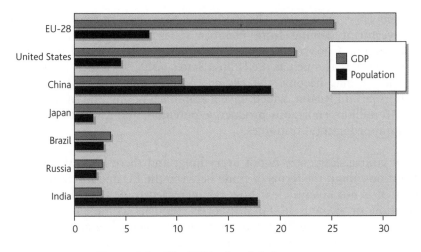

Figure 9.1 *The EU in the global economy*

Sources: Population figures for 2010 from UN Population Division at
http://www.esa.un.org/esa/population. Economic figures for 2011 from World Development
Indicators database at http://www.worldbank.com. All figures retrieved April 2013.

or China (see Figures 9.1 and 9.2). Trade – argues Orbie (2009) –
has become the EU's 'most powerful external policy domain'.

• In spite of the EU's recent economic problems, the personal wealth
of Europeans – combined with the largely open European single
market – means that the EU is the wealthiest market in the world.
China and India may have many more people but they are on
average much poorer; German per capita gross national income is
nearly nine times greater than that of China and more than 30 times
greater than that of India (see Appendix 1).

• Eighteen of the 28 member states (which among them account for
74 per cent of the GDP and 66 per cent of the population of the EU)
have a shared currency that is the only substantial competitor with
the US dollar in terms of credibility and influence – China and India
have nothing that comes close to comparing. At least until the eurozone problems broke in 2009, the euro was drawing new attention
as a challenger to the status of the US dollar, with suggestions that it
might eventually become the primary international reserve currency
(Chinn and Frankel, 2005). Some of the euro's problems have been
offset by declining faith in the dollar, based in part on the snow-
balling US national debt, and in part on questions about American
economic leadership in the world.

• As we saw in Chapter 7, the EU has become the biggest mergers and
acquisitions market in the world, a trend that has helped create new
European multinationals with a global presence comparable only to

their US counterparts. The EU is now the source of two-thirds of all investment coming from member states of the Organization for Economic Cooperation and Development (OECD), and more than three times as much as the United States (OECD website, 2010).
- The EU has become the engine of economic growth for Eastern Europe and Russia, which have a combined population of more than 240 million, enormous productive potential, and a wealth of largely untapped natural resources.

Of course, large size is not everything, and there have always been questions about the terms of trade between the EU and its trading partners. It is not always clear how far increased trade contributes to job creation or growth in GDP, poorer countries complain that trade agreements with the EU often create more dependency and give better terms to wealthy European farmers and industrialists, there are often signs of protectionist leanings in EU approaches to trade (particularly in the wake of the eurozone crisis), and there are questions about how far trade benefits powerful interests in EU states as compared to the average person. But these concerns are not unique to the European case, and even if the global trading system has many flaws, the EU working together as a unit continues to achieve more than if its 28 member states negotiated separately.

The global economic presence of the EU has been built on the foundations of the single market and the Common Commercial Policy, to which end the EU has built a complex network of multilateral and bilateral trading networks and agreements. Some of these are based on proximity (agreements with Eastern Europe and Mediterranean states), some on former colonial ties (see the section on development cooperation below), and some on expediency (agreements with the United States and Japan). Its influence is also reflected in the numbers: the EU is both the biggest importer and exporter in the world, both of merchandise and of commercial services (see Figure 9.2).

The growth of EU trade power has also been helped by an institutional structure that promotes common positions among the member states. The Commission generates policy initiatives, is responsible for investigating and taking action against unfair trading practices, and makes suggestions to the Council of the EU when it thinks that agreements need to be negotiated with other countries or international organizations. Most importantly, once the member states have agreed a position among themselves, the Commission is left to negotiate external trade agreements on behalf of the EU as a whole. So if Henry Kissinger was to ask to whom he should speak in Europe regarding trade matters, the answer would be clear.

The power of the EU is particularly clear in the role it has played in global trade negotiations. In 1948, the General Agreement on Tariffs

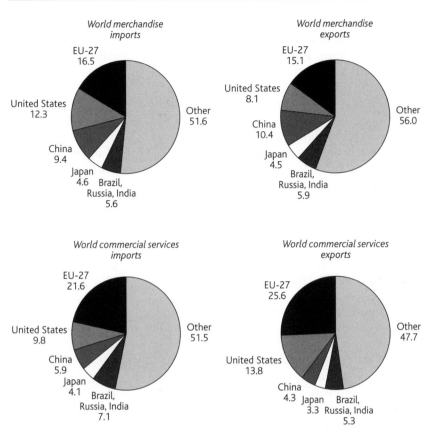

Figure 9.2 *The EU as a trading power*

Sources: Trade figures for 2011 (excluding data for intra-EU trade) from the WTO at http://www.wto.org (retrieved June 2013).

and Trade (GATT) was founded to oversee a programme aimed at removing trade restrictions and liberalizing trade; it was replaced in 1995 by the World Trade Organization (WTO). The GATT/WTO negotiations have taken place in successive rounds in which the EU states negotiate as a group, and are typically represented by the European commissioner for trade. The round that began in 2001 in Doha, Qatar, was designed to open up world markets for agricultural and manufactured goods. By 2006 they had stalled because rich and poor countries could not agree over farm subsidies and import taxes. The poor countries accused the EU in particular of supporting and protecting its farmers through CAP export subsidies (which has made European farmers more competitive and productive), and of 'dumping' their produce cheaply in poor countries, undermining the efforts of local farmers. (The United States was also criticized for its subsidies, particularly to cotton farmers.)

But more telling as a measure of EU trading power has been the frequency with which it has been at odds with the United States, the other giant at the table. If a country adopts a trade policy measure or takes an action that is considered to be a breach of a WTO agreement, the dispute can be taken to the WTO, which investigates and issues a judgement that is binding upon member states. The EU and the United States have brought more cases before the WTO than anyone else, and in many instances the disputes have been between the EU and the United States; they have tussled in recent years over hormone-treated beef, banana imports, trade with Cuba, tariffs on steel, subsidies to aircraft manufacturers, intellectual property rights, trade in services, and the tax regimes of third countries (Billiet, 2005).

Relations with the United States

The transatlantic relationship is – in economic, security and political terms – the most important in the world. But it has blown hot and cold, which is perhaps only to be expected given that the EU and the United States are both major allies and major competitors (see McGuire and Smith, 2008: ch. 1). Relations were strong after the Second World War, the United States having played a critical role in ridding Europe of Nazism, then guaranteeing European reconstruction and integration with the investments it made under the Marshall Plan and the security umbrella it provided for Western Europe during the cold war. US administrations saw integration as a way of helping the region recover from the ravages of war and of improving European (and American) security in the face of the Soviet threat.

Relations cooled in the early 1960s with Charles de Gaulle's concerns about American influence in Europe, and continued to cool as the United States and its European allies fell out over Vietnam, and over West German diplomatic overtures to Eastern Europe. The 1971 collapse of the Bretton Woods system – precipitated by the decision of the Nixon administration to cut the dollar's final links with gold – emphasized to many Europeans the unwillingness of the United States always to take heed of European opinion on critical issues. The Community was by then catching up with the United States in economic wealth, it traded less with the United States and more with Eastern Europe, and disagreement over the Arab–Israeli issue in the 1970s was followed by the revival of the Western European anti-nuclear movement in the early 1980s, both placing a further strain on transatlantic relations.

The end of the Soviet hegemony in Eastern Europe in the late 1980s led to a new volatility in Europe that encouraged the administration of

George H.W. Bush to call for stronger transatlantic ties on political matters. The result was the signature in November 1990 of a Transatlantic Declaration committing the United States and the Community to regular high-level meetings. Contacts were taken a step further in 1995 with the adoption of a New Transatlantic Agenda and a Joint EU–US Action Plan under which both sides agreed to move from consultation to joint action aimed at promoting peace and democracy around the world, expanding world trade, and improving transatlantic ties. Biannual meetings have since taken place between the presidents of the United States, the Commission and the European Council, between the US Secretary of State and EU foreign ministers, and between the Commission and members of the US cabinet.

The EU and the United States today are each other's major trade partners, and the largest sources and destinations of foreign direct investment. They hold common views on the merits of democracy and capitalism, but divisions of opinion have become more common and more substantial with time. This has been partly a result of the reassertion of European economic power since the end of the cold war, and partly a result of the relative decline of US influence in the wake of the Iraqi controversy and the global financial crisis of 2007–10. But it can also be explained by the fact that Americans and Europeans often have different values: Americans place more emphasis on military power than Europeans, unilateralism plays a greater role in their calculations than the multilateralist tendencies of the Europeans, the often unapologetic support given by the United States to Israel says much about the different worldviews of Americans and Europeans, and the two sides have quite different thoughts about the responsibilities of government (Europeans are more willing to support state-run health-care and education systems, for example) and about a string of more focused issues, including capital punishment, climate change, the work of the UN, and the links between religion and politics. The significance of the differences is disputed, with Judt (2005a) and McCormick (2007: ch. 7) making the case that they are important, while Blinken (2001) and Baldwin (2009) make the case that they are overstated.

The fallout over Iraq raised many new questions about the health of the transatlantic relationship that have not yet been answered (see, for example, Kopstein and Steinmo, 2008). At one level, the dispute could be dismissed as just another of the many that have coloured US–European relations since 1945, and perhaps as more reflective of the short-term goals and values of the Bush administration than of long-term US policy on Europe. But the depth of public opposition to US policy was remarkable, as was the division among the leaders of the EU's four major powers: Germany, Britain, France and Italy. For some, the dispute represented the rapidly changing world-views of the United States and the EU, and an opportunity for the EU to assert its often different analyses of –

and prescriptions for – global problems (see Box 9.3). In this sense, the war on terrorism may ultimately be seen as emblematic of a fundamental change not just in the nature of the transatlantic relationship, but in the setting of priorities on international issues.

After several false starts dating back to the 1990s, June 2013 saw the launch of what promised to be the most substantial economic project ever in the history of transatlantic relations: the completion by 2015 of a free trade agreement between the United States and the EU. The supporters of the Transatlantic Trade and Investment Partnership (TTIP) promised that it would create many new jobs and increase GDP on both sides of the Atlantic at a time when national economies were still suffering the effects of the global financial and eurozone crises. But critics charged that the transatlantic market was already one of the biggest and most open in the world, that the negotiations would be dominated by corporate lobbyists, that perhaps an improved security relationship was more important, and that it would be hard to get the Europeans to capitulate on their tighter standards on matters such as genetically modified food (see Kuttner, 2013).

Relations with the neighbourhood

If there are many questions about the global influence of the EU, there are far fewer about its impact on its immediate neighbourhood, where four distinct rings of influence can be identified:

- States that have joined the EU over the last decade, their stories adding to the widely held contention that enlargement has been the most successful of the EU's foreign policy initiatives.
- States that have short-term potential to either become members of the EU (including Macedonia and Montenegro) or have at least established strong economic links with the EU (notably Norway and Switzerland).
- States that have longer-term prospects of joining the EU (including Albania, Serbia, the Ukraine and Turkey).
- States that do not qualify for membership but cannot escape the gravitational pull of the EU (North Africa, Russia and much of the Middle East) (see Map 9.1).

In each of these rings the EU plays a critical role in the making of economic policy, while further afield its activities have critical implications for the spread of democracy and capitalism.

The Community was quick to take a leading role in responding to the fallout from the end of the cold war, coordinating western economic aid to the east and creating in 1990 the European Bank for

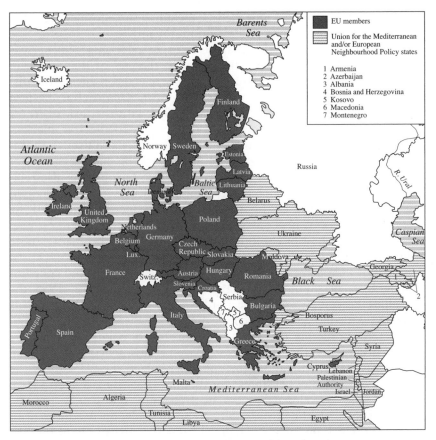

Map 9.1   *The EU and its neighbourhood*

Reconstruction and Development (EBRD), which has since channelled public money from the EU, the United States and Japan into development of the private sector in the east. The EU subsequently signed trade and cooperation agreements with almost every Eastern European state, several billion dollars in loans were made available by the European Investment Bank, and several programmes were launched to help east European economic and social reform. More significantly, the end of the cold war generated several requests from Eastern Europe for associate or full membership of the EU. Europe Agreements were signed with several, arranging for the integration of Eastern European economies with those of the EU through the staged removal of barriers to trade in industrial and agricultural goods, and to the movement of workers. The Treaty of Amsterdam paved the way for eastward expansion, membership negotiations began in 1998 with the Czech Republic, Estonia, Hungary, Poland and Slovenia, and the 2004–13 enlargements brought 13 new members into the EU, including three former republics of the Soviet Union: Estonia, Latvia and Lithuania.

The significance (and the challenge) of eastern enlargement was considerable. It gave final confirmation to the end of the cold war, giving new meaning to the definition of Europe and reducing the distinctions between *Europe* and the *European Union*. But Eastern European governments and citizens struggled with the task of transforming their economies from central planning to the free market, and their political systems from one-party authoritarianism to multiparty democracy, and faced the daunting task of making sure that domestic laws were adapted to EU law. Eastern Europe was also relatively poor: while the 12 countries that joined in 2004–07 increased the population of the EU by 20 per cent, they increased its GDP by less than 5 per cent. In the west, meanwhile, an 'enlargement fatigue' set in, raising questions about how long it would be before more countries would join the EU.

Alongside enlargement, the EU has pursued agreements and cooperation with its neighbours that have different intentions. In 1995 the Barcelona Process (formally the Euro-Mediterranean Partnership) was launched with the goal of strengthening ties between the EU and all other states bordering the Mediterranean. It was handicapped by the lack of progress on the Middle East peace process, by concerns among some partner countries about the dominant role of the EU, and by the inclusion of the many EU states that do not border the Mediterranean. In 2008 the Barcelona Process evolved into the Union for the Mediterranean, intended originally to focus only on Mediterranean states, but which ultimately expanded to include the whole of the EU; it now has 43 members: the 28 EU states and 15 neighbouring states. Meanwhile the European Neighbourhood Policy was launched in 2004, encouraging a relationship that the EU describes as 'privileged', and with the goals of promoting democracy, human rights, the rule of law, good governance, and market economics. Both initiatives include a mix of states with prospects for joining the EU and those without.

Even if there are still many doubts about the substance and potential for success of the EU foreign and security policies as a whole, few now question the critical and dominating role that EU policy has had in ensuring the spread of democracy and free-market ideas to the former Soviet bloc (Leonard, 2005:56, 103–4). The EU's leading role in this area has not only helped define EU foreign policy, but has also made the EU a major regional political actor. In only three cases can major qualifications be added:

- While it has a far greater interest than the United States in seeing peace in the Middle East (given its proximity, its oil interests and its concerns about illegal immigration and terrorism), it has played only

Box 9.3   The changing global balance of power

The tensions of the cold war may have meant that the world lived under the constant threat of war between American and Soviet client states, and – far more seriously – of nuclear war between the super-powers. However, it also had the advantage (if it can be considered as such) of imposing some predictability in the global balance of power. Since the end of the cold war, that predictability has largely gone, and we live today in a world where the balance of political, economic and military power is constantly changing. The United States is still the most powerful actor in the system, but many questions hang over its economic future, the effectiveness of its military power is increasingly questioned, and the focus of its geopolitical interests may be shifting from Europe and Russia to Asia. Post-Soviet Russia, meanwhile, sends mixed messages to the rest of the world, the Middle East continues to be a source of tensions and concerns, Africa may or may not be emerging from the dependency and underdevelopment of the cold war years, and we are seeing the rise of new powers such as China, India, Brazil and Indonesia.

The EU must plan accordingly, but questions continue to be asked about its ability to exert itself as a global actor. Progress on developing a European foreign policy has been halting, as a security actor its shape on the global radar is at best fuzzy, and it continues to face numerous internal problems, including high unemployment, stodgy markets, worries about immigration, a backlash against integration, and the ongoing fallout from the eurozone crisis. The acronym BRIC was coined by the economist Jim O'Neill in 2005 to encapsulate the rising presence of Brazil, Russia, India and China (and some have suggested that an S should be added at the end to include South Africa) (see O'Neill, 2011, for an elaboration of the idea). But while handy for headline writers, it suggests that these countries have more in common than is in fact the case. The BRICs mainly came well out of the global financial crisis, and they have undoubtedly provided more market competition for the EU and the United States, but they also offer large new opportunities for exports and investments from the EU.

If there are many uncertainties about how the story of European integration is going to unfold in the next few years, there are also uncertainties about how the international political and economic system will evolve, and what role the EU will play in that system. The EU has expanded its ties with China and Latin America, and its relationship with the United States is losing some of its military qualities in favour of more economic cooperation. But the future remains uncertain and the development of the EU as a global actor is surrounded by doubt.

a supporting role and has been unable to exert much influence on Israel (see Pardo and Peters, 2009).

- The story of EU–Russian relations has not been a happy one (Antonenko and Pinnick, 2005). During the 1990s the Russians looking for the respectability and economic opportunities that would come from a good relationship with the EU, while the EU looked for Russian support for eastern enlargement, and needed some of the oil and natural gas that Russia has in abundance. But neither side fully trusts the other, and the EU has to balance staying on good terms with Russia against its criticism of the remnants of Russian authoritarianism.
- The EU has had little influence on bringing change to Belarus, the last remaining outpost of Soviet-style authoritarianism in Europe and a close ally of Russia.

Development cooperation

The long history of European colonialism has left the EU with a heritage of close economic and political ties to the South: Latin America, South Asia and Africa. Several of the founding members of the Community – notably France and Belgium – still had colonies when the Treaty of Rome was signed, and when Britain joined the Community in 1973 it brought more mainly former colonies into the equation. As a result, the South has been a significant factor in the external relations of the EU, the core of the relationship being a programme of aid and trade promotion involving several dozen former European colonies in Africa, the Caribbean and the Pacific – the so-called ACP states.

EU development aid policies have been based partly on remedying quality of life issues such as poverty and hunger, but there are also less altruistic motives: Africa in particular is a key source of illegal immigrants to the EU, and the EU continues to rely on the South as a source of oil and of key raw materials such as rubber, copper and uranium. The EU aid programme has several aspects. As well as allowing all Southern states to export industrial products to the EU tariff- and duty-free (subject to some limitations on volume), the EU provides food and emergency aid, and sponsors development projects undertaken by NGOs. The EU has also negotiated a series of cooperative agreements with the ACP countries, mainly non-Asian former colonies of Britain and France. These began with the 1963 and 1969 Yaoundé Conventions (named for the capital of Cameroon, where they were signed), which gave 18 former colonies preferential access to Community markets. The 18 in turn allowed limited duty-free or quota-free access by the EC to their markets. The provision of trade concessions was expanded by the four Lomé Conventions (named after the capital of Togo), which were signed in 1975, 1979, 1984 and 1989.

Lomé IV, which covered the period 1990–2000 and was revised in 1995, had three main elements. First, it provided financial aid to 71 ACP states under the European Development Fund, in the form mainly of grants for development projects and low-interest loans. Second, it provided free access to the EU for products originating in ACP countries, with the exception of agricultural products covered by CAP. About 95 per cent of ACP exports entered the EU duty-free, compared to just 10 per cent of agricultural goods from other countries, and other goods were subject to tariffs in the range of 17–23 per cent. Finally, it offered an insurance fund for ACP exports called Stabex, designed to offset falls in the value of 50 specified ACP agricultural exports. If prices fell below a certain level, Stabex made up the deficit. If they went above that level, ACP countries invested the profits in the fund for future use.

Opinions were mixed about the effects of the Yaoundé and Lomé conventions. On the one hand, they helped build closer commercial ties between the EU and the ACP states, and there was an overall increase in the volume of ACP exports to Europe from the 1960s to the 1990s. But the conventions were widely criticized for promoting economic dependence, and for perpetuating the flow of low-profit raw materials from the ACP to the EU, and the flow of high-profit manufactured goods from the EU to the ACP. Questions were also raised about the extent to which they helped the ACP states invest in their human capital, and helped them develop greater economic independence.

Other problems were structural. Stabex did not help countries that did not produce the specified commodities, payments from the European Development Fund were small by the time the fund had been divided among 71 countries, the ACP programme excluded the larger Southern states that had negotiated separate agreements with the EU (for example, India and China), too little attention was paid to the environmental implications of the focus on cash crops for export, and the programme neither helped deal with the ACP debt crisis nor really much changed the relationship between the EU and the ACP states.

The biggest problem was internal to the ACP states themselves. They mostly failed to diversify their exports, to invest in infrastructure, to build up a more skilled labour force, and to become more competitive in the world market. The EU provided them with a generous set of trade preferences, and yet imports from the ACP as a share of the EU total fell from 6.7 per cent in 1976 to just 3 per cent in 1998. Oil, diamonds, gold, and other industrially related products accounted for about two-thirds of ACP exports to the EU, the balance being made up by agricultural products (30 per cent) and fish (5 per cent). Four countries – Nigeria, Côte d'Ivoire, Cameroon and Mauritius – between them accounted for more than 40 per cent of EU imports from the ACP countries. At the same time, economic growth in many sub-Saharan African states was sluggish, and there was very little trade taking place among African ACP states.

A new agreement was signed in Cotonou, Benin, in 2000, designed to run for 20 years with revisions every five years. It added seven more countries to the ACP group (including Cuba), places a stronger requirement on ACP states to improve domestic political, economic and social conditions, and emphasizes the importance of human rights and democracy. Its objectives include the promotion of the interests of the private sector, gender equality, sustainable environmental management, and the replacement of trade preferences with a progressive and reciprocal removal of trade barriers. Whether this will be enough to address the structural problems of the ACP programme remains to be seen.

Meanwhile, the EU has become the biggest source of official development assistance in the world, collectively accounting for 54 per cent of the total of $126 billion given in 2012 by the 25 members of the Development Assistance Committee of the OECD (compared to 22 per cent from the United States and 8 per cent from Japan) (OECD website, 2013). Most EU aid (15 per cent of which is channelled through the EU) goes to sub-Saharan Africa, but an increasing proportion is going to Latin America. The EU also the world's biggest provider of emergency humanitarian aid (disbursing €1.1 billion in 2011), much of which has gone in recent years to the victims of conflicts in Afghanistan, Côte d'Ivoire, Libya and Sudan, of flooding in Pakistan and Peru, of droughts in the Horn of Africa and Central America, and of earthquakes and tropical storms in Japan and Southeast Asia. It has also become the second largest provider of food aid in the world after the United States, supplying food worth nearly €511 million in 2011.

Conclusions

The process of European integration was born as a way to help Western Europe rebuild after the Second World War, and to remove the historical causes of conflict in the region. It began life with an introverted domestic agenda, leaving leadership on wider foreign and security policy issues to the United States. With the end of the cold war, the clear security threat posed by the Soviet Union was replaced by economic concerns, by regional security problems such as those in the Balkans and the Middle East, and by less easily defined threats such as nationalist pressures in Russia, the movement of political refugees, the spread of nuclear weapons, the implications of new technology, and environmental problems. Meanwhile globalization proceeded under the auspices of the WTO, and the wealth and competitiveness of China and India continued to grow, altering the balance of global economic power.

The EC/EU had no choice but to become more extroverted, and integration has since had implications not just for Europe but for Europe's relations with the rest of the world. While the EEC initially focused on bringing down the barriers to internal trade, it soon became involved in external trade matters, and the EU by the 1990s had turned its attention squarely to common foreign and security policies. Problems were experienced along the way, and the EU become notorious for its often confused and bumbling responses to international problems, but cooperation acquired more consistency and substance, and the development of common foreign and security policies has become one of the core endeavours of European integration.

Events in 2001–04 were to prove a critical turning point. The September 2001 terrorist attacks in the United States were followed by the US-led invasion of Iraq in 2003, while the EU was coincidentally launching its new single currency, expanding its membership deep into Eastern Europe, and upgrading its common foreign, security and defence policies. The new economic power of the EU combined with growing criticism of US global leadership to make it clear that entirely new expectations were being directed at the EU. Where once Europeans followed the lead of the Americans, if not always willingly, it has become more clear of late that they are out of step with the United States not just on such immediate problems as international terrorism and peace in the Middle East, but also on a wide variety of longer-term issues relating to trade, security, the environment, and more.

The changes of the last few years have made it clear that the EU must work to give its international identity clearer definition, to assert itself on the global stage, and to build political influence. Europe may never achieve the qualities of a military power that are so overtly on show in the United States, and increasingly in China, but it has few aspirations in that direction; it is more adept at using soft power, and at building on its political, economic and diplomatic advantages. The eurozone crisis has thrown a large rock into the pond of the EU's aspirations, and for now – at least – it presents a rather confused and confusing image to the outside world. But given changes in the international system, the pressures to give that image more clarity and sharpness continue to grow.

Conclusions

Two contradictory forces have been at work in Europe since 1945. On the one hand, there has been a remarkable effort to put the continent's troubled history behind it, and to create the conditions under which internal conflict and competition might be replaced by perpetual peace and cooperation. Europe has, in that time, enjoyed the longest spell of generalized peace in its recorded history, and has witnessed dramatic overall growth in economic prosperity (short-term downturns notwithstanding), along with active cooperation in almost every significant field of public policy. There are multiple explanations for these changes, including the cold-war role of the United States in providing security guarantees and investment opportunities, a new climate of international cooperation, and the twin effects of globalization and the rise of new technologies. But at the core of the changes has been the impact of European integration; without the opportunities for political, economic and social change offered by the EEC/EU, the history of postwar Europe would have been quite different.

On the other hand, the process of integration has been accompanied by numerous crises and missteps, and a hardening climate of cynicism, resistance and even outright hostility. Doubters and critics have seized every opportunity to claim that the EU is in trouble, that the idea of European unity is dead, that European leaders are fatally divided, and even – in some cases – that everyone would be better off if the member states of the EU went their own way. The EU has come to be typecast as a source of problems, its critics ready and willing to play up the bad news in everything from disagreements on new treaties to failed foreign policy initiatives, worries about the democratic deficit, sluggish economic growth, declining birth rates, ageing populations, negative votes in national referenda, and even the symbolism of delivery problems in 2008–11 with the Airbus A380 super-jumbo. The crisis in the eurozone has surpassed them all, sparking an unparalleled orgy of scepticism and dismissal.

There are many competing explanations for the pall of doubt that has long hung over the European experiment: fears for the loss of national sovereignty and identity, worries about the creation of a new level of government lacking the obvious and typical lines of democratic accountability, concerns about the effects that integration might have on the relative power and influence of big and small EU states, the difficulty that many Europeans have with understanding the EU, fear of the unknown, and a failure by many to stand back from immediate and short-term problems, and to look instead at long-term trends.

In spite of all the doubts, this book argues that the rise of the EU has been one of the most important international developments since 1945, while also one of the least understood. For many years, regional integration was little more than a gleam in the eye of a few pan-Europeanists and a huddle of technocrats in Brussels, and it presented a rather dull and uninspiring face to the world. But it has taken on a new personality and significance since the end of the cold war, and particularly in the wake of the March 2003 US-led invasion of Iraq, and the twin blows of the global financial and eurozone crises. The former had the dual effect of stirring up many lingering doubts in Europe about the wisdom and motives of American global leadership, while also suggesting to many the need for independent and coordinated European foreign policies. The latter emphasized just how poorly prepared the EU was as a whole to deal with critical economic challenges, and just how far the levels of faith in the merits of the European experiment have fallen. But the EU is more than the euro, and no matter how long the problems in fixing the euro continue to linger, it is important to remember that European integration has brought numerous positive change in many other areas of endeavour.

Consider, first, the impact of the single-market programme. The most obvious effect of bringing down borders has been to help create the wealthiest marketplace in the world, with more than 500 million consumers. It is not yet complete, to be sure, but long gone are the days when 'Europe' revolved around squabbles over farm subsidies. The barriers to the free movement of people, money, goods and services have largely gone, giving corporations an expanded market in which to sell their goods and services, affording consumers access to a wider array of products, removing many of the costly and time-wasting differences relating to cross-border trade, and allowing Europeans increased freedom to move around their region, whether out of economic need or for personal choice. The freedoms of the new Europe have been underpinned by the euro, which in spite of its problems has not only made it easier for goods and services to cross national boundaries, but – once those problems are resolved – promises to give the EU a new level of influence over international economic and monetary policies.

Consider, second, the impact of the eastward expansion of the EU. For many years, the EU was an exercise in cooperation among the capitalist economies of Western Europe. Eastern Europe still suffered the effects of nearly 50 years of Soviet domination, with a tradition of single-party politics and central planning. But when countries such as Poland, Hungary, Romania, the Czech Republic and, most notably, three former Soviet republics (Estonia, Latvia and Lithuania) joined the EU in 2004–07, it not only brought a final emphatic end to cold-war attitudes, but meant that for the first time in several generations it was possible to talk about 'Europe' as a whole, rather than always qualifying the label with 'Western' and 'Eastern'. Enlargement increased the size of the European marketplace and opened Eastern Europe to investment from the west, helping free eastern economies and underpinning the process of democratization. Doubters charge that enlargement came too soon and threatened to overextend the EU, perhaps even undermining its new global economic role. They also continue to point to the problems of adjustment that Eastern European member states must inevitably face, but we should not forget what integration meant to countries such as Ireland, Greece, Portugal and Spain (at least before the eurozone crisis).

Consider, third, the impact of common policies on the member states of the EU. The development of common European laws has not always been met with enthusiasm by Europeans, but it has been much easier for sceptics to point at the costs of the relatively trivial – common sets of weights and measures, uniform shapes and sizes for fruits and vegetables, and so on – than to consider the longer-term benefits of removing technical barriers to the single market, and of allowing states with progressive laws (for example, on environmental protection) to change procedures in states that had previously lagged behind. Common agricultural, social and regional policies have helped European farmers become more productive, have helped the EU to direct new investment to those parts of the continent in greatest need, have helped build transport networks that have underpinned the single market, and have removed many of the bumps and hollows in the economic playing field.

Consider, finally, the impact of the changing global role of the EU. Throughout the cold war, Western Europe mainly followed the lead of the United States in the struggle against the Soviet Union; it was understood that the United States was the dominating partner in the alliance in both security and economic terms, and while the two sides often disagreed on policy, the Europeans were rarely in a position to provide much more than symbolic opposition. The relationship began to change with the end of the cold war, when it became clear that the US protective shield in Western Europe was no longer essential, and that the resurgent European economy was offering real competition to the Americans. The Europeans embarrassed themselves in the Gulf and in the Balkans, but as much as anything these underlined the need for more effective European foreign policies. Transatlantic differences were brought home most clearly by Iraq in 2003, which showed that the wisdom of US policy could not be assumed and that it was sometimes right and proper for allies to disagree in public. Europeans finally realized that they could and should offer their own analyses of international threats and challenges. They are still working on making themselves heard politically, but their achievements on the trade front show what is possible.

The combined effects of the global financial crisis, the eurozone crisis, and the growing backlash against European integration have served to cast considerable doubts over where the EU is headed. Some argue that it will survive these problems, learn from them, and emerge stronger, if humbled. Others argue that the crises have been too damaging and that questions now hang over the entire exercise of European integration. And still others feel that substantial reform is needed if the EU is to continue (the more sceptical perspective being that the exercise is fundamentally flawed and that an exit from the EU is the only option). There is no question that the EU today faces enormous challenges, and it will be interesting to see where they lead over the next few years.

Appendix 1

Europe in Numbers

	Area (000 sq. km)	Population (million)	Gross domestic product ($billion)	Per capita gross national income ($)
European Union (28)				
Germany	357	82.3	3,601	44,270
France	549	62.8	2,773	42,420
UK	244	62.0	2,445	37,840
Italy	301	60.6	2,194	35,290
Spain	505	46.1	1,477	30,890
Netherlands	42	16.6	836	49,650
Sweden	450	9.4	540	53,150
Poland	313	38.3	514	12,480
Belgium	31	10.7	514	45,990
Austria	84	8.4	418	48,190
Denmark	43	5.6	334	60,120
Greece	132	11.4	290	24,480
Finland	338	5.4	263	47,770
Portugal	92	10.7	237	21,210
Czech Republic	79	10.5	217	18,620
Ireland	70	4.5	217	39,930
Romania	238	21.5	180	7,910
Hungary	93	10.0	140	12,730
Slovakia	49	5.5	96	16,070
Croatia	57	4.4	62	13,530
Luxembourg	3	0.5	59	77,580
Bulgaria	111	7.5	54	6,530
Slovenia	20	2.0	50	23,610
Lithuania	65	3.3	43	12,280
Latvia	65	2.3	28	12,350
Cyprus	9	1.1	25	29,450
Estonia	45	1.3	22	15,260
Malta	0.3	0.4	9	18,620
Total	4,386	505.1	17,638	34,033

Note: countries in bold are part of the eurozone.

	Area (000 sq.km)	Population (million)	Gross domestic product ($billion)	Per capita gross national income ($)
Non-EU Europe (16)				
Turkey	784	72.8	775	10,410
Switzerland	41	7.7	659	76,400
Norway	324	4.9	486	88,890
Ukraine	604	45.4	165	3,130
Azerbaijan	87	9.2	63	5,290
Belarus	208	9.6	55	5,830
Serbia	88	9.9	46	5,690
Bosnia/Herzegovina	51	3.8	18	4,780
Georgia	70	4.4	14	2,860
Iceland	103	0.3	14	34,820
Albania	29	3.2	13	3,980
Armenia	30	3.1	10	3,360
Macedonia	26	2.1	10	4,730
Moldova	34	3.6	7	1,980
Kosovo	11	1.8	6	3,520
Montenegro	14	0.6	5	7,140
Total	*2,504*	*182.4*	*2,346*	

* Estimates

	Area (000 sq.km)	Population (million)	Gross domestic product ($billion)	Per capita gross national income ($)
Other				
United States	9,364	310.4	14,991	48,620
China	9,600	1,341.3	7,318	4,940
Japan	378	126.5	5,867	44,900
Brazil	8,515	195.0	2,477	10,720
Russia	17,098	143.0	1,858	10,730
India	3,287	1,224.6	1,848	1,410
Indonesia	1,919	239.9	846	2,940
WORLD	134,593	6,895.9	69,980	9,511

Sources: Area figures from Food and Agriculture Organization of the UN at http://faostat.fao.org. Population figures for 2010 from UN Population Division at http://www.esa.un.org/esa/population. Economic figures for 2011 from World Development Indicators database at http://www.world-bank.com.

Notes: States are ranked by GDP. All figures retrieved April 2013.

Appendix 2

A Chronology of European Integration

1944	July	Bretton Woods conference
1945	May	Germany surrenders; European war ends
	October	Creation of United Nations (UN)
1947	June	Announcement of Marshall Plan
1948	January	Creation of Benelux customs union
	April	Organization for European Economic Cooperation founded
1949	April	North Atlantic Treaty signed
	May	Council of Europe founded
1950	May	Publication of Schuman Declaration
1951	April	Treaty of Paris signed, creating the European Coal and Steel Community (ECSC)
1952	March	Nordic Council founded
	May	Signature of draft treaty creating the European Defence Community (EDC)
	July	Treaty of Paris comes into force
1953	March	Plans announced for European Political Community (EPC)
1954	August	Plans for EDC and EPC collapse
	October	Creation of Western European Union
1956	June	Negotiations open on creation of European Economic Community (EEC) and Euratom
	October–December	Suez crisis
1957	March	Treaties of Rome signed, creating Euratom and the EEC
1958	January	Treaties of Rome come into force
	February	Benelux Economic Union founded
1960	May	European Free Trade Association (EFTA) begins operations
1961	February	First summit of EEC heads of government
	July–August	Britain, Ireland and Denmark apply to join EEC
1962	April	Norway applies for EEC membership
1963	January	De Gaulle vetoes British membership of the EEC; France and Germany sign Treaty of Friendship and Cooperation
1965	April	Merger treaty signed
	July	Start of empty-chair crisis (resolved January 1966)
1966	May	Britain, Ireland and Denmark apply for the second time to join EEC (Norway follows in July)
1967	November	De Gaulle again vetoes British membership of the Community
1968	July	Agreement of a common external tariff completes the creation of an EEC customs union

1970	June	Membership negotiations open with Britain, Denmark, Ireland and Norway; concluded in January 1972
1971	August	United States leaves gold standard; end of the Bretton Woods system of fixed exchange rates
1972	September	Referendum in Norway rejects EEC membership
1973	January	Britain, Denmark and Ireland join the Community, bringing membership to nine
1975	March	First meeting of European Council in Dublin; creation of the European Regional Development Fund (ERDF)
	June	Greece applies to join Community
1977	March	Portugal applies to join Community
	July	Spain applies to join Community
1978	December	European Council establishes European Monetary System (EMS)
1979	March	EMS comes into operation; death of Jean Monnet
	June	First direct elections to the European Parliament
1981	January	Greece joins the Community, bringing membership to ten
1984	January	Free trade area established between EFTA and the EEC
1985	June	Schengen agreement signed by France, Germany and Benelux states
	December	European Council agrees to drawing up of Single European Act (SEA)
1986	January	Portugal and Spain join Community, bringing membership to 12
	February	SEA signed in Luxembourg
1987	April	Turkey applies to join Community
	July	SEA comes into force
1989	April	Delors report on economic and monetary union
	July	Austria applies to join Community
	December	Adoption of Social Charter by 11 EC member states
1990	July	Cyprus and Malta apply to join Community
	August	Iraqi invasion of Kuwait
	October	German reunification brings former East Germany into the Community
1991	June	Outbreak of war in Yugoslavia
	July	Sweden applies to join Community
1992	February	Treaty on European Union (Maastricht treaty) signed
	March	Finland applies to join Community
	May	Switzerland applies to join Community
	June	Danish referendum rejects terms of Maastricht
	November	Norway applies again for Community membership
1993	May	Second Danish referendum accepts terms of Maastricht
	November	Treaty on European Union comes into force. European Community becomes a pillar of the new European Union

1994	January	Creation of the European Economic Area (EEA)
	March	Hungary applies to join EU
	April	Poland applies to join EU
	May	Opening of Channel Tunnel, linking Britain and France
	June–November	Referenda in Austria, Finland and Sweden accept EU membership, but Norwegians again say no
1995	January	Austria, Finland and Sweden join the European Union, bringing membership to 15
	March	Schengen agreement comes into force
	July	Europol Convention signed
	October–December	Bulgaria, Estonia, Latvia and Lithuania apply to join EU
	December	Dayton peace accords end war in Yugoslavia
1996	January	Czech Republic applies to join EU
	June	Slovenia applies to join EU
1997	October	Treaty of Amsterdam signed
1998	June	Establishment of European Central Bank (ECB)
1999	January	Launch of the euro in 11 member states
	May	Treaty of Amsterdam comes into force
2000	September	Danish referendum rejects adoption of euro
2001	February	Treaty of Nice signed
	March	Swiss referendum rejects EU membership
	June	Irish referendum rejects terms of Nice
2002	January	Euro coins and notes begin circulating in 12 member states
	February	Opening of Convention on the Future of Europe
	October	Second Irish referendum accepts terms of Nice
2003	February	Treaty of Nice comes into force
	March	US-led invasion of Iraq sparks the most serious fallout in postwar transatlantic relations
	July	Publication of draft treaty establishing a constitution for Europe
	September	Swedish referendum rejects adoption of euro
2004	May	Cyprus, Czech Republic, Estonia, Hungary, Latvia, Lithuania, Malta, Poland, Slovenia, Slovakia join the EU, bringing membership to 25
	June	European Council accepts terms of draft constitutional treaty
	October	European leaders sign the treaty on the European constitution
	November	Lithuania becomes the first EU member to ratify the constitution
2005	May	French referendum rejects constitution
	June	Dutch referendum rejects constitution
2007	January	Bulgaria and Romania join the EU, bringing membership to 27; Slovenia becomes 13th country to adopt the euro
	December	Treaty of Lisbon signed
2008	January	Cyprus and Malta adopt the euro
	June	Irish referendum rejects terms of Lisbon

2009	January	Slovakia adopts the euro
	October	Second Irish referendum accepts terms of Lisbon
	November	Treaty of Lisbon comes into force
	November–December	Breaking of budget crisis in Greece
2010	December	Launch of European External Action Service
2011	January	Estonia adopts the euro
2012	October	European Union awarded the Nobel Peace Prize
2013	January	British Prime Minister David Cameron announces intention to hold referendum on UK membership of the EU in 2016
	June	Negotiations begin on a transatlantic free-trade agreement
	July	Croatia joins the EU, bringing membership to 28
2014	January	Latvia adopts the euro

Appendix 3

Specialized Institutions of the European Union

Advisory bodies

European Economic and Social Committee (Brussels, founded 1957)
Committee of the Regions (Brussels, 1994)

Executive agencies

Education, Audiovisual and Culture Executive Agency (Brussels, 2006)
European Research Council Executive Agency (Brussels, 2007)
Executive Agency for Competitiveness and Innovation (Brussels, 2003)
Executive Agency for Health and Consumers (Luxembourg, 2005)
Research Executive Agency (Brussels, 2009)
Trans-European Transport Network Executive Agency (Brussels, 2006)

Financial institutions

European Investment Bank (Luxembourg, 1958)
European System of Financial Supervision:
   European Banking Authority (London, 2011)
   European Insurance and Occupational Pensions Authority
     (Frankfurt, 2011)
   European Securities and Markets Authority (Paris, 2011)
   European Systemic Risk Board (Frankfurt, 2010)

Justice and policing

European Agency for the Management of Operational Cooperation at
   the External
   Borders (FRONTEX) (Warsaw, 2004)
European Anti-Fraud Office (Brussels, 1999)
European Police College (Bramshill, UK, 2005)
European Police Office (Europol)(The Hague, Netherlands, 1999)
Judicial Cooperation Unit (The Hague, Netherlands, 2002)

Security and foreign affairs

European Defence Agency (Brussels, 2004)

European External Action Service (Brussels, 2010)
European Union Institute for Security Studies (Paris, 2002)
European Union Satellite Centre (Madrid, 2002)

Other policy agencies

Agency for the Cooperation of Energy Regulators (Ljubljana, Slovenia, 2011)
Body of European Regulators for Electronic Communications (Riga, Latvia, 2010)
Community Plant Variety Office (Angers, France, 1995)
European Agency for Safety and Health at Work (Bilbao, Spain, 1994)
European Data Protection Supervisor (Brussels, 2001)
European IT Agency (Tallinn, Estonia, 2012)
European Asylum Support Office (Valletta, Malta, 2011)
European Aviation Safety Agency (Cologne, Germany, 2002)
European Centre for Disease Prevention and Control (Stockholm, 2005)
European Centre for the Development of Vocational Training (Thessaloniki, Greece, 1975)
European Chemicals Agency (Helsinki, 2007)
European Environment Agency (Copenhagen, 1990)
European Fisheries Control Agency (Vigo, Spain, 2005)
European Food Safety Authority (Parma, Italy, 2002)
European Foundation for the Improvement of Living and Working Conditions (Dublin, 1975)
European GNSS Agency (Prague, 2004)
European Institute for Gender Equality (Vilnius, Lithuania, 2010)
European Institute of Innovation and Technology (Budapest, 2008)
European Maritime Safety Agency (Lisbon, 2002)
European Medicines Agency (London, 1995)
European Monitoring Centre for Drugs and Drug Addiction (Lisbon, 1995)
European Network and Information Security Agency (Heraklion, Greece, 2004)
European Railway Agency (Valenciennes, France, 2004)
European Training Foundation (Turin, Italy, 1994)
European Union Agency for Fundamental Rights (Vienna, 2007)
Office for Harmonisation in the Internal Market (Alicante, Spain, 1996)
Translation Centre for the Bodies of the EU (Luxembourg, 1994)

Appendix 4

Sources of Further Information

Publishing on the EU has grown exponentially in the last few years, with the number of new books, journal articles and websites increasing to match the pace of change in the EU itself, and of expanding interest in EU affairs. As a result, the following list of sources can offer no more than a sample of what is currently available. For new titles, monitor acquisitions at your nearest library, watch the catalogues of the publishers with the best lists on the European Union (including Lynne Rienner, Oxford University Press, Palgrave Macmillan, Routledge and Rowman & Littlefield), and search online book dealers such as Amazon.

Books

For general introductions to the history, institutions and policies of the EU, see Cini and Pérez-Solórzano Borragán (2013), Bomberg, Peterson and Corbett (2012), Bache, George and Bulmer (2011), Hix and Høyland (2011), Lelieveldt and Princen (2011), McCormick (2011), Staab (2011), Dinan (2010), Ginsberg (2010), Nugent (2010) and Yesilada and Wood (2009). Edited collections on developments in the EU include Meunier and McNamara (2007), and Jabko and Parsons (2005).

The best summaries of integration theory are offered by Wiener and Diez (2009) and by Rosamond (2000). An assessment of the key debates about the political identity of the EU is offered by Magnette (2005), and an illuminating set of discussions about the comparative character of European federalism can be found in Menon and Schain (2006) and Burgess (2000). Discussions about the meaning of Europe can be found in Wiesner and Schmidt-Gleim (2104), Dunkerley *et al.* (2002), Pagden (2002) and Heffernan (2000).

For histories of the EU, see Gilbert (2011), Blair (2010), Dedman (2010), Eichengreen (2007), Dinan (2004), Gilbert (2003), Gillingham (2003), Henig (2002) and Stirk and Weigall (1999). For general histories of postwar Europe, see Judt (2005b) and Hitchcock (2004), and for a history of postwar transatlantic relations see Lundestad (2003).

For general surveys of EU institutions and decision making, see Peterson and Shackleton (2013). Regarding specific institutions:

- The Commission is covered by Ellinas and Suleiman (2012), Kassim *et al.* (2012), Cini (2007), Spence (2006) and Smith (2004).
- The Council of the EU is assessed by Naurin and Wallace (2008), Hayes-Renshaw and Wallace (2006) and Westlake and Galloway (2004).
- Parliament is the subject of studies by Corbett, Jacobs and Shackleton (2011) and Judge and Earnshaw (2008), and EP committees are assessed by Whitaker (2010).
- Remarkably, Werts (2008) is the only up-to-date book-length study of the European Council currently available.
- See Lasok (2005) for a general survey of the European Court of Justice, and for more political analysis see Alter (2009), Sweet (2004) and Conant (2002). For an explanation of the EU legal system, see Kaczorowska (2013), Horspool and Humphreys (2012) and Hartley (2010).
- The work of the European Central Bank has been reviewed by Howarth and Loedel (2005).

In-depth surveys of the European Parliament elections in 2004 and 2009 can be found in Lodge (2005 and 2010), while Hobolt (2009) and Szczerbiak and Taggart (2005) offer surveys of referenda on European questions. Lindberg, Rasmussen and Warntjen (2009) look at the role of political parties in the EU, while studies of the two major political groups in the European Parliament are offered by Arvanitopoulos (2010) and Lightfoot (2005). For analyses of lobbying at the EU level, see Coen and Richardson (2009) and Pedler (2002). Taggart and Szczerbiak (2008) offer the most thorough study of euroscepticism to date.

Studies of the relationship between the EU and its member states can be found in Zeff and Pirro (2014) and Bulmer and Lequesne (2013). For studies of EU policy in general, see Buonanno and Nugent (2013), Wallace, Pollack and Young (2010) and Richardson (2006). Assessments of economic policy and the single market can be found in Baldwin and Wyplosz (2012), de Grauwe (2012), Neal (2007) and McDonald and Dearden (2005), while Marsh (2011), Chang (2008) and Hosli (2005) have written about the euro. There has been extensive coverage of the eurozone crisis, including James (2012), Lapavitsas (2012) and Lynn (2011).

Publication on specific areas of EU policy has been on the rise in recent years, with studies of agriculture (Hill, 2012 and Cardwell, 2004), cohesion (Baun and Marek, 2008 and Leonardi, 2005), competition (Cini and McGowan, 2009 and Lyons, 2009), development (Holland and Doidge, 2012 and Mold, 2007), employment (Gold, 2009), energy (Morata and Sandoval, 2012 and Birchfield and Duffield, 2011), the environment (Jordan and Adelle, 2013 and Knill and Liefferink, 2007), immigration (Boswell and Geddes, 2010 and Geddes, 2008), justice and home affairs (Holzhacker and Luff, 2013, Kaunert, 2011 and Mitsilegas, Monar and Rees, 2003), social policy (Hantrais, 2007) and terrorism (Kaunert and Léonard, 2013 and von Hippel, 2005).

In spite of all the debates about the problems related to EU foreign and security policy, it has been the subject of a burgeoning literature. For example, see Bindi and Angelescu (2012), Cameron (2012), Hill and Smith (2011), Orbie (2009), Keukeleire and MacNaughtan (2008), Smith (2008) and Bretherton and Vogler (2005). For security and defence policy, see Koutrakos (2013), Marsh and Rees (2011), Howorth (2007) and Jones (2007), and for trade policy see Bungenberg and Herrmann (2013). One particular area of recent growth has been assessments of the transatlantic relationship: for example, see Croci and Verdun (2013) and McGuire and Smith (2008), as well as Kagan (2003).

Periodicals and EU publications

The Economist. A weekly news magazine that has stories and statistics on world politics, including a section on Europe (and occasional special supplements on the EU). Selected headline stories can be found on *The Economist* website at http://www.economist.com.

The Economist also publishes two series of quarterly reports that are treasure-houses of information, but they are expensive, and not every library carries them: *Economist Intelligence Unit Country Reports* (these cover almost every country in the world, and include a series on the European Union), and *European Policy Analyst*. Both provide detailed political and economic news and information.

Online news. There are many websites offering up-to-the-minute coverage of EU affairs, including the following:

E! Sharp at http://esharp.eu
EU Business at http://www.eubusiness.com
EU Observer at http://euobserver.com
EurActiv at http://www.euractiv.com
European Voice at http://www.europeanvoice.com
New Europe at http://www.neurope.eu

Academic journals. A wide range of these deal either wholly or partially with the European Union, including the following:

Common Market Law Review
Comparative European Politics

European Foreign Affairs Review
European Journal of International Relations
European Journal of Political Research
European Union Politics
International Organization
Journal of European Social Policy
Journal of Common Market Studies
Journal of European Integration
Journal of European Public Policy
Parliamentary Affairs
West European Politics

Official sources. There are several of these, all of which are available through the Europa website at http://europa.eu.

Websites

The variety of useful websites changes often, as do their URLs, so instead of listing useful sites here, I keep them updated on my website at http://johnmccormick.eu (which also includes my blog). My Twitter posts can be found at @JohnMcCormickEU, and I welcome questions, thoughts or responses to material in this book, or to my tweets.

Palgrave Macmillan also has a website for books in the European Union series which provides information on key developments and links to other internet sources. The URL is http://www.palgrave.com/products/Series.aspx?s=EU.

Bibliography

Allen, David (1996) 'Competition Policy: Policing the Single Market', in Helen Wallace and William Wallace (eds), *Policy-Making in the European Union*, 3rd edn (Oxford: Oxford University Press).

Alter, Karen J. (2009) *The European Court's Political Power: Selected Essays* (Oxford: Oxford University Press).

Andersen, Svein S. and Kjell A. Eliassen (eds) (1995) *The European Union: How Democratic Is It?* (London: Sage).

Andersen, Svein S. and Nick Sitter (2006) 'Differentiated Integration: What Is It and How Much Can the EU Accommodate?', *Journal of European Integration* 28(4): 313–30.

Anderson, Scott (1992) 'Western Europe and the Gulf War', in Reinhardt Rummel (ed.), *Toward Political Union: Planning a Common Foreign and Security Policy in the European Community* (Boulder, CO: Westview).

Antonenko, Oksana and Kathryn Pinnick (eds) (2005) *Russia and the European Union* (London: Routledge).

Armstrong, Harvey (1993) 'Community Regional Policy', in Juliet Lodge (ed.), *The European Community and the Challenge of the Future* (London: Continuum and New York: Palgrave Macmillan).

Arvanitopoulos, Constantine (ed.) (2010) *Reforming Europe: The Role of the Centre-Right* (New York: Springer).

Asmus, Ronald, Philip P. Everts and Pierangelo Isernia (2003) 'Power, War and Public Opinion: Thoughts on the Nature and Structure of the Trans-Atlantic Divide' (Washington, DC: German Marshall Fund), September.

Bache, Ian and Matthew Flinders (2004) *Multi-Level Governance* (Oxford: Oxford University Press).

Bache, Ian, Stephen George and Simon Bulmer (eds) (2011) *Politics in the European Union*, 3rd edn (Oxford: Oxford University Press).

Baldwin, Peter (2009) *The Narcissism of Minor Differences: How America and Europe are Alike* (New York: Oxford University Press).

Baldwin, Richard and Charles Wyplosz (2012) *The Economics of European Integration*, 4th edn (Maidenhead: McGraw-Hill).

Balme, Richard and Didier Chabanet (2008) *European Governance and Democracy: Power and Protest in the EU* (Lanham, MD: Rowman & Littlefield).

Bardi, Luciano (2002) 'Transnational Trends: The Evolution of the European Party System', in Bernard Steunenberg and Jacques Thomassen (eds), *The European Parliament: Moving Toward Democracy in the EU* (Lanham, MD: Rowman & Littlefield).

Barnes, Ian and Pamela M. Barnes (1995) *The Enlarged European Union* (London: Longman).

Baun, Michael and Dan Marek (eds) (2008) *EU Cohesion Policy after Enlargement* (Basingstoke: Palgrave Macmillan).

Beck, Ulrich and Edgar Grande (2007) *Cosmopolitan Europe* (Cambridge: Polity Press).

Billiet, Stijn (2005) 'The EC and WTO Dispute Settlement: The Initiation of Trade Disputes by the EC', *European Foreign Affairs Review* 10(2): 197–214.

Bindi, Federiga and Irina Angelescu (eds) (2012) *The Foreign Policy of the European Union: Assessing Europe's Role in the World*, 2nd edn (Washington, DC: Brookings Institution).

Birchfield, Vicki L. and John S. Duffield (eds) (2011) *Toward a Common European Union Energy Policy* (Basingstoke: Palgrave Macmillan).

Blair, Alasdair (2010) *The European Union Since 1945*, 2nd edn (Harlow: Longman).

Blinken, Antony J. (2001) 'The False Crisis Over the Atlantic', *Foreign Affairs* 80(3): 35–48.

Bomberg, Elizabeth, John Peterson and Richard Corbett (eds) (2012) *The European Union: How Does it Work?* 3rd edn (Oxford: Oxford University Press).

Booker, Christopher and Richard North (2005) *The Great Deception: Can the European Union Survive?*, rev. edn (London: Continuum).

Boswell, Christina and Andrew Geddes (2010) *Migration and Mobility in the European Union* (Basingstoke: Palgrave Macmillan).

Bretherton, Charlotte and John Vogler (2005) *The European Union as a Global Actor*, 2nd edn (London: Routledge).

Bugge, Peter (1995) 'The Nation Supreme: The Idea of Europe 1914–1945', in Kevin Wilson and Jan van der Dussen (eds), *The History of the Idea of Europe* (London: Routledge).

Bulmer, Simon and Christian Lequesne (eds) (2013) *The Member States of the European Union*, 2nd edn (Oxford: Oxford University Press).

Bungenberg, Marc and Christoph Herrmann (eds) (2013) *Common Commercial Policy after Lisbon* (Heidelberg: Springer).

Buonanno, Laurie and Neill Nugent (2013) *Policies and Policy Processes of the European Union* (Basingstoke: Palgrave Macmillan).

Burgess, Michael (2000) *Federalism and European Union: The Building of Europe, 1950–2000* (London: Routledge).

Burgess, Michael (2006) *Comparative Federalism: Theory and Practice* (London: Routledge).

Cameron, Fraser (2012) *An Introduction to European Foreign Policy*, 2nd edn (Abingdon: Routledge).

Cardwell, Michael (2004) *The European Model of Agriculture* (Oxford: Oxford University Press).

Carr, William (1987) *A History of Germany, 1815–1985*, 3rd edn (London: Edward Arnold).

Chang, Michelle (2008) *Monetary Integration in the European Union* (Basingstoke: Palgrave Macmillan).

Chinn, Menzie and Jeffery Frankel (2005) 'Will the Euro Eventually Surpass the Dollar as the Leading International Reserve Currency?', Washington, DC, National Bureau of Economic Research Working Paper 11510, July.

Chryssochoou, Dimitris I. (2000) *Democracy in the European Union* (London: I.B. Tauris).

Cini, Michelle (2007) *From Integration to Integrity: Administrative Ethics and Reform in the European Commission* (Manchester: Manchester University Press).

Cini, Michelle and Lee McGowan (2009) *Competition Policy in the European Union*, 2nd edn (London: Palgrave Macmillan).

Cini, Michelle and Nieves Pérez-Solórzano Borragán (eds) (2013) *European Union Politics*, 4th edn (Oxford: Oxford University Press).

Clover, Charles (2005) *The End of the Line: How Overfishing is Changing the World and What We Eat* (London: Ebury Press).

Coen, David and Jeremy Richardson (eds) (2009), *Lobbying the European Union: Institutions, Actors, and Issues* (Oxford: Oxford University Press).

Conant, Lisa (2002) *Justice Contained: Law and Politics in the European Union* (Ithaca, NY: Cornell University Press).

Connelly, Tony (2009) *Don't Mention the Wars: A Journey through European Stereotypes* (Dublin: New Island).

Corbett, Richard, Francis Jacobs and Michael Shackleton (2011) *The European Parliament*, 8th edn (London: John Harper).

Cornell, Tim and John Matthews (1982) *Atlas of the Roman World* (Oxford: Phaidon).

Croci, Osvaldo and Amy Verdun (eds) (2013) *The Transatlantic Divide: Foreign and Security Policies in the Atlantic Alliance from Kosovo to Iraq* (Manchester: Manchester University Press).

Dahrendorf, Ralf (1988) *The Modern Social Conflict* (London: Weidenfeld & Nicolson).

de Grauwe, Paul (2012) *The Economics of Monetary Union*, 9th edn (Oxford: Oxford University Press).

Dedman, Martin J. (ed.) (2010) *The Origins and Development of the European Union 1945–2008* (Abingdon: Routledge).

Delanty, Gerard (1995) *Inventing Europe: Idea, Identity, Reality* (Basingstoke and New York: Palgrave Macmillan).

den Boer, Pim (1995) 'Europe to 1914: The Making of an Idea', in Kevin Wilson and Jan van der Dussen (eds), *The History of the Idea of Europe* (London: Routledge).

de Rougemont, Denis (1966) *The Idea of Europe* (London: Macmillan).

Dinan, Desmond (2004) *Europe Recast: A History of European Union* (Boulder, CO: Lynne Rienner and Basingstoke: Palgrave Macmillan).

Dinan, Desmond (2010) *Ever Closer Union: An Introduction to European Integration*, 4th edn (Boulder, CO: Lynne Rienner and Basingstoke: Palgrave Macmillan).

Dunkerley, David, Lesley Hodgson, Stanislaw Konopacki, Tony Spybey and Andrew Thompson (2002) *Changing Europe: Identities, Nations and Citizens* (London: Routledge).

Dye, Thomas (2010) *Understanding Public Policy*, 13th edn (New York: Pearson).

Dye, Thomas and Harmon Zeigler (2000) *The Irony of Democracy* (Fort Worth, TX: Harcourt Brace).

Edwards, Geoffrey and David Spence (eds) (2006) *The European Commission*, 3rd edn (London: John Harper).

Eichengreen, Barry (2007) *The European Economy Since 1945: Coordinated Capitalism and Beyond* (Princeton, NJ: Princeton University Press).

Ellinas, Antonis A. and Ezra Suleiman (2012) *The European Commission and Bureaucratic Autonomy: Europe's Custodians* (Cambridge: Cambridge University Press).

Eriksen, Erik Oddvar, John Erik Fossum and Agustín José Menéndez (eds) (2004), in their introduction to *Developing a Constitution for Europe* (London: Routledge).

Etzioni, Amitai (ed.) (1998) *The Essential Communitarian Reader* (Lanham, MD: Rowman & Littlefield).

Eurobarometer polls can be found on the Europa website at http://europa. eu.int/comm/public_opinion/index_en.htm.

European Commission (1985) *Completing the Internal Market* (The Cockfield Report), COM(85)310 (Brussels: European Commission).

European Commission (2001a) *European Governance: A White Paper*, COM428 (Brussels: European Commission).

European Commission (2001b) 'Interim Report from the Commission to the Stockholm European Council: Improving and Simplifying the Regulatory Environment', COM130 Final (Brussels: European Commission).

European Commission (2008) *European Agencies: The Way Forward* (Luxembourg: CEC).

Europol (2013) *EU Terrorism Situation and Trend Report 2013* (The Hague: Europol).

Eurostat (2007) *Europe in Figures: Eurostat Yearbook 2006–07* (Brussels: European Commission).

Fligstein, Neil (2008) *Euroclash: The EU, European Identity, and the Future of Europe* (Oxford: Oxford University Press).

Forsyth, Murray (1981) *Unions of States: The Theory and Practice of Confederation* (Leicester: Leicester University Press).

Franklin, Mark (1996) 'European Elections and the European Voter', in Jeremy Richardson (ed.), *European Union: Power and Policy-Making* (London: Routledge).

Geddes, Anthony (2008) *Immigration and European Integration: Towards Fortress Europe?* 2nd edn (Manchester: Manchester University Press).

Geyer, Robert and Beverly Springer (1998) 'EU Social Policy after Maastricht: The Works Council Directive and the British Opt-Out', in Pierre-Henri Laurent and Marc Maresceau (eds), *The State of the European Union*, vol. 4 (Boulder, CO: Lynne Rienner).

Giegerich, Bastian and William Wallace (2004) 'Not Such a Soft Power: The External Deployment of European Forces', *Survival* 46(2): 163–82.

Giersch, Herbert (1985) *Eurosclerosis* (Kiel: Institut für Weltwirtschaft).

Gilbert, Mark (2003) *Surpassing Realism: The Politics of European Integration since 1945* (Lanham, MD: Rowman & Littlefield).

Gilbert, Mark (2011) *European Integration: A Concise History* (Lanham, MD: Rowman & Littlefield).

Gill, Graeme (2003) *The Nature and Development of the Modern State* (Basingstoke: Palgrave Macmillan).

Gillingham, John (1991; reissued 2002) *Coal, Steel, and the Rebirth of Europe, 1945–1955* (Cambridge: Cambridge University Press).

Gillingham, John (2003) *European Integration, 1950–2003: Superstate or New Market Economy?* (Cambridge and New York: Cambridge University Press).

Ginsberg, Roy H. (2001) *The European Union in International Politics: Baptism by Fire* (Lanham, MD: Rowman & Littlefield).

Ginsberg, Roy H. (2010) *Demystifying the European Union: The Enduring Logic of Regional Integration*, 2nd edn (Lanham, MD: Rowman & Littlefield).

Gold, Michael (2009) *Employment Policy in the European Union* (Basingstoke: Palgrave Macmillan).

Grabbe, Heather (2004) 'What the New Member States Bring into the European Union', in Neill Nugent (ed.), *European Union Enlargement* (Basingstoke and New York: Palgrave Macmillan).

Grant, Wyn (1997) *The Common Agricultural Policy* (Basingstoke and New York: Palgrave Macmillan).

Graziano, Paolo and Maarten P. Vink (eds) (2007) *Europeanization: New Research Agendas* (Basingstoke: Palgrave Macmillan).

Greenwood, Justin (2011) *Interest Representation in the European Union*, 3rd edn (Basingstoke: Palgrave Macmillan).

Greer, Steven (2006) *The European Convention on Human Rights: Achievements, Problems and Prospects* (Cambridge: Cambridge University Press).

Haas, Ernst B. (1958) *The Uniting of Europe: Political, Social, and Economic Forces, 1950–57* (Stanford, CA: Stanford University Press).

Habermas, Jürgen and Jacques Derrida (2003 [2005]) 'February 15, or What Binds Europe Together: Plea for a Common Foreign Policy, Beginning in Core Europe', *Frankfurter Allgemeine Zeitung*, 31 May. Reproduced in Daniel Levy, Max Pensky and John Torpey (eds), *Old Europe, New Europe, Core Europe* (London: Verso, 2005).

Hantrais, Linda (2007) *Social Policy in the European Union*, 3rd edn (Basingstoke: Palgrave Macmillan).

Harmsen, Robert and Menno Spiering (2004) 'Introduction: Euroscepticism and the Evolution of European Political Debate', in Robert Harmsen and Menno Spiering (eds) *Euroscepticism: Party Politics, National Identity and European Integration* (Amsterdam: Rodopi).

Hartley, T.C. (2010) *The Foundations of European Union Law*, 7th edn (Oxford: Oxford University Press).

Hay, Colin, Michael Lister and David Marsh (eds) (2006) *The State: Theories and Issues* (Basingstoke: Palgrave Macmillan).

Hay, David (1957) *Europe: The Emergence of an Idea* (Edinburgh: Edinburgh University Press).

Hayes-Renshaw, Fiona and Helen Wallace (2006) *The Council of Ministers*, 2nd edn (Basingstoke: Palgrave Macmillan).

Heater, Derek (1992) *The Idea of European Unity* (London: Continuum and New York: Palgrave Macmillan).

Heater, Derek (2004) *Citizenship: The Civic Ideal in World History, Politics and Education*, 3rd edn (Manchester: Manchester University Press).

Heath, Anthony, Iain McLean, Bridget Taylor and John Curticel (1999) 'Between First and Second Order: A Comparison of Voting Behaviour in

European and Local Elections in Britain', *European Journal of Political Research*, 35(3): 389–414.

Heffernan, Michael (2000) *The Meaning of Europe: Geography and Geopolitics* (London: Edward Arnold).

Heidenreich, Martin and Gabriele Bischoff (2008) 'The Open Method of Co-ordination: A Way to the Europeanization of Social and Employment Policies?', *Journal of Common Market Studies* 46(3): 497–532.

Heisler, Martin O., with Robert B. Kvavik (1973) 'Patterns of European Politics: The European Polity Model', in Martin O. Heisler (ed.), *Politics in Europe: Structures and Processes in Some Postindustrial Democracies* (New York: David McKay).

Henig, Stanley (2002) *The Uniting of Europe: From Consolidation to Enlargement* (London: Routledge).

Hill, Berkeley (2012) *Understanding the Common Agricultural Policy* (Abingdon: Earthscan).

Hill, Christopher and Michael Smith (eds) (2011) *International Relations and the European Union*, 2nd edn (Oxford: Oxford University Press).

Hill, Steven (2010) *Europe's Promise: Why the European Way is the Best Hope in an Insecure Age* (Berkeley: University of California Press).

Hitchcock, William I. (2004) *The Struggle for Europe: The Turbulent History of a Divided Continent* (New York: Anchor Books).

Hix, Simon (2005) *The Political System of the European Union*, 2nd edn (Basingstoke and New York: Palgrave Macmillan).

Hix, Simon and Bjørn Høyland (2011) *The Political System of the European Union*, 3rd edn (Basingstoke: Palgrave Macmillan).

Hobolt, Sara Binzer (2009) *Europe in Question: Referendums on European Integration* (Oxford: Oxford University Press).

Hobsbawm, Eric (1991) *The Age of Empire 1848–1875* (London: Cardinal).

Hoffman, Stanley (1964) 'The European Process at Atlantic Crosspurposes', *Journal of Common Market Studies* 3: 85–101.

Hogan, Michael J. (1987) *The Marshall Plan: America, Britain, and the Reconstruction of Western Europe, 1947–52* (New York: Cambridge University Press).

Holland, Martin and Mathew Doidge (2012) *Development Policy of the European Union* (Basingstoke: Palgrave Macmillan).

Holzhacker, Ronald L. and Paul Luff (eds) (2013) *Freedom, Security, and Justice in the European Union* (Heidelberg: Springer).

Horspool, Margot and Matthew Humphreys (2012) *European Union Law* (Oxford: Oxford University Press).

Hosli, Madeleine O. (2005) *The Euro: A Concise Introduction to European Monetary Integration* (Boulder, CO: Lynne Rienner).

Howarth, David and Peter Loedel (2005) *The European Central Bank: The New European Leviathan?* 2nd edn (Basingstoke: Palgrave Macmillan).

Howorth, Jolyon (2003) 'Foreign and Defence Policy Cooperation', in John Peterson and Mark A. Pollack (eds), *Europe, America, Bush: Transatlantic Relations in the Twenty-First Century* (London: Routledge).

Howorth, Jolyon (2007) *Security and Defence Policy in the European Union* (Basingstoke: Palgrave Macmillan).

Human Security Report Project (2011), *Human Security Report 2009–10: The Causes of Peace and the Shrinking Costs of War* (New York: Oxford University Press).

Hutton, Will (2003) *The World We're In* (London: Abacus).

International Institute for Strategic Studies (2013) *The Military Balance 2013* (London: Routledge).

Ivaldi, Gilles (2006) 'Beyond France's 2005 Referendum on the European Constitutional Treaty', *West European Politics* 29(1): 47–69.

Jabko, Nicolas and Craig Parsons (eds) (2005) *The State of the European Union, Vol. 7: With US or Against US? European Trends in American Perspective* (Oxford and New York: Oxford University Press).

James, Harold (2012) *Making the European Monetary Union* (Cambridge, MA: Harvard University Press).

Jones, Seth G. (2007) *The Rise of European Security Cooperation* (Cambridge: Cambridge University Press).

Jordan, Andrew and Camilla Adelle (eds) (2013) *Environmental Policy in the European Union: Actors, Institutions and Processes*, 3rd edn (London: Earthscan).

Jordan, Andrew, Dave Huitma, Harro van Asselt and Frans Berkhout (eds) (2010) *Climate Change Policy in the European Union: Confronting the Dilemmas of Mitigation and Adaptation?* (Cambridge: Cambridge University Press).

Judge, David and David Earnshaw (2008) *The European Parliament*, 2nd edn (Basingstoke: Palgrave Macmillan).

Judt, Tony (2005a) 'Europe vs. America', *New York Review of Books* 52:2, 10 February.

Judt, Tony (2005b) *Postwar: A History of Europe since 1945* (New York: Penguin).

Kaczorowska, Alina (2013) *European Union Law* (Abingdon: Routledge).

Kagan, Robert (2003) *Of Paradise and Power: America and Europe in the New World Order* (New York: Alfred A. Knopf).

Kassim, Hussein *et al.* (2012) *The European Commission of the Twenty-First Century* (Oxford: Oxford University Press).

Kaunert, Christian (2011) *European Internal Security: Towards Supranational Governance in the Area of Freedom, Security and Justice* (Manchester: Manchester University Press).

Kaunert, Christian and Sarah Léonard (eds) (2013) *European Security, Terrorism and Intelligence: Tackling New Security Challenges in Europe* (Basingstoke: Palgrave Macmillan).

Keating, Michael and Liesbet Hooghe (1996) 'By-passing the Nation State? Regions and the EU Policy Process', in Jeremy Richardson (ed.), *European Union: Power and Policy-Making* (London: Routledge).

Keohane, Robert O. and Stanley Hoffmann (eds) (1991) *The New European Community: Decisionmaking and Institutional Change* (Boulder, CO: Westview).

Keukeleire, Stephan and Jennifer MacNaughtan (2008) *The Foreign Policy of the European Union* (Basingstoke: Palgrave Macmillan).

Knill, Christoph and Duncan Liefferink (2007) *Environmental Politics in the European Union: Policy-making, Implementation and Patterns of Multilevel Governance* (Manchester: Manchester University Press).

Kopecký, Petr and Cas Mudde (2002) 'The Two Sides of Euroscepticism: Party Positions on European Integration in East Central Europe', *European Union Politics* 3(3): 297–326.

Kopstein, Jeffrey and Sven Steinmo (eds) (2008) *Growing Apart? America and Europe in the Twenty-First Century* (New York: Cambridge University Press).

Kuttner, Robert (2013) 'Economy Sick, Politics Deadlocked? How About a Trade Deal!?', *Huffington Post*, 4 March.

Koutrakos, Panos (2013) *The EU Common Security and Defence Policy* (Oxford: Oxford University Press).

Laffan, Brigid and Johannes Lindner (2010) 'The Budget: Who Gets What, When and How?', in Helen Wallace, Mark A. Pollack and Alasdair R. Young (eds), *Policy-Making in the European Union*, 6th edn (Oxford: Oxford University Press).

Lapavitsas, Costas (2012) *Crisis in the Eurozone* (London: Verso).

Lasok, K.P.E. (2005) *Law and Institutions of the European Communities*, 7th edn (Oxford: Oxford University Press).

Lasok, K.P.E. (2007) *European Court Practice and Procedure*, 3rd ed. (Haywards Heath: Tottel).

Lavenex, Sandra (2010) 'Justice and Home Affairs: Communitarization with Hesitation', in Helen Wallace, Mark A. Pollack and Alasdair R. Young (eds), *Policy-Making in the European Union*, 6th edn (Oxford: Oxford University Press).

Layton, Christopher (1971) *Cross-Frontier Mergers in Europe* (Bath: Bath University Press).

Layton, Lyndsey (2008) 'Chemical Law Has Global Impact', *Washington Post*, 12 June.

Lelieveldt, Herman and Sebastiaan Princen (2011) *The Politics of the European Union* (Cambridge: Cambridge University Press).

Leonard, Mark (2005) *Why Europe will Run the 21st Century* (London: Fourth Estate).

Lequesne, Christian (2004) *The Politics of Fisheries in the European Union* (Manchester: Manchester University Press).

Lewis, David P. (1993) *The Road to Europe: History, Institutions and Prospects of European Integration 1945–1993* (New York: Peter Lang).

Leonardi, Robert (2005) *Cohesion Policy in the European Union: The Building of Europe* (Basingstoke: Palgrave Macmillan).

Lightfoot, Simon (2005) *Europeanizing Social Democracy? The Rise of the Party of European Socialists* (Abingdon: Routledge).

Lijphart, Arend (1971) 'Comparative Politics and the Comparative Method', *American Political Science Review* 65(3): 682–93.

Lindberg, Bjørn, Anne Rasmussen and Andreas Warntjen (eds) (2009) *The Role of Political Parties in the European Union* (London: Routledge).

Lindberg, Leon N. (1963) *The Political Dynamics of European Economic Integration* (Stanford: Stanford University Press).

Lindberg, Leon N. and Stuart A. Scheingold (1970) *Europe's Would-Be Polity: Patterns of Change in the European Community* (Englewood Cliffs, NJ: Prentice Hall).

Lindberg, Leon N. and Stuart A. Scheingold (1971) *Regional Integration: Theory and Research* (Cambridge, MA: Harvard University Press).

Lindblom, Charles (1959) 'The Science of "Muddling Through"', *Public Administration Review* 19(2): 79–88.

Lister, Frederick K. (1996) *The European Union, the United Nations, and the Revival of Confederal Governance* (Westport, CT: Greenwood).

Lodge, Juliet (ed.) (2005) *The 2004 Elections to the European Parliament* (Basingstoke: Palgrave Macmillan).

Lodge, Juliet (ed.) (2010) *The 2009 Elections to the European Parliament* (Basingstoke: Palgrave Macmillan).

Lundestad, Geir (2003) *The United States and Western Europe Since 1945: From 'Empire' by Invitation to Transatlantic Drift* (Oxford: Oxford University Press).

Lynn, Mathew (2011) *Bust: Greece, the Euro, and the Sovereign Debt Crisis* (Hoboken, NJ: John Wiley).

Lyons, Bruce (2009) *Cases in European Competition Policy* (Cambridge: Cambridge University Press).

Magnette, Paul (2005) *What is the European Union? Nature and Prospects* (Basingstoke: Palgrave Macmillan).

Mair, Peter (2001) 'The Limited Impact of Europe on National Party Systems', in Simon Hix and Klaus H. Goetz (eds), *Europeanised Politics? European Integration and National Political Systems* (London: Frank Cass).

Majone, Giandomenico (2006) 'Federation, Confederation, and Mixed Government: An EU–US Comparison', in Anand Menon and Martin Schain (eds), *Comparative Federalism: The European Union and the United States in Comparative Perspective* (Oxford: Oxford University Press).

Marks, Gary (1993) 'Structural Policy and Multi-level Governance in the EC', in Alan Cafruny and Glenda Rosenthal (eds), *The State of the European Community*, vol. 2 (Boulder, CO: Lynne Rienner).

Marsh, David (2011) *The Euro: The Politics of the New Global Currency*, 2nd edn (New Haven, CT: Yale University Press).

Marsh, Steve and Wyn Rees (2011) *The European Union in the Security of Europe: From Cold War to Terror War* (Abingdon: Routledge).

Mazey, Sonia and Jeremy Richardson (1996) 'The Logic of Organisation: Interest Groups', in Jeremy Richardson (ed.), *European Union: Power and Policy-Making* (London: Routledge).

Mazey, Sonia and Jeremy Richardson (1997) 'The Commission and the Lobby', in Geoffrey Edwards and David Spence (eds), *The European Commission*, 2nd edn (London: Cartermill).

McCormick, John (1995) *The Global Environmental Movement*, 2nd edn (London: John Wiley).

McCormick, John (2007) *The European Superpower* (Basingstoke: Palgrave Macmillan).

McCormick, John (2010) *Europeanism* (Oxford: Oxford University Press).

McCormick, John (2011) *European Union Politics* (Basingstoke: Palgrave Macmillan).

McDonald, Frank and Stephen Dearden (eds) (2005) *European Economic Integration*, 4th edn (New York and Harlow: Prentice Hall Financial Times).

McGuire, Steven and Michael Smith (2008) *The European Union and the United States* (Basingstoke: Palgrave Macmillan).

Menon, Anand and Martin Schain (eds) (2006) *Comparative Federalism: The European Union and the United States in Comparative Perspective* (Oxford: Oxford University Press).

Mettler, Ann and Sylwia Stępień (2012) 'Why European SMEs need the digital single market', on EurActiv at http://www.euractiv.com, 23 April.

Meunier, Sophie and Kathleen R. McNamara (eds) (2007) *Making History: European Integration and Institutional Change at Fifty* (Oxford: Oxford University Press).

Milward, Alan S. (1984) *The Reconstruction of Western Europe, 1945–51* (Berkeley: University of California Press).

Mitrany, David (1966) *A Working Peace System* (Chicago, IL: Quadrangle).

Mitsilegas, Valsamis, Jörg Monar and Wyn Rees (2003) *The European Union and Internal Security: Guardian of the People?* (Basingstoke: Palgrave Macmillan).

Mold, Andrew (ed.) (2007) *EU Development Policy in a Changing World: Challenges for the 21st Century* (Amsterdam: Amsterdam University Press).

Monnet, Jean (1978) *Memoirs* (Garden City, NY: Doubleday).

Morata, Francesc and Israel Solorio Sandoval (eds) (2012) *European Energy Policy: An Environmental Approach* (Cheltenham: Edward Elgar).

Moravcsik, Andrew (1998) *The Choice for Europe* (Ithaca, NY: Cornell University Press).

Moravcsik, Andrew (2002) 'In Defence of the 'Democratic Deficit': Reassessing Legitimacy in the European Union', *Journal of Common Market Studies* 40(4): 603–24.

Moravcsik, Andrew (2007) 'The European Constitutional Settlement', in Sophie Meunier and Kathleen R. McNamara (eds), *Making History: European Integration and Institutional Change at Fifty* (Oxford: Oxford University Press).

Morris, Chris (2005) *The New Turkey: The Quiet Revolution on the Edge of Europe* (London: Granta).

Müller, Jan-Werner (2007) *Constitutional Patriotism* (Princeton: Princeton University Press).

Naurin, Daniel and Helen Wallace (eds) (2008) *Unveiling the Council of the European Union: Games Governments Play in Brussels* (Basingstoke: Palgrave Macmillan).

Neal, Larry (2007) *The Economics of Europe and the European Union* (Cambridge and New York: Cambridge University Press).

Nugent, Neill (2001) *The European Commission* (Basingstoke and New York: Palgrave Macmillan).

Nugent, Neill (2010) *The Government and Politics of the European Union*, 7th edn (Basingstoke: Palgrave Macmillan).

Nye, Joseph S. (1971) 'Comparing Common Markets: A Revised Neofunctionalist Model', in Leon N. Lindberg and Stuart A. Scheingold (eds), *Regional Integration: Theory and Research* (Cambridge, MA: Harvard University Press).

Nye, Joseph (2004) *Soft Power: The Means to Success in World Politics* (New York: Public Affairs).

OECD website (2013) http://www.oecd.org.

O'Neill, Jim (2011) *The Growth Map: Economic Opportunity in the BRICs and Beyond* (London: Penguin).

Orbie, Jan (ed.) (2009) *Europe's Global Role: External Policies of the European Union* (Aldershot: Ashgate).

Pagden, Anthony (ed.) (2002) *The Idea of Europe: From Antiquity to the European Union* (Cambridge: Cambridge University Press).

Page, Edward C. (2003) 'Europeanization and the Persistence of Administrative Systems', in Jack Hayward and Anand Menon (eds), *Governing Europe* (Oxford: Oxford University Press).

Palmer, Michael (1968) *European Unity: A Survey of European Organizations* (London: George Allen & Unwin).

Pardo, Sharon and Joel Peters (2009) *Uneasy Neighbors: Israel and the European Union* (Lanham, MD: Lexington Books).

Parsons, Craig A. and Timothy M. Smeeding (eds) (2006) *Immigration and the Transformation of Europe* (Cambridge: Cambridge University Press).

Pedler, Robin (2002) *European Union Lobbying: Changes in the Arena* (Basingstoke: Palgrave Macmillan).

Peters, B. Guy (1992) 'Bureaucratic Politics and the Institutions of the European Community', in Alberta Sbragia (ed.), *Euro-Politics: Institutions and Policy-making in the 'New' European Community* (Washington, DC: Brookings Institution).

Peters, B. Guy (2001) 'Agenda-Setting in the European Union', in Jeremy Richardson (ed.), *European Union: Power and Policy-Making*, 2nd edn (New York: Routledge).

Peterson, John (2003) 'The US and Europe in the Balkans', in John Peterson and Mark A. Pollack (eds), *Europe, America, Bush: Transatlantic Relations in the Twenty-First Century* (London: Routledge).

Peterson, John and Michael Shackleton (eds) (2013) *The Institutions of the European Union*, 3rd edn (Oxford: Oxford University Press).

Pew Research Centre Global Attitudes Survey web site (2013) http://www.pewglobal.org.

Philippon, Thomas and Nicolas Véron (2008) 'Financing Europe's Fast Movers', Policy Brief 2008/01 (Brussels: Breugel), January.

Popkin, Samuel L. (1994) *The Reasoning Voter: Communication and Persuasion in Presidential Campaigns* (Chicago: University Of Chicago Press).

Prestowitz, Clyde (2003) *Rogue Nation: American Unilateralism and the Failure of Good Intentions* (New York: Basic Books).

Puchala, Donald J. (1975) 'Domestic Politics and Regional Harmonization in the European Communities', *World Politics* 27(4): 496–520.

Pye, Lucien (1966) *Aspects of Political Development* (Boston, MA: Little, Brown).

Reiff, K. and H. Schmitt (1980) 'Nine Second-Order National Elections: A Conceptual Framework for the Analysis of European Election Results', *European Journal of Political Research* 8(1): 3–44.

Richardson, Jeremy (ed.) (2006) *European Union: Power and Policy-Making*, 3rd edn (London and New York: Routledge).

Rieger, Elmar (2005) 'Agricultural Policy: Constrained Reforms', in Helen Wallace, William Wallace and Mark A. Pollack (eds), *Policy-Making in the European Union*, 5th edn (Oxford: Oxford University Press).

Rifkin, Jeremy (2004) *The European Dream: How Europe's Vision of the Future is Quietly Eclipsing the American Dream* (New York: Tarcher/Penguin).

Rittberger, Berthold (2005) *Building Europe's Parliament: Democratic Representation Beyond the Nation-State* (Oxford: Oxford University Press).

Rosamond, Ben (2000) *Theories of European Integration* (Basingstoke and New York: Palgrave Macmillan).

Ross, George (1995) *Jacques Delors and European Integration* (New York: Oxford University Press).

Rumford, Chris (ed.) (2007) *Cosmopolitanism and Europe* (Liverpool: Liverpool University Press).

Salmon, Trevor and Sir William Nicoll (eds) (1997) *Building European Union: A Documentary History and Analysis* (Manchester: Manchester University Press).

Sapir, André *et al.* (2004) *An Agenda for a Growing Europe: Making the EU Economic System Deliver* (Oxford: Oxford University Press).

Sbragia, Alberta (1992) 'Thinking about the European Future: The Uses of Comparison', in Alberta Sbragia (ed.), *Euro-Politics: Institutions and Policymaking in the 'New' European Community* (Washington, DC: Brookings Institution).

Schlesinger, Philip and François Foret (2006) 'Political Roof and Sacred Canopy?', *European Journal of Social Theory* 9(1): 59–81.

Silver, Nate (2012) *The Signal and the Noise: Why So Many Predictions Fail – But Some Don't* (New York: Penguin).

Sitter, N. and S. S. Andersen (2006) 'Differentiated Integration: What is it and How Much Can the EU Accommodate?', *Journal of European Integration* 28(4): 313–30.

Slaughter, Anne-Marie (2011) 'War and Law in the 21st Century: Adapting to the Changing Face of Conflict', *Europe's World* 19: 32–7.

Smith, Andy (ed.) (2004) *Politics and the European Commission: Actors, Interdependence, Legitimacy* (London: Routledge).

Smith, Graham (1999) *The Post-Soviet States: Mapping the Politics of Transition* (London: Edward Arnold).

Smith, Karen E. (2008) *European Union Foreign Policy in a Changing World*, 2nd edn (Cambridge: Polity).

Smith, Michael (2006) 'The Commission and External Relations', in David Spence (ed.), *The European Commission*, 3rd edn (London: John Harper).

Sniderman, Paul M., Richard A. Brody and Philip E. Tetlock (1991) *Reasoning and Choice: Explorations in Political Psychology* (New York: Cambridge University Press).

Snyder, Francis (2003) 'The Unfinished Constitution of the European Union: Principles, Processes and Culture', in J.H.H. Weiler and Marlene Wind (eds), *European Constitutionalism Beyond the State* (Cambridge: Cambridge University Press).

Sørensen, Georg (2004) *The Transformation of the State: Beyond the Myth of Retreat* (Basingstoke: Palgrave Macmillan).

Soros, George (2012) Remarks at the Festival of Economics, Trento, Italy, 2 June, at http://www.georgesoros.com/interviews-speeches/entry/remarks_at_the_festival_of_economics_trento_italy.

Spence, David (ed.) (2006) *The European Commission*, 3rd edn (London: John Harper).

Staab, Andreas (2011) *The European Union Explained: Institutions, Actors, Global Impact*, 2nd edn (Bloomington: Indiana University Press).

Stacey, Jeffrey (2010) *Integrating Europe: Informal Politics & Institutional Change* (Oxford: Oxford University Press).

Stirk, Peter M.R. and David Weigall (eds) (1999) *The Origins and Development of European Integration: A Reader and Commentary* (London: Pinter).

Strange, Susan (1996) *The Retreat of the State: The Diffusion of Power in the World Economy* (Cambridge: Cambridge University Press).

Sweet, Alec Stone (2004) *The Judicial Construction of Europe* (New York: Oxford University Press).

Szczerbiak, Aleks and Paul Taggart (eds) (2005) *EU Enlargement and Referendums* (Abingdon: Routledge).

Taggart, Paul and Aleks Szczerbiak (2004) 'Supporting the Union? Euroscepticism and the Politics of European Integration', in Maria Green Cowles and Desmond Dinan (eds), *Developments in the European Union 2* (Basingstoke: Palgrave Macmillan).

Taggart, Paul and Aleks Szczerbiak (eds) (2008), *Opposing Europe? The Comparative Party Politics of Euroscepticism, Vols 1 and 2* (Oxford: Oxford University Press).

Tetlock, Philip E. (2005) *Expert Political Judgment: How Good Is It? How Can We Know?* (Princeton, NJ: Princeton University Press).

Tsoukalis, Loukas (1997) *The New European Economy Revisited: The Politics and Economics of Integration*, 3rd edn (Oxford: Oxford University Press).

Turner, Barry (2006) *Suez 1956: The Inside Story of the First Oil War* (London: Hodder & Stoughton).

United Nations Framework Convention on Climate Change website (2007) http://unfccc.int.

United Nations, Department of Economic and Social Affairs, Population Division (2009) *Trends in International Migrant Stock: The 2008 Revision*, United Nations database, POP/DB/MIG/Stock/Rev.2008.

United Nations High Commissioner for Refugees website (2013) http://www.unhcr.org.

Urwin, Derek (1995) *The Community of Europe*, 2nd edn (London: Longman).

van Creveld, Martin (1999) *The Rise and Decline of the State* (Cambridge: Cambridge University Press).

van Eekelen, Willem (1990) 'WEU and the Gulf Crisis', *Survival* 32(6): 519–32.

Vasileva, Katya (2010) 'Foreigners living in the EU are diverse and largely younger than the nationals of the EU Member States', Eurostat Statistics in Focus 45/2010 (Brussels: Eurostat).

von Hippel, Karin (ed.) (2005) *Europe Confronts Terrorism* (Basingstoke: Palgrave Macmillan).

Walkenhorst, Heiko (2008) 'Explaining Change in EU Education Policy', *Journal of European Public Policy* 15(4): 567–87.

Wallace, Anthony (2004) 'Completing the Single Market: The Lisbon Strategy', in Maria Green Cowles and Desmond Dinan (eds), *Developments in the European Union 2* (Basingstoke: Palgrave Macmillan).

Wallace, Helen, Mark A. Pollack and Alasdair R. Young (eds) (2010) *Policy-Making in the European Union*, 6th edn (Oxford: Oxford University Press).

Wallace, William (1990) *The Transformation of Western Europe* (London: Royal Institute of International Affairs).

Waltz, Kenneth N. (2008) *Realism and International Politics* (Abingdon: Routledge).

Watts, Ronald J. (2008) *Comparing Federal Systems*, 3rd edn (Montreal: Institute of Intergovernmental Relations).

Weigall, David and Peter Stirk (eds) (1992) *The Origins and Development of the European Community* (London: Pinter).

Werts, Jan (2008) *The European Council* (London: John Harper).

Westlake, Martin and David Galloway (2004) *The Council of the European Union*, 3rd edn (London: John Harper).

Wexler, Immanuel (1983) *The Marshall Plan Revisited: The European Recovery Program in Economic Perspective* (Westport, CT: Greenwood).

Whitaker, Richard (2010) *The European Parliament's Committees* (London: Routledge).

Wiener, Antje and Thomas Diez (eds) (2009) *European Integration Theory*, 2nd edn (Oxford: Oxford University Press).

Wiesner, Claudia and Mieke Schmidt-Gleim (eds) (2104), *The Meanings of Europe: Changes and Exchanges of a Contested Concept* (Abingdon: Routledge).

Wolff, Sarah, Nicole Wichmann and Gregory Mounier (eds) (2009) *The External Dimension of Justice and Home Affairs: A Different Security Agenda for the European Union?* (Abingdon: Routledge).

World Trade Organization website (2013) http://www.wto.org.

Wurzel, Rüdiger and James Connelly (eds) (2010) *The European Union as a Leader in International Climate Change Politics* (Abingdon: Routledge).

Yesilada, Birol A. and David M. Wood (2009) *The Emerging European Union*, 5th edn (New York: Pearson).

Young, Alasdair R. (2010) 'The European Policy Process in Comparative Perspective', in Helen Wallace, Mark A. Pollack and Alasdair R. Young (eds), *Policy-Making in the European Union*, 6th edn (Oxford: Oxford University Press).

Zeff, Eleanor and Ellen B. Pirro (eds) (2014) *The European Union and the Member States*, 3rd edn (Boulder, CO: Lynne Rienner).

Zurcher, Arnold J. (1958) *The Struggle to Unite Europe, 1940–58* (New York: New York University Press).

Index